W9-BXG-587

# LOVE THY NEIGHBOR AS THYSELF

## U. S. CATHOLIC BISHOPS SPEAK AGAINST RACISM

JANUARY 1997—JUNE 2000

Committee on African American Catholics
National Conference of Catholic Bishops

United States Catholic Conference
Washington, D.C.

At the November 1998 General Meeting of the U.S. Catholic bishops, the Committee on African American Catholics, under the chairmanship of Bishop George V. Murry, SJ, invited all bishops to increase their efforts in combating racism. *Love Thy Neighbor as Thyself: U.S. Catholic Bishops Speak Against Racism* highlights the variety of ways the bishops have taken the lead in confronting the issue of racism and responding to it. The purpose of this publication is to prompt efforts that act as a blueprint for initiatives for the rest of the Catholic community. *Love Thy Neighbor as Thyself* has been reviewed by Bishop J. Terry Steib, SVD, chairman of the Committee on African American Catholics, and is authorized for publication by the undersigned.

Monsignor Dennis M. Schnurr
General Secretary
NCCB/USCC

Photo Credits: Cover (from left to right, clockwise): *The Catholic Telegraph*; Michael Hoyt; P. C. Piazza, *Acadiana Catholic*. Inside: Bob Roller/CNS (p. iii); National Coalition for Burned Churches (p. 7); Steve Skjold (pp. 9, 11); Rick Reinhard (pp. 12, 80, 122, 132); Karen Callaway (pp. 22, 64, 104); Michael Hoyt (pp. 27, 32, 58, 76); National Black Catholic Clergy Caucus (p. 24); Cathy Joyce (pp. 45, 90); Neil Jacobs/CNS (p. 78); Corbis Corp. Digital (p. 85); Archdiocese of St. Louis (pp. 94, 96, 97); Florent Flipper/Unicorn Stock Photos (p. 109); Chris Sheridan (pp. 111, 113); National Black Catholic Congress (p. 142); NCCB/USCC (p. 149)

Special thanks to Bishop Moses B. Anderson, SSE, for providing the mitre used on the back cover.

First Printing, January 2001

ISBN 1-57455-393-3

LIFT EVERY VOICE AND SING

TILL EARTH AND HEAVEN RING,

RING WITH THE HARMONIES OF LIBERTY.

—"LIFT EVERY VOICE AND SING"

# TABLE OF CONTENTS

# PREFACE

At the November 1998 General Meeting of the U.S. Catholic bishops, the Committee on African American Catholics invited the bishops to increase their efforts in combating racism. Issuing a call for the bishops to take action at this time was a result of such high-profile events as the dragging death of James Byrd, an African American man in Jasper, Texas; the shooting of a young African from Guinea, Amadou Diallo; and the ongoing burning of churches and defiling of synagogues and mosques.

This compendium of articles shows great diversity and vastly different approaches of the bishops, but nonetheless stresses their solidarity against the forces of evil and dehumanization.

The challenge now is to get every Catholic involved in combating racism where it exists. As followers of Jesus Christ, it goes against our faith to sit on the sidelines and do nothing to stamp out the sin of racism. Let us lead by example in eliminating this sin that divides the human family. May this collection of articles help to open our minds and encourage our hearts to take action so that all will be free.

Most Rev. George V. Murry, SJ
Bishop of St. Thomas
Chairman, Committee on African American Catholics

PART ONE:

ORAL REPORT AND PANELISTS ON RACISM,

NATIONAL CONFERENCE OF CATHOLIC BISHOPS'

GENERAL MEETING

# Oral Report *by* Committee *on* African American Catholics, National Conference *of* Catholic Bishops' General Meeting

## BY MOST REV. GEORGE V. MURRY, SJ

NOVEMBER 1998

My Brother Bishops,

For over one hundred years, the American bishops have spoken out about the evils of racism. Taking the form of a pastoral letter, for example, the entire body of bishops; individual letters, for example, bishops to the people in their diocese; or courageous actions to promote social justice, our predecessors and ourselves have attempted to change attitudes and actions rooted in racism.

Unfortunately, concrete facts such as the number of racial hate group websites on the Internet, lack of economic opportunities, White flight, government neglect and at times an official code of silence at the small amount of money we spend on education in our own poor communities, not to mention blatantly violent, racially motivated attacks, lead most observers to conclude that racism is alive, and indeed, thriving. How can we, as leaders in the Church, combat racism? This morning, the Committee on African American Catholics hopes to reopen that discussion. We have invited four bishops to describe what they have seen, heard, or experienced of racism. Our

panelists are Bishop Curtis Guillory, SVD (African Americans), Bishop John Cummins (Asians), Bishop Paul Zipfel (Native Americans) and Bishop Gerry Barnes (Latinos).

After, we will open the discussion to the floor and focus on racism, vis-à-vis African Americans as a paradigm of racism, in the hope that we can gain insight into this very American problem and find new and productive ways to lead our brothers and sisters who hold racist beliefs to conversion in Christ.

[After discussion] I thank you for this discussion and in the name of the Committee on African American Catholics, I urge each diocesan bishop to publish a letter on racism, conversion and reconciliation during Lent.

I thank the panelists for the participation, the staff for their work, and especially the Committee for their personal commitment to this important mission. ■

Most Rev. George V. Murry, SJ, *is the bishop of St. Thomas, Virgin Islands, and the former chairman of the bishops' Committee on African American Catholics.*

## DISCUSSION OPENS POSSIBILITY OF FURTHER BISHOPS' ACTION ON RACISM

BY PATRICIA ZAPOR, CATHOLIC NEWS SERVICE • NOVEMBER 1998

WASHINGTON (CNS)—In what was described as an opening discussion on racism, U.S. bishops acknowledged that they see racism in their dioceses and in church institutions.

In a November 18 session during their annual meeting, Bishop George V. Murry, SJ, chairman of the Committee on African American Catholics, asked his fellow bishops to talk about some of the race-related problems in their dioceses and what efforts they think are needed to address them.

After the hour-long discussion, Bishop Murry, who is the coadjutor of St. Thomas, Virgin Islands, asked his fellow bishops to consider publishing a letter on racism, conversion and reconciliation during the coming Lenten season.

African Americans, Asians, Hispanics and Native Americans all have reason to feel at times that they are treated as less than full members of society and the Church, said some bishops. Four bishops discussed racism in the Church as it affects those particular groups, then a dozen or so bishops talked about what they see happening in their own dioceses.

"As much as we would like to think the question of racism is behind us, it still exists," said Auxiliary Bishop Curtis J. Guillory of Galveston-Houston.

Bishop Paul A. Zipfel of Bismarck, North Dakota, said in his years living in an area with a large Native American population he has come to realize how little most of the rest of the country understands about treaty rights, native customs and the limited opportunities for employment and education on Indian reservations.

Bishop Gerald R. Barnes of San Bernardino, California, chairman of the Hispanic Affairs Committee, said as the Hispanic population grows and shifts into other parts of the country, people who never paid much attention to Hispanics are getting an "Alamo feeling" of being "completely surrounded."

Bishop John S. Cummins of Oakland, California, talked about the difficulties of trying to approach "Asians" as a

single entity when people falling under the label range from Mongolian to Chinese to Filipinos and Indians.

In comments from the floor, Archbishop James P. Keleher of Kansas City, Kansas, said he has seen dramatic changes in people's attitudes toward other races as a result of small faith groups such as those used in the Renew 2000 program. "That is an environment where hearts can change," he said. "I've seen it happen."

Boston Cardinal Bernard F. Law suggested the bishops' conference broaden its agenda and take on the full spectrum of racism, beginning with the Church's own history.

He said he recently read a new history of the Archdiocese of Boston which addresses the Church's less-than-admirable role in the slavery debate of the last century. "Our own history is—and should be—painful to learn," he said.

Bishop John H. Ricard of Pensacola-Tallahassee, Florida, described a program he helped start in the Baltimore Archdiocese, where he served as an auxiliary before he was appointed to the Florida diocese in 1997.

It brought together first pastors and then parishioners from inner-city and suburban parishes to discuss the types of problems each had. The program has been successful in easing tensions between the two groups, he said, and might be a model for other communities.

Bishop Murry also hosted a November 15 workshop for the bishops on African American Catholics and racism, where presenters talked about how they see race-based conflicts as deacons, priests and lay Catholics.

At a press conference following the November 18 discussion, Bishop Murry said his committee has considered proposing a new pastoral letter on racism from the bishops' conference, but decided to first get the body of bishops talking about the issue.

The U.S. bishops called racism a sin in their 1979 pastoral letter *Brothers and Sisters to Us: U.S. Bishops' Pastoral Letter on Racism in Our Day*.

# Address *to the* United States Catholic Conference *for* Their Dialogue *on* Racism

BY MOST REV. CURTIS J. GUILLORY, SVD

NOVEMBER 1998

I. Twenty years ago this conference promulgated the pastoral letter *Brothers and Sisters to Us: U.S. Bishops' Pastoral Letter on Racism in Our Day*, which stated that racism is a sin because it blots out the image of God and divides the human family. It also provides ideas and programs on how to eradicate racism.

Certainly, much progress has been accomplished. Hopefully, in our discussion, some of you will, in your diocese and archdiocese, talk about what you are doing that is effective in eradicating racism.

Yet as much as we would like to believe that the question of racism in society and in the Church is behind us, ongoing racial incidents continue to remind us that it is a scar in our society and Church that we must face. Examples are blatant incidents such as the brutal killing of James Byrd in Jasper, Texas, or in Independence, Virginia, where a White man by the name of Emmett Cresel Jr. set Garrett Johnson, a Black man, on fire and then beheaded him. Then there were the church burnings last summer. Though they were not all racially motivated, too many were.

Those are the blatant incidents of racism that get media attention and quick condemnation by people of faith and goodwill. However, there are the more subtle incidents of racism that take place in society and the Church. There is the African American youth who is eyed or followed in the mall or stores. There is the well-dressed African American male who is unable to get a cab, not because he cannot pay for the ride, but simply because he is Black. Only 2 percent of people of color have decision making positions in dioceses and archdioceses. There are 140 websites pushing racial hatred and many of these are directed

toward children, the belief being that if you capture the mind of children you have them forever. There is the African American woman who extends her hand at the kiss of peace at a Eucharistic celebration and is refused the kiss of peace. Such subtle forms of racism are in many ways much harder to deal with since for the most part, they are only known by the victim and the perpetrator.

II. Beyond Tolerance to Reconciliation. In its report to the president, after hearings on race throughout the country, the President's Advisory Commission on Race said that the president should call on the nation to be more tolerant of race. In the minds of many, tolerance is the goal in racial relations. However, for Christians and Catholics in particular, the goal goes beyond to the deeper level of actual reconciliation.

The Gospel of Jesus Christ and the social teachings of the Church call upon us as teachers and as believers to go beyond tolerance. Tolerance might be the beginning but it is not the end. Tolerance of another means accommodation, existing at a comfortable distance, or co-existing with the other. Tolerance calls one to deal with another of a different ethnic or racial background as required by the law. However, as you so well know, the law does not change hearts. The Church today is being called upon to change hearts with the Word of God, the social teachings of the Church and programs geared toward understanding and respect for the privilege of difference. In Galatians (3:28) "Since everyone of you that has been baptized has been clothed in Christ, there can be neither Jew nor Greek, there can be neither slave or free man, there can be neither male nor female—for you are all one in Christ Jesus." Paul calls us to go beyond tolerance. He calls us to dialogue, to engage in conversation, in extended interaction. He calls us to be reconciled about the past, embrace the reconciled past and be strengthened to face the future.

It is important to mention and to praise the voice of the conference and that of individual bishops who have put out documents urging acceptance and reconciliation. However, in spite of the progress that has been made, much needs to be done. We are not necessarily advocating new programs, but much good could be done if we revisited and implemented what we have already written: documents such as *Brothers and Sisters to Us, Economic Justice For All* and *Love One Another.* These and others such as the Vatican's *Towards a Fraternal Society* are just as relevant today as they were when they were first released.

In his 1994 Apostolic Letter *On the Coming of the Third Millennium,* the Holy Father said that while the great jubilee year of the year 2000 is to be a time of joyful celebration, the joy should be based on forgiveness and reconciliation.

The time has come for us to help our people engage in honest and constructive dialogue that will lead to this reconciliation, trust and understanding. There are those who feel there are no racial problems. Others see race in every incident. Still others, and perhaps the majority of people, want to deal with this scar, but do not know how or where to begin. When Mr. Byrd's sister was asked by a reporter about how she felt toward the three men who had brutally killed her brother, she responded that she and her family forgave them because they were not brought up to hate. What an example for us as we strive to forgive! Armed with the Word of God and the social teachings of the Church, we must help our people so that Jesus' prayer, "That they might all be one," can indeed be a reality. And so let us not grow weary or tired in our own efforts to eradicate racism and to promote true peace and reconciliation among those we serve. ∎

Most. Rev. Curtis J. Guillory, SVD, *is the bishop of Beaumont, Texas, and the chairman of the bishops' Committee on World Mission.*

# Remarks *on the* Asian Experience

### BY MOST REV. JOHN S. CUMMINS

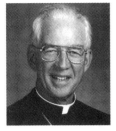

NOVEMBER 1998

I. Our city of Oakland has a Chinatown a century and a half old. It is a circumscribed downtown neighborhood, which exists as testimony to the history of residential and occupational restrictions on the Chinese in the area.

II. This downtown site rests in the context of the state of California. Despite the contribution of the Chinese to the building of railroads, farms, wineries and cities, California in the 1860s barred Chinese children from attending public schools. They were not allowed to testify in court against those of European descent. In 1882, California led the United States Congress to pass a Chinese Exclusion Act prohibiting Chinese laborers from entering the United States and Chinese immigrants already present from becoming United States citizens. That law lasted from 1882 until it was repealed in 1943.

III. Chinese are one illustration of the Asian experience in the United States. That word "Asia" represents a very big world. As someone has said, "from the Bosporus to Vladivostok" and from Indonesia to Korea. For us in particular, that word includes

some of the most ancient Christian churches in the Near and Middle East and in India, predominantly Oriental Rite, and the youngest churches as well. We further add, that from the perspective of our Migration and Refugee Services Committee, the pastoral category includes not just Asian, but Pacific Islanders as well.

IV. The United States' experience records these acts of exclusion. It witnesses too, the inability of Filipino workers in the early part of the century to bring their wives with them. There are marks of burdensome labor practices in California and Hawaii, affecting very much the Japanese and Filipinos. Through the years Asians have suffered from very low immigration quotas.

That represents the past. There are newer elements in the present. Though often seen as an "acceptable minority," a label Asians feel patronizing, many from Asia still feel the glass ceiling of opportunity in so many areas of life. We can add to this also a sense of concern among recently arrived Moslems, whether they will receive acceptance in this country.

V. I would add two current comments. One of these is from history and heritage. There has existed, even to the present, a class preference in many Asian communities, often economically based, clearly social, distinguishing and discriminating. The wisdom of Paul VI, in *Evangelii Nuntiandi*, can be heard: "All cultures are in need of evangelization."

Secondly, many first-generation Asians were rural and uneducated. They accepted their disadvantaged status because they wanted a better life for the generations to come. Today we see a much more assertive leadership in Asian communities, even in better-educated new arrivals. Second and third generations here have benefited from educational opportunity and have entered professions, technical fields and in more recent times, politics. Part of that rising self-awareness belongs to our Asian Catholics. These represent two million members of the Church, who seek, albeit politely, recognition, felt by some long overdue, on the part of the church leadership. They seek acknowledgment of their presence, participation and generous contribution to the life of the Church in this country. ■

Most Rev. John S. Cummins *is the bishop of Oakland, California, and the chairman of the bishops' Committee on Science and Human Values.*

# Remarks *on the* Native American Prospective

## BY MOST REV. PAUL A. ZIPFEL

NOVEMBER 1998

Although I have been in the diocese of Bismarck, North Dakota, for a little less than two years, it has become clear to me that there is both subtle and not-so-subtle discrimination directed at the Native American population.

I would like to suggest some signs of this discrimination that still exist today.

Because so many people do not understand the Treaty Rights that have existed for years, they make the judgment that support of the Native American is nothing more than welfare. As a result the American Indian is often seen as irresponsible and lazy.

Because of the segregation that the reservation brings about, people of other races have little understanding of customs and traditions of our Indian brothers and sisters. In addition, there is little interest in learning about them.

Although efforts are being made by both church and state, many Native Americans have limited opportunities for effective education and health care. Attempts to move into communities outside the reservation can result in unfounded fear. Most feel very unwelcome when they are the minority race.

In my estimation there is much denial of the racism that exists in our own communities. People either don't see it or don't want to see it. When we don't see the problem, there is little chance that it can be corrected. ∎

Most Rev. Paul A. Zipfel *is the bishop of Bismark, North Dakota, and the chairman of the bishops' Committee on Home Missions.*

# Remarks *on the* Hispanic/Latino Prospective

### BY MOST REV. GERALD R. BARNES

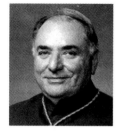

NOVEMBER 1998

Racism toward the Hispanic/Latino community is a historic and well-documented fact in the United States. One can read the history of the different regions of this country to see that violence and hatred have been directed toward Latinos. Today we see the effects of racism in the political and economic arena, in education, in social concerns, and in our Church.

In the political arena, race is being used to promote anti-Latino sentiments, particularly in statewide initiatives like California's Proposition 187. Other similar initiatives—like affirmative action, anti-bilingual education, and the English Only Movement—are being promoted throughout the United States, and the Latino community is the target of many of these efforts. These initiatives divide the greater community and harm the image of the Latino by promoting negative stereotypes.

Economically, Hispanics have an annual market value of $372 billion, and yet in many communities they are red-lined and denied credit by a variety of businesses, making it difficult for them to secure loans, to buy insurance, to purchase homes and automobiles. When our economy meets difficult times, it is often the Latino immigrant that is used as the scapegoat.

In many of our communities, Hispanics have the highest high school drop-out rate, and only 10 percent of Hispanics have a college degree. Recent changes in federal and state laws may keep Latinos and other minority groups from attending colleges and universities.

In society, we see Latinos incarcerated in large numbers and we do not see an end in sight. There is also an increase in the number of incidents of violence against Latinos and immigrants. This can be attributed to the constant racist and anti-immigrant hysteria fomented by opportunistic politicians. And federal enforcement agencies are creating strategies to seek out the undocumented, while intimidating and at times ignoring the rights of Latinos, 95 percent of whom are U.S. citizens or legal residents. The victims are usually poor and do not have the skills to file complaints or lawsuits.

In the Church, many Hispanic Catholics struggle to be accepted and welcomed by some pastors and by parishioners. It was not too long ago that in some churches Latinos were relegated to the church's basement for Mass, sacramental preparation, and other services. Or, Mass was scheduled during hours of the day that were inconvenient to families. In the area of vocations, with thirty million Latinos in the United States, there are only about five-hundred born Hispanic priests.

My father was among those who had to attend Mass in the basement of his parish church because he was "Mexican" and "Mexicans" were not allowed to worship in the church. My father was a third-generation U.S. citizen.

As bishop, I have witnessed and heard church employees refer to a competent sixty-year-old Latina secretary as "the little Mexican girl." When asked why certain programs were not offered to Latinos, the response was "they can't be taught." Latinos were not counted as parishioners for fear that the parish would have to offer them services; or when services were requested by Latinos, responses were made "What more do they want, they already have a Mass?" [And when asked if] diocesan and parish programs designed for leadership people might be offered in Spanish, a response is given "You don't understand, this is only for leaders."

The point is *what is the source of this struggle for the Latino population*, and why? I believe it to be the effect of racism in society. ∎

Most Rev. Gerald R. Barnes *is the bishop of San Bernardino, California.*

# PART TWO:
## CATHOLIC SOCIAL TEACHING

# Racial Harmony:
# A Statement *of the* Catholic Bishops *of* Louisiana

CATHOLIC BISHOPS OF LOUISIANA

Most Rev. Gregory M. Aymond, Most Rev. Dominic Carmon, SVD, Most Rev. William B. Friend,
Most Rev. Alfred C. Hughes, Most Rev. Sam G. Jacobs, Most Rev. Michael Jarrell,
Most Rev. Edward J. O'Donnell, Most Rev. Francis B. Schulte, and Most Rev. Jude Speyrer

FEBRUARY 1997

The teaching of the Roman Catholic Church on racism is clear.[1] Racism is morally wrong. To persist obstinately in this stance is unchristian.

Racism is the theory or practice which assumes that one race or ethnic stock is superior to another. It denies the equal dignity of all the members of the human family.

Sacred Scripture testifies that God created us with an equal dignity and destiny (Gn 1:26). After sin introduced division and oppression, the Lord Jesus restored at least in principle equality and respect for neighbor and foreigner, man and woman. He restored the unity of all in one people and one body. He taught us to recognize His face in every brother and sister. St. Paul in reflecting on this wrote that in Christ Jesus there is no male or female, no Greek or Roman, no slave or free person (Gal 3:28). We share a common dignity in Jesus Christ. Through the Holy Spirit we enjoy communion with the triune God and are bonded with one another as brothers and sisters. We are now called to realize in practice God's original created plan, restored in Christ Jesus.

Racism continues to exist in our time despite Christian teaching. We should remember, however, that racism as an ideology is a rather late phenomenon in history.

Only at the end of the eighteenth century was the word "race" used for the first time to classify human beings biologically.

The theories about essential differences of a hereditary biological nature led to fostering at that time and subsequently a racist ideology which in turn served as a convenient tool to justify the practice already in use by slave traders and profiteers. The oppression of others can flourish only when the basic truths of God's creative action are forgotten. This was dramatically demonstrated again in the 1930s and 1940s when a genetic concept of race became popular.

Contemporary scientific research on the degree of genetic variations in people indicates that almost all genetic diversity is accounted for by variation within populations, rather than by differences between populations. Individual variations in human DNA profiles overwhelm any interpopulation differences, no matter how the populations are ethnically or racially classified. Therefore, the superiority or inferiority of races cannot be substantiated by genetics.

In 1984 the Catholic Bishops of Louisiana insisted, "There is no ethnic hierarchy among the children of God; ethnic gifts deserve the same reverence and respect that we hold for life itself." We also lamented that racism still affected our country, our state and even our Church. Twice since then, in 1989 and 1990, the Church in Louisiana has condemned all forms or expressions of racism.

Let us then make it clear again. To hold that one race is inherently superior to another is a serious sin. To persist obstinately in this stance is incompatible with God's original creation and our redemption in Christ Jesus.

In a sense it is easy and natural to observe certain physical differences which exist among people. Are we wrong to notice such differences? We answer: In our lives together as members of different ethnic and family backgrounds it is natural for us to notice differences which may exist among us. We are helped in our own personal growth and development when we can appreciate and learn from such differences. It is only when we presume to boast of having superiority over others, or judge unfairly, or discriminate against their basic rights as human persons that we offend. Moreover, the absence of personal fault for the level of racism does not absolve us of all responsibility. Social harm demands a social remedy.

It is our conviction that the people of Louisiana truly want to promote racial harmony. Citizens, Black and White, live side by side in a number of neighborhoods, attend community schools, and work together in constructive ways. In the Catholic Church, some African Americans prefer to remain in historically Black parishes, others are welcomed into territorial parishes. There is a helpful twinning of some Black parishes with territorial parishes. Vietnamese, Hispanic, and other immigrant peoples are being welcomed as well.

We also know, however, that recent political campaigns have been tinged with slightly veiled racial rhetoric. The media coverage of events can sometimes give undue attention to more extreme racial positions.

Some unsolved crimes involving the burning of African American churches arouse anxieties about the possibility of racial motivation. Prejudices against immigrants can also degenerate into xenophobia or even racial hatred. There are also many subtle ways in which racial attitudes and prejudices can influence feelings, judgments and actions in us all.

Sacred Scripture offers us a graced corrective. If we place ourselves humbly and sincerely before the revelation which God gives to us in Sacred Scripture and pray for the gift of His Holy Spirit to help us to understand, we will be strengthened in the understanding of God's way and given the grace to live it. Hence we recommend for this purpose reflections on the Sacred Scriptures.[2]

It is our hope that the pondering of God's Word will then lead to an inner conversion of heart and some constructive initiatives.

## CONCLUSION

The good news of the victory of Jesus Christ over sin and death encourages us to proclaim anew this call to conversion and His invitation to new life. We cannot tolerate racism. We cannot allow fears and hatreds to drive us apart.

We repent and ask for forgiveness for any failures in the past or present and the grace to recognize the seriousness of this injustice and to resist it more strongly and forthrightly. We pledge with God's grace to be more faithful to the deeper and fuller implications of the gospel message entrusted to us. We seek to promote the reconciliation that God offers to us in Christ Jesus. We want to work with all people of good will. We seek collaboration with the faithful of other religions.

We thank God who has made us all in His image and likeness, called us to call Him our Father and to live as brothers and sisters in one family. We rejoice in the gift of His Son, Jesus Christ, who has given us the

grace to know repentance and the forgiveness of our sins and the grace to live new life in Him. May the faith and love of Mary the Mother of Jesus and the Mother of the Church inspire and help us through the Holy Spirit to live truly as brothers and sisters of her Son, Jesus Christ. ■

Most Rev. Gregory M. Aymond *is the bishop of Austin, Texas, and a former auxiliary bishop of New Orleans, Louisiana;* Most Rev. Dominic Carmon, SVD, *is an auxiliary bishop of New Orleans, Louisiana;* Most Rev. William B. Friend *is the bishop of Shreveport, Louisiana, and the secretary of the National Conference of Catholic Bishops;* Most Rev. Alfred C. Hughes *is the bishop of Baton Rouge, Louisiana;* Most Rev. Sam G. Jacobs *is the bishop of Alexandria, Louisiana;* Most Rev. Michael Jarrell *is the bishop of Houma-Thibodaux, Louisiana;* Most Rev. Edward J. O'Donnell *is the bishop of Lafayette, Louisiana;* Most Rev. Francis B. Schulte *is the archbishop of New Orleans, Louisiana;* and Most Rev. Jude Speyrer *is the former bishop of Lake Charles, Louisiana.*

**NOTES**

1    *The Church and Racism: A Statement of the Pontifical Commission on Peace and Justice,* 1988; National Conference of Catholic Bishops [NCCB], *Brothers and Sisters to Us: U.S. Bishops' Pastoral Letter on Racism in Our Day,* 1979; Catholic Black Bishops, *What We Have Seen and Heard,* 1984; NCCB, *For the Love of One Another,* 1989; and a series of statements on racism by Louisiana's bishops in 1984, 1989 and 1990.

2    For example: Mt 22:1-14 (Guests at a banquet), Mk 12:28-31 (Great Commandment), Jn 15:12 (Love one another), Acts 10:1-48 (Story of Cornelius), Rom 13:10 (Love fulfills law), 1 Cor 12:12-31 (Mystical Body), Gal 3:26-28 ( . . . no Jew or Greek . . .), Eph 4:1-15 (Support Body of Christ in love), Eph 4:31-32 (Get rid of anger), 1 Jn 2:7-11 (One who hates his brother is in darkness), 1 Jn 4:20-21 (Whoever loves God must love his brother).

# Racism: A Tarnished Reflection *of* Ourselves

BY MOST REV. JAMES A. GRIFFIN

MAY 1997

I want to write to you about something which I believe disfigures the face of society, the Church and individuals: racism. Recent events in our world, our country and our local community remind us that despite our efforts and our progress, racism remains with us. This is true in spite of some advances over the last three or four decades to correct this unjust situation. We still see racism in inferior schooling for minority children, discriminatory treatment toward minority workers and the unfair practices of business and industry. We hear it in racial slurs, belittling references to minorities and outright insults directed to persons because of their race.

Racism is a serious sin. It is a refusal to accept God's creative plan—that all human beings are made in his image and likeness, that all persons have the same heavenly Father, regardless of their race or nationality. The teaching of Jesus Christ, "you shall love your neighbor as yourself," is intended to be inclusive, extending even to those whom we reject because of their ethnic or racial differences (see Lk 10:25-37). The Catholic Church proclaims that all races are children of God and brothers and sisters to one another. In doing this, she remains true to Gospel faith and Christian tradition.

This Gospel truth is echoed in our country's Declaration of Independence: "We hold these truths to be self-evident, that all men are created equal, that they are endowed by their Creator with certain unalienable rights, that among these are life, liberty and the pursuit of happiness."

This basic principle is spelled out in the Constitution and in repeated legislative enactments over the past two hundred years. We can rightly say that racism is un-American and contrary to the laws of our nation. We must recognize that overt acts of racism are criminal.

We are all responsible for our society. We must each contribute in our own way to the molding of the society of which we are a part. We must also ensure the rights of all other members of society to do the same. Only when all people are free to influence the development of culture and society can that society become everything it can be and which we want it to be for the sake of the common good, for our own sakes and for future generations.

Blatant forms of racist practices can be readily known and condemned. It is the subtle forms that elude our perception. Before public acts occur, racism resides in the mind and heart. Prejudicial attitudes and feelings exist which at times are not so easily recognized. These can give rise to racist talk and racist activities, and ultimately to racist practices throughout our society.

Racism flows from personal attitudes and actions into the human world around us; it becomes a social evil. Our social institutions and structures are affected. None seems to escape: families and schools, public institutions and governmental programs, large corporations and small businesses, even our own church communities. As responsible members of our society, we are obliged to do our part to eradicate racism from this society—from the whole and from each of its component parts.

## RACISM IN THE CHURCH

As a church, we must examine and confront the subtle forms of racism of which we are guilty. The Catholic Church in the United States is an overwhelmingly White church. As the bishops' Committee on African American Catholics stated, "History reveals that racism has played a powerful role in discouraging African Americans from the Catholic Church as a spiritual home." It is therefore vitally important that predominantly White parishes learn to worship and live as open invitations to people of all races. We need to change our hospitality habits in order to become a true gathering of believers. We must face the challenge of liberating ourselves from the bonds of racism. Racism, as a sin, harms not only the victim but the sinner too. We are held bound by our prejudices and our fears of letting go of control and power. Perhaps racism does not register as a "sin" in "my parish"—but it can be present. We must name and confess our prejudices in order to be freed from them. How does your parish welcome the stranger and celebrate diversity?

Those reading this letter who are Catholic must remember that we find our unity with Christ and one another in the Eucharist. Each time I distribute holy communion to various congregations around the diocese, I am made aware of our unity in diversity. The faces of those receiving Christ are of all colors and yet all hunger after the same Lord. In this hunger is the key to our unity.

## RACISM'S PERSONAL ROOTS

If we are to remove the sin and crime of racism from our midst, we must start with the self. All social sin begins in the choices of individuals to be unjust and is sustained by our blindness to those initial choices. As St. John says, "If we say we have no sin we deceive ourselves." We can say the same thing about prejudices: We all have them, though we may never have faced them honestly.

In order to overcome this blindness, I ask each of you to make a personal review of any prejudices you might hold. To confront our prejudices, we need to conduct a rigorous self-examination of our attitudes. With the teaching of the Church on human dignity as our "compass," we also need another tool, a mirror in which to examine ourselves. I would suggest that every individual ask himself/herself the following questions as a kind of "morality mirror" in which to see his or her own prejudices:

—What prejudices do I now have? Can I identify the sources of those prejudices?

—What prejudices have I taken from my family and home life?

—What prejudices have I formed or accepted as a result of my experiences in life or from the media?

—How do my prejudices manifest themselves in my everyday living?

—How would I feel were I confronted by people who hold the same prejudices about me that I do about others?

—What one action can I take to begin to combat or remove the major prejudices in my life?

—What further action can I take to work on behalf of victims of racism, whether they be children, young people or adults?

This aspect of taking concrete action is especially important; if we can convince ourselves and others to act as if we truly believe in the equality and dignity of every person of every race, we will find that this action will change our belief. Consistently acting in a certain way begins to form beliefs—or, as may be the case, to "reform" beliefs—and changing our beliefs reforms our behavior.

Personal conversion and pastoral charity are necessary, but this conversion from prejudice must be linked to a sharing of power and influence with minority people. In this move to share power and influence, citizens in the majority race signal that racism is not to be tolerated. We cannot let economic fears deter us from acting justly. We cannot cling to power and control when doing so results in the perpetuation of racism and oppression.

In closing I want to address and challenge specific groups of citizens:

—To parents: I remind you that you are the first and best teachers of your children. By word, but even more by example, you form their moral intelligence. Be sure that respect for all sisters and brothers is part of the framework of your teaching. Seek ways to provide your children with positive experiences of many ethnic groups.

—To religious leaders: Be that prophetic voice to challenge the consciences and actions of your people on this issue of racism. Ask them to reflect seriously on what it means to be sisters and brothers, children of God. Pinpoint the real issues that your parish or congregation must address regarding racism.

—To government officials and community leaders: Do not allow the ugly head of racism to arise in our community. Above all, do not allow members of your staff to "trade" on this issue of racism for political gain.

—To business leaders: The "bottom line" cannot be the sole criterion of your profession. Business must be guided by ethics and principles, chief among which must be respect for every individual regardless of race and opportunity for every employee to rise to his or her full potential with no limits or exclusionary practices based on race.

—To teachers: You mold the future of our community. You have the best chance to eradicate the roots of racism from families and communities. You have the opportunity to plant the seeds of racial fairness in the hearts of our children. Please make the most of this opportunity.

—To all men and women of good will: The value of each of us is dependent on the value which we place on others. Once we make or allow the judgment that any other is expendable or to be limited in opportunity because of race, we open the door to the same fate befalling ourselves based on the same or other irrational criteria. Let us defend our own human dignity by defending the human dignity of every one of our sisters and brothers. Among other things, this means adopting an attitude of "zero tolerance" of racist comments or activity taking place even when you are not directly involved or affected. Do not turn your back in indifference or seek to take the easy way out.

To write of our shortcomings and to confess our failures is never easy or attractive, but this is the only way to face and eradicate racism in our midst. In this Easter season, I ask you to join me in prayer, reflection and action. I also ask you to carry with you and often refer to the "morality mirror" on this subject of racism which accompanies this letter. I close by reminding you of the final words of the pastoral letter on racism issued by the U.S. bishops in 1979. These same words were quoted in our subsequent pastoral, *For the Love of One Another* (1989):

There must be no turning back along the road of justice, no sighing for bygone times of privilege, no nostalgia for simple solutions from another age. For we are children of the age to come, when the first shall be last and the last first, when blessed are they who serve Christ the Lord in all his brothers and sisters, especially those who are poor and suffer injustice. ∎

Most Rev. James A. Griffin *is the bishop of Columbus, Ohio.*

# Racial Intolerance *in the* U.S. Catholic Church: A Healing History, A Hopeful Future

## BY MOST REV. WILTON D. GREGORY

SPRING 1998

In one of the closing scenes of Steven Spielberg's *Amistad*, Capt. Fitzgerald fires upon the vacant fortress in Lomboko on the Galinas Bay in Sierra Leone, destroying the place from which slaves were loaded onto ships headed to the Americas. This emotional moment is cathartic for most of the audience. The business of slavery is now universally considered unsavory! However, the enduring bequest of slavery in the United States still leaves a misery that is not so easily dismissed. That legacy needs reconciliation, and the Catholic Church must exercise its mission at the repository of reconciliation.

The bishops of the United States have issued a number of pastoral statements on the topic of racism and racial intolerance. Over the years, these statements have grown increasingly direct and forceful. They have also revealed a changing focus from charity toward people of color to a serious realization of the personal and universal consequence that slavery has left on this nation and [on] all others who were participants in the business of slavery.

Unfortunately, in the last century, American Catholic bishops chose not to take a formal position condemning slavery, fearing perhaps that such a choice would result in dividing Catholic people along the extraor-

dinary complex matters that would eventually result in a four-year civil war dividing the nation into warring camps. Perhaps the Catholic Church, immigrant community that it was, could not have chosen another path. Who will ever know the numbers of African American Catholics we might have had if the Catholic Church had publicly and enthusiastically chosen to be identified with the anti-slavery movement? When the American bishops began addressing the needs of the newly freed Black Americans, they were generous in their language: "I think it is our most urgent duty to discuss the future status of the Negro. . . . Four million of these unfortunate beings are thrown on our charity, and they silently but eloquently appeal to us for help. We have a golden opportunity to reap a harvest of souls, which neglected, may not return" (Archbishop Martin Spalding, 1866). Sadly, the American bishops' words proved more generous than effective in reaping that harvest of souls. The sentiments, as noble as they sound, did not yet see racism as a malady that disgraces both those who hate and those who are hated.

More than a century later, at the beginning of the Civil Rights Movement, the American bishops issued a document disavowing segregation, but urging prudence to bring about the end of segregation. The statement was issued at a moment in time when the social forces of our society were in the midst of radical change. The bishops, as pastors, urged a judicious path toward integration. They had not yet felt the urgency that civil rights would impose on the nation: "We may well deplore a gradualism that is merely a cloak for inaction. But we equally deplore rash impetuosity that would sacrifice the achievements of decades in ill-timed and ill-considered ventures" (U.S. bishops' statement, November 14, 1958).

Clearly by 1968, the mood of the country and of the bishops had changed. Civil unrest was commonplace, and the threat of violence was growing more certain, especially after the assassination of Dr. King. Now, the bishops began to speak with persistence and a passion that was new and greatly needed: "There is no place for complacency and inertia. The hour is late and the need is critical. Let us act while there is still time for collaborative peaceful solutions. We must show concern, we must give ground for hope. In the name of God, our Father—and we do not lightly invoke His name—let us prove to all men that we are truly aware that we are a single human family on the unity of which depend our best hope for our progress and our peace" (U.S. bishops' statement, April 25, 1968).

However, in 1979, under the courageous leadership of Bishop Joseph A. Francis, SVD, the fifth African American bishop in the nation, the Catholic bishops confronted racism head-on with the issuance of *Brothers and Sisters to Us: U.S. Bishops' Pastoral Letter on Racism in Our Day*. This landmark document dared to challenge the Church itself to conversion and healing from the sin of racism: "How great, therefore, is that sin of racism which wakens the Church's witness as the universal sign of unity among all peoples! How great the scandal given by racist Catholics who would make the body of Christ, the Church, a sign of racial oppression!" Yet all too often the Church in our country has been for many a "White Church," a racist institution.

As we prepare for the new millennium of Christianity, we stand at a hopeful juncture where the Church can fulfill the nobility of its mission and live out the dignity of its documented history. Those in leadership in tomorrow's Church will be judged by a higher standard—one that is rooted in the Gospel and the Catholic Church's ability to reconcile and heal the sins of humanity. There is no turning back! ∎

Most Rev. Wilton D. Gregory *is the bishop of Belleville, Illinois, and the vice president of the National Conference of Catholic Bishops.*

# "As I Have Done *for* You ...":
# A Pastoral Letter *on* Social Justice Concerns *(Excerpt)*

BY MOST REV. JOHN F. KINNEY

AUGUST 1998

Editors' Note: This pastoral letter in its entirety can be found on the website of the Diocese of St. Cloud at www.stclouddiocese.org/bishop/socpast.htm.

## INTRODUCTION

Then the righteous will answer him, "Lord, when was it that we saw you hungry and gave you food, or thirsty and gave you something to drink? And when was it that we saw you a stranger and welcomed you, or naked and gave you clothing? And when was it that we saw you sick or in prison and visited you?" And the king will answer them, "Truly I tell you, just as you did it to one of the least of these who are members of my family, you did it to me." (Mt 25:37-40)

In Jesus' parable of the last judgment (Mt 25) the righteous were surprised at the king's reply.

The surprise was not in hearing that they would be judged by their acts of love, mercy and justice. Rather, they were surprised at where these acts of mercy and justice were to be done: among those who were hungry, thirsty and in need of clothing; among strangers, prisoners and the sick; among those who lacked the basic necessities of life; among those who were least able to return the kindness.

In John's Gospel we read of Jesus washing the feet of his disciples (13:1-11). Jesus then tells them that they should do to one another as he has done to them (v. 15). A little later (v. 34) Jesus tells his disciples:

*I give you a new commandment that you love one another. Just as I have loved you, you also should love one another.*

The Gospels could not be clearer. To be followers of Jesus Christ—to be Christians—means above all that we love one another, precisely because God has loved us. To love as Jesus loves calls us to serve anyone in need—without questioning, without judging, without expecting a reward:

*Do to one another as I have done to you.*

Our Catholic Church always has taught that we have a special obligation to those who are poor, to those in our community and around the world who are most in need. Pope John Paul II often reminds us that this obligation calls for more than charity. He challenges us to do more, to go beyond charity, to examine who are the poor and why they are poor. The pope challenges us to change whatever it is that causes or toler-

ates poverty in our own country and throughout the world.[1]

As your bishop I offer this pastoral letter as a continuing reflection upon our Holy Father's challenge. I believe we are a generous people. My three years in the Diocese of St. Cloud convince me that the people of central Minnesota do care about their neighbors and are willing to help one another. I also believe we could do more—as individuals and as parishes. I invite every parishioner to reflect with me upon Jesus' ministry to the poor and what it means for us in the Diocese of St. Cloud. I ask you to join with me in seeking a better understanding of the needs of persons within our diocese and how we might best respond.

## OUR DIOCESE: ITS CHANGING FACE

The needs of individuals and families in central Minnesota are many and varied. Some are recurring with every generation; others seem to accompany the growing diversity of this geographical area. In either case, it is helpful to identify specific areas of concern and need to which both parishes and individuals can respond.

### Our Heritage

Ours is a diocese with a rich history that continues to enhance the Church today. People of deep faith built both communities and churches. It was this same faith that directed our predecessors to look out for one another. Extended families and limited mobility made it easier to experience community, belonging and the love that each of us needs. A predominantly European population made it easier to recognize and respond to one another's needs. Some parishes were established as ethnic or national churches to better care for an immigrant population. From the earliest days of our diocese we note how parish life, programs and organizations were set up to meet the total needs of the parishioners.

Our diocese is often characterized as stable and with a relatively homogeneous population. In recent decades that has been the case. But the earliest years found settlers arriving from many different European nations with different languages, foods and customs. A history of the diocese shows that for many years the various ethnic groups—especially German, Polish, Irish and French Canadians—struggled to get along together.[2] Today we again experience the richness of growing diversity and with it the challenge of truly being the "People of God."

### Growing Diversity

The sixteen counties of the Diocese of St. Cloud represent communities undergoing changes in populations and in economics. These changes lead to an increasing diversity among the people, the parishes and the towns—a diversity that creates both opportunities and challenges. Some of our counties (such as Sherburne) are among the fastest growing counties in Minnesota. Other counties, notably on the western side of the diocese, experience net population losses. Rural areas more distant from St. Cloud struggle to maintain a stable population, while resort and recreational areas see significant population growth. Some communities have a high percentage of elderly citizens; others observe the steady departure of young adults. Regarding economics, we note that when our diocese was founded in 1889, the vast majority of the people in central Minnesota made their living through farming. Today only about 12 percent of the working people in this diocese are involved in agriculture. Manufacturing, retail, health services, education— each count more employees than agriculture.[3] Even within agriculture we see a continuing movement towards fewer but larger farming operations.

Changes within the population of central Minnesota and within its economy offer exciting opportunities for each of us to respond to Jesus' command:

*Do to one another as I have done to you.*

These changes, creating their own new needs, provide each of our parishes with rich opportunities to be more fully the Church. Individual Christians and local faith communities are well-positioned to recognize and respond to these needs.

Indeed, the growing diversity within our diocese can be viewed as a challenge to each of us and to all of our parishes. It is a challenge that asks how well we carry out the social implications of the Gospel of Jesus Christ. Do we welcome new residents into our parish or community? Do we hear the cries of our young people in a confusing and frightening world? Do we help persons of racial minority groups feel welcome in our communities? Do we appreciate the gifts that elderly persons can offer to both communities and parishes? Do we try to understand and respond to the needs of the poor? Do we recognize how economic changes affect people and communities?

We may view these as opportunities or challenges. Either way, as followers of Jesus and as communities professing faith in Jesus Christ, we are called to reach out to those in need:

*Just as I have loved you,*
*you also should love one another.*

It hardly needs saying that among the more serious areas of concern in our diocese is that of racial minority population groups. The total racial minority population here is relatively small. But the numbers are changing, and as they change they challenge us to examine carefully our own feelings and attitudes about persons from different racial groups. In recent years public attention has focused upon undocumented workers of Hispanic background as well as the fishing rights of Native Americans. While the issues involved are always complex, the tone of the public debate surrounding them often reveals a not-too-

subtle racism. In recent months the City of St. Cloud has witnessed overt acts of racism directed toward members of the African American and Asian communities. We must be clear on this point: Christianity does not condone racism and discrimination in any form—neither the actions themselves nor the silent acceptance of them within the majority population. To be a Christian means that we speak out against such behavior within our own communities. Let us recognize that among the needs of minority groups in central Minnesota none is greater than the need to be accepted, respected and treated as people of dignity.

## *The Church's Social Teaching*

The Church has a vital interest in areas of social concern. The joys and sorrows, the hopes and fears of the People of God relate directly to the proclamation of the Gospel of Jesus Christ. Jesus proclaimed the Good News to the poor, release to the captives, sight to the blind and freedom to the oppressed (Lk 4:18-19). Throughout his ministry Jesus addressed the daily physical needs of people—especially those who were poor, those who were struggling in any way, those who were vulnerable. The Church that Jesus founded also reaches out, as part of its central mission, to people with these same needs.

It is not for the Church to resolve complex problems facing individuals and communities in central Minnesota or anywhere else. But the Church can offer guidance to individual Christians and to Catholic parishes that are themselves in positions to respond to needs in their areas. For the past one hundred years the Church has been developing its teaching on social, economic and political issues.[4] This teaching offers fundamental principles about the human person and about society.[5]

## *Dignity/Sacredness of the Human Person*

Every human being is created by God, redeemed by Jesus Christ and called to communion with God.[6] For this reason every person has a sacred dignity. Each of us has a special place within God's creation. Each of us is so loved by God that the only possible response we can offer is to love God in return and to love and respect all that God has created.

In this sacred dignity all humans are equal. Respect for the dignity of others allows for no distinctions or discrimination based on gender, race, language, religion or social conditions. Respect for the dignity of others is not compatible with oppressive economic and social differences within God's human family. The dignity of the human person means that all life is sacred. Christians respect the lives of all humans and extend this respect to all of creation. Life is a loving gift of the Creator. Our response—always and everywhere—must be to show loving respect for such a gift. The dignity of the human person is the foundation of the Church's teaching about people and about how we organize our society.

## CONCLUSION

I ask every Catholic in the Diocese of St. Cloud—and every person of good will—to reflect upon the biblical text with which I began this pastoral letter. In Jesus' parable of the Last Judgment the Son of Man tells those awaiting judgment that he stood before them every day of their lives:

> For I was hungry and you gave me food,
> I was thirsty and you gave me something to drink,
> I was a stranger and you welcomed me,
> I was naked and you gave me clothing,
> I was sick and you took care of me,
> I was in prison and you visited me. (Mt 25:35-36)

A lesson of this parable is that Jesus is present in the suffering, the hurts and the everyday needs of people around us. Another rather harsh lesson is that some of us see these needs and act, and some of us don't. Perhaps the most important lesson in this parable is that to be a Christian—to be a disciple of Jesus Christ—means that we serve everyone in need— without questioning, without judging, without expecting a reward. Catholic social teaching can help us live this critical lesson of the parable in our own time and setting. That teaching shows us how to reach out in our communities and around the world today to all who are hungry and thirsty, to all who are strangers or in need of clothing, to all who are ill or in prison. Our diocesan Social Concerns Office is ready to help parishes and individuals respond to that challenge of our faith. As Christians we are called to love one another as Jesus has loved us. This love must show itself in daily acts of charity and in the more difficult work of justice. May all of us take up the wonderful challenge to do for one another as Christ has done for us. ■

*Most Rev. John F. Kinney is the bishop of St. Cloud, Minnesota.*

**NOTES**

1   *On Social Concerns*, 42.1. *On the Hundredth Anniversary of "Rerum Novarum,"* 28.2; 52.1.

2   Yzermans, Vincent A. *The Spirit in Central Minnesota: A Centennial Narrative of the Church of Saint Cloud 1889-1989* (St. Cloud, Minn.: Sentinel Printing, 1989).

3   1990 Census: State of Minnesota. *Employment Profiles: Employment by Industry* (Datanet. MN PLANNING.)

4   The papal documents on social justice, from *Rerum Novarum* (1891) through *Centesimus Annus* (1991), can be found in *Proclaiming Justice & Peace*, edited by Michael Walsh and Brian Davies (Mystic, Conn.: Twenty-Third Publications, 1991). Many of these documents can be purchased individually from Catholic bookstores, the U.S. Catholic Conference, or from the diocesan Social Concerns Office. The latter also are places where one can purchase social documents of the United States Catholic bishops.

5   This section offers a summary of the core principles of Catholic social teaching. A recent publication of the U.S. Catholic bishops presents these same principles in a longer list that includes "key themes which are at the heart of our Catholic social tradition." That document, *Sharing Catholic Social Teaching: Challenges and Directions*, calls for the inclusion of our social teaching at every level of Catholic education and faith formation.

6   *Pastoral Constitution on the Church in the Modern World*, 19; 24.1; 29.

# Homily *at* Holy Ghost Parish, Opelousas, Louisiana

## BY HIS EMINENCE PIO CARDINAL LAGHI

NOVEMBER 1998

In the words of the Letter to the Ephesians, Saint Paul invited us to carry out the service that Christ has entrusted to each one of us: "to build up the body of Christ, till we become one in faith, and in the knowledge of God's Son, and form that perfect man who is Christ come to full stature."

The Church, the Mystical Body of Christ, in this Diocese of Lafayette, and, particularly in this parish dedicated to the Holy Spirit, arose, put down roots and developed through time with great vigor, producing many visible fruits: a remarkable number of seminarians, young people proud of their faith and willing to speak openly about it and practice it, vibrant family life, and strong leadership among African American and other Black people. Almost half of the African American bishops who serve the Church in the United States call this area home. You know that the Church esteems and honors all cultures; she respects them in all her evangelizing efforts among the various peoples. At the first Pentecost, those present heard the apostles speaking in their own languages. With the guidance of the Holy Spirit, the Catholic Church tries to bring the Gospel convincingly and understandably to people of all races and conditions, of all languages and cultures.

"It is important to realize"—said Pope John Paul II on September 12, 1987, addressing a meeting of Black Catholic Leaders at the Superdome in New Orleans—"that there is no Black Church, no White Church, no American Church; but there is, and must be, the one Church of Jesus Christ, a home for Blacks, Whites, Americans, every culture and race." And he added: "What I said on another occasion, I willingly repeat: The Church is Catholic . . . because she is able to present in every human context the revealed truth, preserved by her intact in its divine content, in such a way as to bring it into contact with the lofty thoughts and just expectations of every individual and every people" (*Slavorum Apostoli*, no. 18).

[Holy Ghost Parish] bears the name of the third person of the Most Holy Trinity, dedicated to the Holy Spirit. It is very significant for you and your community that Pope John Paul II, to prepare us for the celebration of the Great Jubilee of the Year 2000 of the Incarnation, wished that this year 1998, "be dedicated to the Holy Spirit, soul of the Christian people. Looking to him, Christians will discover his action especially in the sacrament of Confirmation and will strive to make the most of the numerous charisms and services that he inspires in the ecclesial community."

The Prophet Isaiah, in today's first reading [Phil 4:10-19], lists some services that we are called to provide for those who suffer, for those who are, or feel themselves to be, prisoners and wish to be freed, for those who wish to be comforted, and those who strive for peace. Saint Paul, writing to the Ephesians, mentions the roles to be carried out, charisms that Christ entrusts to us: evangelization, care of souls, teaching: all at the service of others. It is always the Holy Spirit who sparks us to service, and makes us capable of carrying out these charges.

The Mystery of the Incarnation was fulfilled "by the work of the Holy Spirit": by the work of that Spirit who, of one being with the Father and the Son, is, in the absolute mystery of the One and Triune God, the Person-love, the uncreated gift, who is the source of every gift that comes from God in the order of creation, and the direct principle of our sanctification in the order of grace. It is he who, dwelling in us, makes us live with God and in God. As Saint Paul writes, the Holy Spirit prays in us and with us, he guides us and

leads us to the point where it is no longer we who live, but rather Christ who lives in us. This leads us to conclude, with the theologian Von Balthasar, that: "Our most intimate actions of believing, loving, hoping, our most personal and free resolutions, and our availability for the service of others: all that we think, love, and do is penetrated by the Holy Spirit, that it is He who is the final subject of our action, on the foundation of the subject that we are."

I am sure that you are all well aware of the existence of the Holy Spirit, of his presence and action in the Church and in each one of you. If Saint Paul introduced himself to one of you—as he did during his visit to Ephesus—and asked: "Have you received the Holy Spirit?" you would not respond as did the Ephesians: "No, we have never even heard that there is a Holy Spirit." Paul then continued: "Into what,

then, were you baptized?" And they responded, "Into John's baptism." Paul said, "John baptized with the baptism of repentance. . . ." Then, to conclude the story, those present were baptized in the name of the Lord Jesus (Acts 19:1-5).

We profess our faith in the third Person of the Most Holy Trinity affirming: "We believe in the Holy Spirit, the Lord, the Giver of Life, who proceeds from the Father and the Son. With the Father and the Son he is worshiped and glorified. He has spoken through the prophets." With these few words, we shall shortly renew our faith in Him, as we do at every Sunday Eucharist.

Dear brothers and sisters: your Black cultural heritage enriches the Church and makes her witness of universality more complete. In a real way the Church needs you, just as you need the Church, for you are part of the Church and the Church is part of you. I would like to conclude with these words of John Paul II, spoken at that meeting in New Orleans eleven years ago: "As you continue to place this heritage at the service of the whole Church for the spread of the Gospel, the Holy Spirit himself will continue through you his work of evangelization. With a joyful and hopeful heart, I entrust you to the loving care of Mary, Mother of our Savior: may she, who both listened to the word and believed in it, guide your lives and those of future generations of Black Catholics within the one Mystical Body of Christ, the one, holy Catholic and Apostolic Church." ■

His Eminence Pio Cardinal Laghi *is now retired. He is the former prefect of the Congregation for Catholic Education and the former apostolic nuncio to the United States.*

# Letter *to* Catholics: Racism

BY MOST REV. PAUL A. ZIPFEL

NOVEMBER 1998

Dear Sisters and Brothers in the Lord:

I am always amazed that some people with whom I speak seem to deny or choose to ignore the reality of racism that exists in our Church and society today. Despite apparent advances, racism remains. In large part it is only the external appearances which have changed.

Several years ago, I gave a prayerful reflection at a conference on racism. Sadly, it still applies today—right here in our own diocese of Western North Dakota. I thought it might be helpful to share parts of it with you.

WHEN JESUS DREW NEAR AND

SAW THE CITY, HE WEPT OVER IT,

SAYING: "WOULD THAT EVEN

TODAY YOU KNEW THE THINGS

THAT MAKE FOR PEACE! BUT NOW

THEY ARE HID FROM YOUR EYES."

(LK 19:41-42)

Lord, we come before you today with so many differences. Some of us are very articulate in our convictions; others are more reticent in expressing themselves. Some of us feel great resistance to change; others are much more aggressive in our demands. Some of us have years behind us; the lives of others lie ahead. Some of us have experienced the pain of racial prejudice; others have a hard time understanding it at all. Some of us are happy people; others have forgotten how to laugh.

Some of us are awfully sure about how we should approach the issues at hand; others are confused, uncertain, torn this way and that, even anxious about our own uncertainty. Some of us have stored up hate in our hearts; others thrill with love. Lord, we are a diverse lot, aren't we?

Only one thing unites us at this moment, Lord: We are all convinced that racism is a moral evil and that it is destructive of the peace of which you speak. We all feel that there is something tragically wrong when our own people see nothing wrong with systematic discrimination. When human beings are being put down by other "human" beings.

We all weep for it, Lord—even those of us who feel that we will discover no solutions, that although it is not Christian, is not human, the problem will always be with us. We all want peace and justice, not division and prejudice. We feel embarrassed and ashamed about our own ignorance of the subtle ways in which we have oppressed our brothers and sisters even today.

Yes, Lord, we all want peace and justice. The problem is, we are not agreed on how to bring it about. There are those who "know" that the first step is for the minority to accommodate themselves to the majority. There are those who "know" that it is a White problem only. There are those who "know" that further talk will only lead to more frustration. And there are those who are somewhere in between.

We do not know, except in a superficial way, "the things that make for peace." If, as your prophet Isaiah proclaimed, "peace is the fruit of righteousness," and if, as your Council taught, "peace is likewise the fruit of love," then racism is the fruit of unrighteousness, of hate. But I cannot lay that unrighteousness, that hate, only at the feet of others. If I am honest, as I want my neighbor to be, I must look within, to see if the seeds of racism are planted in my heart.

What is there about us that would make anyone marvel and cry "Look how they love?" The seeds of prejudice are within us, from the jealousy of Cain to the hate in my own heart. It is frightening to think that my own lack of love could be part of the problem that we are experiencing within our own diocese. No wonder your Son weeps over our community, saying: "Would that even today you knew the things that make for peace! But now they are hid from your eyes."

Perhaps what we need to ask for is a conversion for ourselves. Change us, Lord. Take hate from us, for we never have a just cause for hatred. If we have bled in the process let the blood we shed be redemptive like your Son's. Each of us knows what it is within us that makes for prejudice. Touch all our hearts with a sense of understanding; for we have sinned, Lord, all of us—we have sinned against peace and justice.

Let me see in each human being a brother or sister and the image of your Christ, that our hearts are open to them as never before, that we are ashamed and weep for our crimes against them. ■

Most Rev. Paul A. Zipfel *is the bishop of Bismark, North Dakota, and the chairman of the bishops' Committee on Home Missions.*

# Homily *in the* Trans World Dome

## BY POPE JOHN PAUL II

JANUARY 1999

IN THIS WAY THE LOVE OF GOD WAS REVEALED TO US: GOD SENT HIS ONLY SON INTO THE WORLD SO THAT WE MIGHT HAVE LIFE THROUGH HIM.

(1 JN 4:9)

Dear brothers and sisters,

1. In the incarnation, God fully reveals himself in the Son who came into the world (cf. *Tertio Millennio Adveniente*, no. 9). Our faith is not simply the result of our searching for God. In Jesus Christ, it is God who comes in person to speak to us and to show us the way to himself.

The incarnation also reveals the truth about man. In Jesus Christ, the Father has spoken the definitive word about our true destiny and the meaning of human history (cf. ibid., 5). "In this is love: not that we have loved God, but that he loved us and sent his Son as an expiation for our sins" (1 Jn 4:10). The apostle is speaking of the love that inspired the Son to become man and to dwell among us. Through Jesus Christ we know how much the Father loves us. In Jesus Christ, by the gift of the Holy Spirit, each one of us can share in the love that is the life of the Blessed Trinity.

St. John goes on: "Whoever acknowledges that Jesus is the Son of God, God remains in him and he in God" (1 Jn 4:15). Through faith in the Son of God made man we abide in the very heart of God: "God is love, and whoever remains in love remains in God and God in him" (1 Jn 4:16). These words open to us the mystery of the Sacred Heart of Jesus: The love and compassion of Jesus is the door through which the eternal love of the Father is poured out on the world. In celebrating this Mass of the Sacred Heart, let us open wide our own hearts to God's saving mercy!

2. In the Gospel reading which we have just heard, St. Luke uses the figure of the Good Shepherd to speak of this divine love. The Good Shepherd is an image dear to Jesus in the Gospels. Answering the Pharisees, who complained that he welcomed sinners by eating with them, the Lord asks them a question: Which of you, having one-hundred sheep and losing one of them, would not leave the ninety-nine in the desert and go after the lost one until he finds it? "And when he does find it, he sets it on his shoulders with great joy and, upon his arrival home, he calls together his friends and neighbors and says to them: 'Rejoice with me because I have found my lost sheep'" (Lk 15:5-6).

This parable highlights the joy of Christ and of our heavenly Father at every sinner who repents. God's love is a love that searches us out. It is a love that saves. This is the love that we find in the heart of Jesus.

3. Once we know the love that is in the heart of Christ, we know that every individual, every family, every people on the face of the earth can place their trust in that heart. We have heard Moses say, "You are a people sacred to the Lord, your God. . . . The Lord set his heart on you and chose you . . . because the Lord loved you" (Dt 7:6-8). From Old Testament times, the core of salvation history is God's unfailing love and election, and our human answer to that love. Our faith is our response to God's love and election.

Three hundred years have passed since December 8, 1698, when the holy sacrifice of the Mass was offered for the first time in what is now the city of St. Louis. It was the feast of the Immaculate Conception of our Blessed Mother, and Fr. Montigny, Fr. Davion and Fr. St. Cosme set up a stone altar on the banks of the Mississippi River and offered Mass. These three centuries have been a history of God's love poured out in this part of the United States and a history of generous response to that love.

In this archdiocese, the commandment of love has called forth an endless series of activities for which—today—we give thanks to our heavenly Father. St. Louis has been the Gateway to the West, but it has also been the gateway of great Christian witness and evangelical service. In fidelity to Christ's command to evangelize, the first pastor of this local church, Bishop Joseph Rosati—who came from the town of Sora, very near Rome—promoted outstanding missionary activity from the beginning. In fact, today we can count forty-six different dioceses in the area which Bishop Rosati served. With great affection I greet your present pastor, dear Archbishop Rigali, my precious collaborator in Rome. In the love of the Lord I greet the entire church in this region.

In this area, numerous religious congregations of men and women have labored for the Gospel with exemplary dedication, generation after generation. Here can be found the American roots of the evangelizing efforts of the Legion of Mary and other associations of the lay apostolate. The work of the Society for the Propagation of the Faith, made possible by the generous support of the people of this archdiocese, is a real sharing in the church's response to Christ's command to evangelize.

From St. Louis, Cardinal Ritter sent the first *fidei donum* priests to Latin America in 1956, giving practical expression to the exchange of gifts which should always be a part of the communion between the churches. This solidarity within the Church was the central theme of last year's Special Assembly for America of the Synod of Bishops, and it is the central idea of the apostolic exhortation *Ecclesia in America*—the Church in America—which I have just signed and issued at the Shrine of Our Lady of Guadalupe in Mexico City.

4. Here, by the grace of God, charitable activities of every kind have been a vibrant part of Catholic life. The St. Vincent de Paul Society has had a privileged place in the archdiocese from the beginning. Catholic Charities have for years performed exceptional work in the name of Jesus Christ. Outstanding Catholic health care services have shown the human face of the loving and compassionate Christ.

Catholic schools have proven to be of priceless value to generations of children, teaching them to know, love and serve God, and preparing them to take their place with responsibility in the community. Parents, teachers, pastors, administrators and entire parishes have sacrificed enormously to maintain the essential character of Catholic education as an authentic ministry of the Church and an evangelical service to the young. The goals of the strategic pastoral plan of the archdiocese—evangelization, conversion, stewardship, Catholic education, service to those in need—have a long tradition here.

Today American Catholics are seriously challenged to know and cherish this immense heritage of holiness and service. Out of that heritage you must draw inspiration and strength for the new evangelization so urgently needed at the approach of the third Christian millennium. In the holiness and service of St. Louis' own St. Philippine Duchesne, and of countless faithful priests, religious and laity since the Church's earliest days in this area, Catholic life has appeared in all its rich and varied splendor. Nothing less is asked of you today.

AS THE NEW MILLENNIUM APPROACHES, THERE REMAINS ANOTHER GREAT CHALLENGE FACING THIS COMMUNITY OF ST. LOUIS, EAST AND WEST OF THE MISSISSIPPI, AND NOT ST. LOUIS ALONE, BUT THE WHOLE COUNTRY: TO PUT AN END TO EVERY FORM OF RACISM, A PLAGUE WHICH YOUR BISHOPS HAVE CALLED ONE OF THE MOST PERSISTENT AND DESTRUCTIVE EVILS OF THE NATION.

5. As the new evangelization unfolds, it must include a special emphasis on the family and the renewal of Christian marriage. In their primary mission of communicating love to each other, of being co-creators with God of human life, and of transmitting the love of God to their children, parents must know that they are fully supported by the Church and by society. The new evangelization must bring a fuller appreciation of the family as the primary and most vital foundation of society, the first school of social virtue and solidarity (cf. *Familiaris Consortio*, no. 42). As the family goes, so goes the nation!

The new evangelization must also bring out the truth that "the Gospel of God's love for man, the Gospel of the dignity of the person and the Gospel of life are a single and indivisible Gospel" (*Evangelium Vitae*, no. 2). As believers, how can we fail to see that abortion, euthanasia and assisted suicide are a terrible rejection of God's gift of life and love? And as believers, how can we fail to feel the duty to surround the sick and those in distress with the warmth of our affection and the support that will help them always to embrace life?

The new evangelization calls for followers of Christ who are unconditionally pro-life: who will proclaim, celebrate and serve the Gospel of life in every situation. A sign of hope is the increasing recognition that the dignity of human life must never be taken away, even in the case of someone who has done great evil. Modern society has the means of protecting itself, without definitively denying criminals the chance to reform (cf. *Evangelium Vitae*, no. 27). I renew the appeal I made most recently at Christmas for a consensus to end the death penalty, which is both cruel and unnecessary.

As the new millennium approaches, there remains another great challenge facing this community of St. Louis, east and west of the Mississippi, and not St. Louis alone, but the whole country: to put an end to every form of racism, a plague which your bishops have called one of the most persistent and destructive evils of the nation.

6. Dear brothers and sisters, the Gospel of God's love, which we are celebrating today, finds its highest expression in the Eucharist. In the Mass and in Eucharistic adoration we meet the merciful love of God that passes through the heart of Jesus Christ. In the name of Jesus, the Good Shepherd, I wish to make an appeal—an appeal to Catholics throughout the United States and wherever my voice or words may reach—especially to those who for one reason or another are separated from the practice of their faith. On the eve of the great jubilee of the 2,000th

anniversary of the incarnation, Christ is seeking you out and inviting you back to the community of faith. Is this not the moment for you to experience the joy of returning to the Father's house? In some cases there may still be obstacles to Eucharistic participation; in some cases there may be memories to be healed; in all cases there is the assurance of God's love and mercy. The Great Jubilee of the Year 2000 will begin with the opening of the Holy Door in St. Peter's Basilica in Rome: This is a powerful symbol of the Church—open to everyone who feels a need for the love and mercy of the heart of Christ. In the Gospel Jesus says, "I am the door; whoever enters through me will be saved, and will come in and go out and find pasture" (cf. Jn 10:9).

Our Christian life can be seen as a great pilgrimage to the house of the Father, which passes through the door that is Jesus Christ. The key to that door is repentance and conversion. The strength to pass through that door comes from our faith and hope and love. For many Catholics, an important part of the journey must be to rediscover the joy of belonging to the Church, to cherish the Church as the Lord has given her to us, as mother and teacher.

Living in the Holy Spirit, the Church looks forward to the millennium as a time of far-reaching spiritual renewal. The Spirit will truly bring about a new springtime of faith if Christian hearts are filled with new attitudes of humility, generosity and openness to his purifying grace. In parishes and communities across this land holiness and Christian service will flourish if "you come to know and believe in the love God has for you" (cf. 1 Jn 4:16).

Mary, mother of mercy, teach the people of St. Louis and of the United States to say yes to your son, our Lord Jesus Christ!

Mother of the Church, on the way to the great jubilee of the third millennium, be the star which safely guides our steps to the Lord!

Virgin of Nazareth, two thousand years ago you brought into the world the incarnate Word: Lead the men and women of the new millennium to the one who is the true light of the world! Amen.

*At the end of Mass, the pope made the following remarks:*

Peace—the peace of Christ—to all: to my brother cardinals and bishops—so many here today—the pastors of the Church in America.

A special greeting to the priests, who carry forward with love the daily pastoral care of God's people. My thanks to you all for this beautiful liturgy!

I appreciate very much your enthusiastic participation and your spirit of prayer.

Again, I express my gratitude to Archbishop Rigali, your pastor, and to everyone who cooperated in preparing this great event.

[In Polish] I cordially greet my fellow Poles in America, particularly those living in St. Louis. I thank you for remembering me in your prayers. God bless you all!

A special word of affection goes to the sick, those in prison and all who suffer in mind and body.

My gratitude and esteem go also to our brothers and sisters who, in a spirit of ecumenical friendship, have shared this wonderful moment with us. ∎

Pope John Paul II—*the 265th pope of the Roman Catholic Church—has been the bishop of Rome since October 16, 1978.*

# Racism: Foreign *to the* Mind *of* Christ

## BY MOST REV. DANIEL E. PILARCZYK

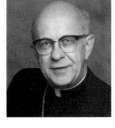

JANUARY 1999

Last November at our annual fall bishops' meeting, we heard a presentation on racism which included four narratives of how people had been mistreated in our country simply because they were African American, Native American, Hispanic or Asian. A discussion followed in which the bishops agreed that racism is a matter of injustice and that, while the Church in our country has made considerable efforts to combat this injustice, we still have a long way to go. At the end of the presentation, the main speaker requested that each bishop offer some teaching on this matter to his people as part of the local church's preparation for the Jubilee Year. What follows are some of my reflections on racism addressed to the faithful of the Archdiocese of Cincinnati on the occasion of this year's observance of Martin Luther King Day January 15.

Because racism is an offense against justice, we first have to be clear about what justice is. The classical definition of justice is "the strong and firm will give to each what is his or her due." Justice is concerned with rights and duties, receiving and owing, claims and obligations. Justice is a complicated thing, but I happen to think that the basics of the Church's teaching about justice can be boiled down to five basic principles—five fundamental insights which are supposed to guide us in giving to each what is his or her due.

The first and most basic principle of justice from a Catholic Christian perspective is that the world is the Lord's and He means each of us to have our share of it. God is the creator and His creation belongs to Him.

Humankind has its part to play, but it is still God's creation, made according to God's plan and for God's purposes. Included in those purposes is the use and enjoyment of creation by God's human creatures—all of them.

The world's goods are not to be used or apportioned out merely as we happen to see fit. We are the Lord's agents and we must use the world and its goods in accord with His plan, His will.

The second foundational principle of justice is the principle of human dignity. Just as all creation exists for God's purposes and belongs to God and may not simply be used up or thrown away, so also human beings exist because God has called them into being on His terms and for His reasons and must be respected as such.

The word dignity means worth or value, and when we speak of the principle of human dignity we mean that every human being has a unique worth or value that nobody can take away and everybody is called to respect. Each of us has a right to receive respect from others and an obligation to give respect to others simply because we are what God has made us to be.

The third fundamental principle of justice is the principle of human responsibility. Human beings are responsible for what goes on in the world. While God is still very much an interested part and intends the world to operate according to the purposes for which it was created, we share responsibility with God for the day-to-day running of it. In the context of justice, this means that we—all of us—are called to work, to the extent that we are able, for the right use and distribution of the world's goods and for the protection of human dignity.

Justice is not just God's project. It's ours, too.
The fourth principle is the principle of human solidarity. Granted that I share responsibility for the right distribution of the world's goods and the protection of human dignity, to what extent and for whom am I responsible? I am responsible for promoting justice in every context that my life touches. Obviously I am responsible for promoting and defending justice for myself, my family, my friends, my fellow workers, my neighbors. But, given the ongoing shrinkage of the world and the increasing connection of one part with the other, not much happens in the world that doesn't have its effect somewhere else. We are all involved together much more than we used to be. Pope John Paul II has said that solidarity is a moral category that involves "a firm and persevering determination to commit oneself to the common good, . . . to the good of all and of each individual, because we are all really responsible for all" (*Solicitudo Rei Socialis*, no. 38).

The fifth principle of justice is care for the poor and the powerless. Why is that a part of justice? For one thing, because the poor and the powerless do not have their rightful share of the blessings of creation that God meant us all to enjoy. Consequently, their fundamental human dignity is threatened. Moreover, because of the situation in which they find themselves, they are not able to exercise a rightful degree of responsibility for themselves and others and often find themselves outside the embrace of human solidarity, whether as doers of justice or as its recipients.

The poor and the powerless live in a situation that is fundamentally unjust. Justice demands that their situation be responded to.

Now, let's look at racism. Racism has been defined as a belief that race is the primary determinant of human traits and capacities and that racial differences produce an inherent superiority or inferiority of a particular race. The racist holds that some people are less human and less valuable than others and the criterion of value is race, nationality or cultural background. How does that square with justice? Obviously it doesn't, and the main disharmony lies in the area of the principle of human dignity. The racist denies the human worth and dignity of those at whom the racism is directed.

Historically racism has worked by simply denying the full humanity of those at whom it is aimed. Black American slaves, Jews in pre-Hitler Germany and Tutsis in Rwanda have been classed as sub-human and therefore able to be treated in any way the racist pleases. This presumption of the racist is manifestly false and constitutes a violation of the principle of human dignity. Whether explicit or implicit, whether a matter of public policy or individual opinion, racism is wrong—factually wrong and morally wrong. But racism involves a disregard of the other principles of justice, too.

If some people are not accorded their full human dignity, they are excluded from sharing in the exercise or the fruits of human responsibility and solidarity. They have no part in the concern that is owed to the poor and the powerless. Most of all, racism violates the very nature of creation. God didn't create different degrees of human beings, and to act as if He did is simply a denial of the goodness of the creative plan of the Lord. By whatever principle of justice we choose to measure, racism is unjust.

Racism is not just a theory, or something that exists only elsewhere. It is a reality. It exists in our country

**UNEQUAL INCARCERATION AND EMPLOYMENT RATES FOR MEN IN THE UNITED STATES**

| Year | Official unemployment statistics for men ages 20 and older | | Official incarceration rates for men ages 18 and older | | Black men's index of economic idleness |
|---|---|---|---|---|---|
| | Black unemployment rate | White unemployment rate | Black incarceration rate | White incarceration rate | Sum of unemployment and incarceration rates |
| 1980 | 12.4% | 5.3% | – | – | – |
| 1983 | 18.1 | 7.9 | – | – | – |
| 1985 | 13.2 | 5.4 | 3.5% | 0.5% | 16.7% |
| 1990 | 10.4 | 4.3 | 5.2 | 0.7 | 15.6 |
| 1995 | 8.8 | 4.3 | 6.6 | 0.9 | 15.4 |
| 1996 | 9.4 | 4.1 | 6.6 | 0.9 | 16.0 |
| 1997 | 8.5 | 3.6 | – | – | – |
| 1998 | 7.4 | 3.2 | – | – | – |
| 1999 | 6.7 | 3.0 | – | – | – |
| 2000 | 6.9 | 2.9 | – | – | – |

Sources: U.S. Department of Labor, Bureau of Labor Statistics, and U.S. Department of Justice, Bureau of Justice Statistics

and our diocese. We had some sad experiences not long ago with racism directed toward Jews and immigrant workers from Latin America. More common is the racism directed by White people toward African Americans.

Black people are generally not as well off in our country as White people. For example, the percentages of poverty and unemployment among Blacks are twice as high as among Whites (see table). These percentages can be explained in many ways, but the fundamental explanation is that historically "they" have been considered "different," that is, inferior, and treated as such by our society.

It may well be that none of us as individuals has deliberately set out to make or keep our social structures this way, but they are this way, and we bear some responsibility for seeing that they change. Then there are our own personal attitudes. Some of these attitudes may have been absorbed unconsciously from the world around us. Some may be "private opinions" that we think don't really matter much in our personal moral life. But whatever their source and however insignificant the effect we may think they have on our behavior, racist ideas do have their influence on us. In countless ways they determine how we look at other people, how we treat them and the extent to which we are willing to go to promote justice and right in their regard.

The Second Vatican Council teaches about racism in its *Declaration on Non-Christian Religions*. Because the Council's teaching is part of our faith, it is important that we take these paragraphs seriously.

We cannot in truthfulness call upon that God who is the Father of all if we refuse to act in a fraternal way toward certain human beings created though they be to God's image. Our relationship with God the Father and our relationship with our human brothers and sisters are so linked together that Scripture says, "The one who does not love does not know God" (1 Jn 4:8). The ground is therefore removed from every theory or practice which leads to a distinction between persons or peoples in the matter of human dignity or rights that flow from it.

As a consequence, the Church rejects, as foreign to the mind of Christ, any discrimination against people or any harassment of them because of their race, color, condition of life or religion (*Nostra Aetate*, no. 5). These are the principles of justice and the teaching about racism that the Church gives us. Our task as followers of Christ is to apply them to our society—and to ourselves. ∎

Most Rev. Daniel E. Pilarczyk *is archbishop of Cincinnati, Ohio.*

# Homily *at* St. Christina Church, Chicago, Illinois

BY HIS EMINENCE FRANCIS CARDINAL GEORGE, OMI

SEPTEMBER 1999

Every family has stories that recall events that shape the life of the family. Growing up I used to hear a story about my sister when she was two years old. It was the first Christmas that she was aware that something special was going on. She was the first grandchild, so my parents and my grandparents decided that they would make this a Christmas that a little two-year-old girl would never forget. They planned and they talked and they bought and they arranged everything so that when my sister came down on Christmas morning she saw a Christmas tree full of lights and beneath that tree, so beautifully decorated, there were all kinds of gifts, presents beautifully wrapped in paper and bows, each one carefully thought out so that everything that she might desire, everything that she would really want, would be there for her that Christmas morning. She set to, and she started to pull out one package after the other and rip open the wrappings and take out a teddy bear, and take out a beautiful dress, and take out some balls, and each time she would say, "Oh, oh, isn't that wonderful." She would put it aside and go with great eagerness to the next one and she did this until finally she came to the end, the last package, the last present, and she turned to take the next and she started to cry. My mother said to her, "Margaret, what's the matter? Why are you crying?" And she said, "No soldiers." No soldiers! Who would have thought that a little two-year-old girl wanted

before anything else that Christmas to have some toy soldiers. But that afternoon they went to my aunt and uncle's place where one of my cousins had gotten one of those sets where you pour liquid lead into a mold. One of the molds was a soldier mold, and so my sister had her soldiers and was delighted with them.

In the Book of Genesis, the first book of holy Scripture, God looks at what He has made, all of creation, taken out of nothingness by his Word. He looks at the light, and it is good. He is delighted in it—like a little child unwrapping presents under a Christmas tree. The delight of God speaks in that first book of holy Scripture, those first chapters in the Book of Genesis. One thing after the other, the light and the darkness, it is good. The heavens and the earth, they are good. The waters and the dry land, they are good. The fish and the animals, they are good. He takes delight in everything that is before him called from nothingness into being by his love. And finally he creates man and woman, and he looks and says, "This is very good." United to God, a delight to God, our first parents lived in that kind of friendship with a God who delighted in his creatures until they sinned and in disobedience fell and lost his friendship, lost that intimacy, no longer walked with him in the garden, no longer were truly closer to him than they were to one another. At the beginning, God delighted at his creation, and shortly after the beginning we spoiled that creation and sin was introduced into the world. Not just a personal bad choice on the part of Adam and Eve, but a cosmic disaster. Everything that had been so wonderful and so delightful now had a darker side, an underside, a sinful side.

The story of the human race continues, a litany of grace and of sin, of good and of evil, until finally at the beginning again, at the beginning of our redemption, as we read in the first chapter of the Gospel according to St. John, God sends light again into the world in the person of His only begotten Son, eternally Son of God born in the time of the Virgin Mary and therefore truly one of us, so that creation is restored. If it was a delight and a marvel to create something out of nothing, how much more marvelous, how much more delightful it is for God to call grace out of sin, good out of evil. God takes delight in his redeemed creation, a true delight, because once again we are restored to friendship with Him. Jesus then tells us that we in turn are to point to him as John the Baptist went before him and pointed to him when it wasn't so clear who He was. "This is the Lamb of God, this is the Light of the World." We take up that refrain in age after age until Jesus comes again in glory: "This is the Lamb of God, this is the Light of the World." In that light we are friends of God, and He takes delight in us. The history of the cosmos and of the whole human race is one of grace and sin, of joy and sorrow. Our personal history in our efforts to remain friends of the Lord, along with all those who have gone before us as his disciples and his friends, his mother Mary, our mother, all the saints who have shown us the way, the paths that they have tried, a path of light, sometimes often in the midst of darkness, all of that is to encourage us so that as we look at our personal history, we will not be overcome with the sorrow of our sinfulness, but we will be overjoyed with the grace of God who brings us into the light of his friendship.

The history of the relations among the races and among the various groups and ethnic communities that form our city is also a history of sorrow and of joy, of sin and of grace. It's a very mixed history. It is something that we embrace tonight as we look at Mount Greenwood

[in the Chicago metropolitan area], and we remember with sorrow recent incidents that are sinful; but we recall with joy our coming together tonight to know that this is not the real community. Here there is reason for God to be delighted: here, in you who pick up the light of Christ and proclaim Jesus as light of the world to all who will hear, to all who will see. God is delighted in you. God takes delight in your love for Him and your love for all that He has made, especially our brothers and sisters, all of them.

What we are not saying tonight, therefore, is that concerns that are close to your heart, concerns for maintaining the equity of a house, for example, are racist. For people of modest means, a house is the investment of their life and it is not racist to be concerned about its value, to be concerned that its value be maintained. That is a good concern because it gives you assurance that you can pass on something to those you love the most. What is racist is to assume that if a neighborhood changes, if into a neighborhood come people of Asian descent or African Americans or Hispanics or poor Whites, then in fact, the value of our homes, the economic security of our life must disappear inevitably, automatically. That is racist. What we are not saying is that a concern, deepest in the hearts of each and every one of us, to live in safety, in personal security, to live with safe streets and with safe parks and with safe schools and with a safe neighborhood, that concern is racist—it is not. It is something desired by everyone and rightfully so. We should live free of violence, and to desire that and to work towards that is wonderful and good. What is racist is to assume that automatically without anything else being said, if people who are different from us, in a different economic class, of a different race, of a different ethnic group, come into our streets and our neighborhood, our personal security must absolutely vanish, no matter what we can do about it. That is a racist judgment. The desires are good. What we do with that desire is good or is bad, depending upon whether the light of our judgment is formed in union with Jesus Christ, our Lord, in the light of faith in Him as Light of the World.

What are we saying, then? That we are to be the light of Christ for one another. That we are able to—in this neighborhood, in this wonderful community, in your homes, in our schools, and in the various parish communities and faith communities of the neighborhood—that we are able to proclaim that what God has made, He has made good; that what Jesus has come to redeem can be full of grace, if indeed we cooperate with the power that the Gospel gives us, the power that is available to us in God's holy word amid the sacraments of the Church.

We received tonight a kind of a sign which is, in its own way, sacramental—a rainbow with a cross. That cross is the cross that saves us, that assures us that Christ's light will remain with us until he comes again. Superimposed upon a rainbow, it reminds us first of all of the covenant with Noah. Remember that story in the Book of Genesis? Remember God's closeness, his intimacy with those whom he has created? The men and women of

every time are shaped by a series of covenants. The new and everlasting covenant is through Jesus Christ our Savior. But before that there was a covenant with King David. There was a covenant with Moses on Mount Sinai. There was a covenant with Abraham that continued in Isaac and Jacob as God chose a people to be his very own, to be light to all the other peoples of the world. But before that, before Abraham, there was a covenant with Noah. After the deluge, God promised that he would never again destroy the human race because of our sinfulness through a flood and that he would, in time, send a Savior to be sure that we could remain in friendship with him no matter what else disturbs our life. Do you remember that in the Book of Genesis the sign of the covenant with Noah was a rainbow? That first great covenant, the beginning of the fulfillment of the promises that God made to a sinful Adam and Eve, is memorialized in a natural sign. Every time it rains and God refreshes the earth so that, with our toil now, we could still be fed and be clothed, we

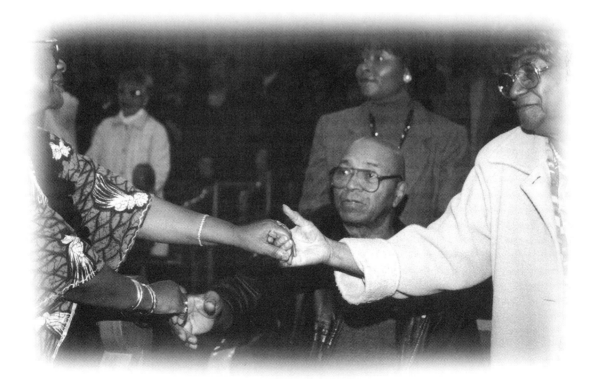

are to recall God's promise to be faithful to us. Every time we see a rainbow and remember the promises that God has made, we should renew our hope, hope now not only for a Savior who has come in Jesus Christ, but hope for the grace and the strength to live according to His light until He comes again in glory.

Here in Mount Greenwood, in our country and in our world, at the turn of a new millennium, God asks us to be light to the world; but he doesn't just ask us, it isn't an empty command. He gives us the strength through Jesus Christ our Savior, through all the reminders that he sends us, that he is with us and that, no matter what else happens, we can rest secure. We have a kind of security more basic than that given us by a political order or an economic order or anything else, a security that comes to us with the grace of God. That security is there if we call upon it.

The rainbow reminds us not only of the first covenant; it reminds us also of how light is refracted into all kinds of colors through a prism. It is the light, the light that God made, that he took delight in, the light renewed in Jesus Christ, the light of the world, that light comes to us in all kinds of colors. The rainbow reminds us of that. The refraction into all the colors of the rainbow reminds us that the human race comes with all kinds of backgrounds, all kinds of colors and all kinds of differences. If we accept them as gifts, presents under the Christmas tree of God's love, and not obstacles to be feared, not impediments to human community, not something that stops our unity as a human race redeemed by Jesus Christ, then we will live as God's creation, God's gift to one another, everyone of those differences, the differences of all the nationalities, Americans and Mexicans and Russians and French and Chinese and Africans of all different nation states, if all those colors, if all those differences are like presents to us, then we understand how marvelously diverse are the gifts of God. How boring a world it would be if everyone was a man or everyone was a woman or if everyone was American or if everyone was Chinese; what a dull, dull place it would

be. If there was only one kind of plant instead of the hundreds of millions of different kinds of plants and species, what a dull place it would be. God would be stingy in his presents.

Difference is a gift, a present to be made public so that it can be shared. If our own gifts are not offered in that way, if you are not a gift to others, able to give yourselves, even to those who perhaps are suspicious of you, then God's love is not burning bright. Jesus is not then the Light of the World, as he wants to be. Share the gifts that you are, the great goodness that God has given you; and in sharing who you are, be willing to accept as a gift, as a present, the presence of those who are very different from you or me in any way. Difference is not something to be feared unless it is made into something fearful. Difference is a gift, for the differences come from a good God who loves us beyond our every imagining and who will give us, if we ask for it, the peace that Christ promises.

Remember all those appearances in the Gospels where Jesus is risen from the dead and his disciples are always huddled somewhere, afraid, up in Galilee, in a closed and locked room in Jerusalem; they're afraid, and the risen Lord comes to them. A Lord full of light, with a body transformed in ways we cannot imagine, truly his body, bearing the wounds of his passion, the gift of himself to us, his own self-sacrifice for our redemption, and yet, totally different, changed, transformed. The first word he always says is, "Do not be afraid. Peace be with you. Do not be afraid." That's what Jesus tells us tonight and every night as his people, "Do not be afraid." The gift of others is something to be accepted, to be loved, to be cherished. The gift of yourself in imitation of the Lord who sacrifices himself for us is something to be given always with joy and with peace, which is the sign of God's kingdom among us. "Do not be afraid." Thank you and God bless you. ∎

His Eminence Francis Cardinal George, OMI, *is the archbishop of Chicago, Illinois.*

# Pastoral Letter: Confronting Racism Today

BY MOST. REV. DONALD W. WUERL

SEPTEMBER 1999

To the Clergy, Religious and Laity of the Church of Pittsburgh:

The love and peace of God be with you.

As we celebrate the Great Jubilee—the beginning of another millennium of grace—we can use this time to reflect on how well we succeed in confronting one of the perduring blights of our society and culture—racism. As we commemorate two thousand years of God's Holy Spirit at work in the hearts of believers in our effort to manifest more clearly here on earth the beginnings of God's kingdom among us, it seems appropriate to look around us and into our own hearts to see how well we demonstrate in our attitudes and actions that "fellowship with the saints" that the Scriptures tell us knows no ethical, cultural, social or racial boundary.

To address racism, it seems to me that we need to recognize two things: that it exists in a variety of forms, some more subtle and others more obvious; and that there is something we can do about it even if we realize that what we say and the steps we take will not result in an immediate solution to a problem that spans generations. We must, however, confront this issue with the conviction that in some small way we can help to resolve it.

These reflections are meant to be a word of encouragement in our effort to work together against the evil of racism that has long diminished our society—and continues to do so—and as an opportunity to share a few examples of some efforts of which we can all be a part.

Where do we start? Before we turn our attention to some forms of action, we need to reaffirm that what we are doing is not only necessary but also good because it is willed by God.

The divisions we face today that are based on the color of one's skin or ethnic background are obviously not a part of God's plan. In the first chapter of the book of Genesis we read at the beginning of the story of creation, "God created man in his image, in the divine image he created him; male and female he created them" (Gn 1:27).

This is the starting point for our reflection. The human race is rooted in the loving, creative act of God who made us and called us to be a family—all God's children—made in God's image and likeness. There is no basis to assert that some are made more in the image of God than others.

In a clear and forceful passage from the *Pastoral Constitution on the Church in the Modern World*, the Second Vatican Council affirms

All women and men are endowed with a rational soul and are created in God's image; they have the same nature and origin and, being redeemed by Christ, they enjoy the same divine calling and destiny; there is here a basic equality between all men and it must be accorded ever greater recognition.

Undoubtedly not all people are alike as regards physical capacity and intellectual and moral powers. But any kind of social or cultural discrimination in basic personal rights on the grounds of sex, race, color, social conditions, language or religion, must be curbed and eradicated as incompatible with God's design. (no. 29)

In whatever form, intolerance of other people because of their race, religion or national origin is ultimately a denial of human dignity. No one is better than another person because of the color of their skin or the place of their birth. What makes us equal before God and what should make us equal before each other is that we are all sisters and brothers of one another, because we are all children of the same loving God who brought us into being.

Racism denies the basic equality and dignity of all people before God and one another. For this reason the United States bishops in their November 1979 pastoral letter on racism, *Brothers and Sisters to Us: U.S. Bishops' Pastoral Letter on Racism in Our Day*, clearly state: "Racism is a sin" (3). It is a sin because it "divides the human family, blots out the image of God among specific members of that family, and violates the fundamental human dignity of those called to be children of the same Father" (3). The letter goes on to remind us that "Racism is the sin that says some human beings are inherently superior and others essentially inferior because of race" (3).

We are called to recognize that racism continues to manifest itself in many ways. It can be personal, institutional or social. What should be a blessing—the diversity of our backgrounds, experiences and cultures—becomes a hindrance to unity and a heavy burden for some to bear. As we struggle to remove the attitudes that nurture racism and the actions that express it, we must show how the differences we find in skin color, national origin or cultural diversity are enriching. Differences mean diversity, not being better or worse. Equality among all men and women does not mean that they must all look, talk, think alike and act in an identical manner. Equality does not mean uniformity. Rather each person should be seen in his or her uniqueness as a reflection of the glory of God and a full, complete member of the human family.

Among Christians the call to unity is greater because it is rooted in grace and, therefore, racism merits even stronger condemnation. Every one who is baptized into Christ Jesus is called to new life in the Lord. Baptism unites us with the Risen Lord and through him with every person who sacramentally has died and risen to new life in Christ. This unity, sacramental and real, brings us together on a level above and beyond the purely physical. It carries that oneness we all share through the natural reality of creation to a higher level—the realm of grace.

In Christ we live in the same Spirit, we share the same new life and are members of one spiritual body. The members of the Church are called to be witnesses to the unity of God's family and, therefore, to be a living testimony to the inclusiveness that is a graced sign of our oneness.

The call to a unity that transcends ethnic ties and racial divisions is difficult for some people to accept. Too often we become comfortable in the enclave of our own familiar world and view others who are different from us, ethnically or because of the color of their skin, as a threat. Nonetheless, to be truly faithful to Christ we must respond to his teaching that we are one in him and, therefore, one with each other.

Intolerance and racism will not go away without a concerted effort on everyone's part. Regularly we must renew the commitment to drive it out of our hearts, our lives and our community. While we may devise all types of politically correct statements to proclaim racial equality, without a change in the basic attitude of the human heart we will never move to that level of oneness that accepts each other for who we are and the likeness we share as images of God.

In the bishops' statement on racism, *Brothers and Sisters to Us*, we read, "To the extent that racial bias affects our personal attitudes and judgments, to the extent that we allow another's race to influence our relationship and limit our openness, to the extent that we see yet close our hearts to our brothers and sisters in need—to that extent we are called to conversion and renewal in love and justice" (10).

Ongoing conversion is an essential part of the Christian vocation. We as a diocese have been involved in a conscious effort at spiritual renewal and revitalization both personal and institutional for a number of years. Our Holy Father in his Apostolic Letter *On the Coming of the Third Millennium* challenges us to place our daily efforts at ongoing conversion in the wider perspective of preparation for the coming celebration of the next millennium. This means that we not only recognize our need to draw every day closer to Christ and become more like him in our attitudes, but that we also do this systematically and even programmatically over a period of time. Our diocesan-wide effort at spiritual renewal also provides us a way to address racism.

In a personal way conversion means examining our attitudes and actions. This includes expressly rejecting racial stereotypes, slurs and jokes. We can also be an influence on co-workers, friends and family members by speaking out on the injustice of racism. Part of personal spiritual development includes a self-conscientious sensitivity to what we say and think. In a positive

manner we can interact with one another in a way which reflects the teaching of Jesus: "Treat others the way you would have them treat you" (Mt 7:12).

In an article entitled "Racism and Respect for Others," I reflected in the *Pittsburgh Catholic* on the "pro-active" stance that we must all adopt if we hope to overcome gradually but decisively the evil that is racism. "The Church must show its opposition to intolerance, whether religious, ethnic or racial, in her teaching and example. The inherent human dignity of every person is a theme that should be increasingly woven into the fabric of the Church's daily proclamation of the gospel. In our schools, religious education programs, adult education efforts and every opportunity available to us, we must continue to weave that thread into the fabric of the life of the Church. We must educate people with God's truth and motivate them with God's love."

Responding to Christ's love calls us to action. We need to move to the level of Christian solidarity. This term often spoken of by our Holy Father as a virtue touches the practical implications of what it means to recognize our unity with others. There is a sense in which solidarity is our commitment to oneness at work in the practical order.

In attempting to focus attention on racism and how we confront it, there have been a number of recent local initiatives. Christian Associates of Southwest Pennsylvania, an ecumenical organization involving twenty-two Christian faith communities in nine counties of southwest Pennsylvania, has encouraged efforts to confront racism among its member churches. The purpose of this initiative is to renew the Church's commitment to address racism, to heighten awareness that it continues to be a problem, and to take practical steps to address it. In conjunction with Carlow College, the Ecumenical Institute on Racism has been established to prepare people to confront racism at every level of our society.

Within the diocese we have made the fight against racism a priority in our programs over the past number of years and continue to address institutional and individual racism. In the past four years diocesan gatherings have been conducted under the direction of the diocesan Office for Black Catholic Ministries and the Department for Social Programs. Priests, religious and laity are being asked to examine their own life situations, their ministries, parishes and the institutions they direct in order to confront any vestige of racism.

The Sunday Eucharist offers a wealth of opportunities to reflect on this issue. The prayers of the faithful can promote social justice and urge the elimination of racism. Homilies can explain why true Christian faith is opposed to prejudice and racist behavior. Parish efforts at evangelization ought to reach out to people of every race, culture and nationality.

We need to be alert to and condemn racism wherever we meet it. In housing, citizens need to insist that the government enforce fair housing statues. In the workplace, recruitment, hiring and promotion policies need to reflect true opportunity. In public education,

we should support the teaching of tolerance and appreciation for each culture. In the public debate on the illnesses of our age, we ought also to insist on the place of religious faith. Without God and the sense of right and wrong that religious convictions engender, we will never adequately confront racism.

The elimination of racism may seem too great a task for any one of us or even for the whole Church. Yet we place our confidence in the Lord. In Christ, we are brothers and sisters to one another. With Christ, we have received the Spirit of justice, love and peace. Through Christ, we are called to envision the new city of God, not built by human hands, but by the love of God poured out in the Savior. On the journey to that "new heaven and new earth," we make our way with faith in God's grace, with hope in our own determination, and above all with love for each other as children of God. ■

Most Rev. Donald W. Wuerl *is the bishop of Pittsburgh, Pennsylvania, and the chairman of the bishops' Committee on Education.*

# Moving Beyond Racism:
# Learning *to* See *with the* Eyes *of* Christ

CATHOLIC BISHOPS OF ILLINOIS

Most Rev. Edwin M. Conway, Most Rev. Thomas G. Doran, His Eminence Francis Cardinal George, OMI,
Most Rev. Raymond E. Goedert, Most Rev. John R. Gorman, Most Rev. Wilton D. Gregory, Most Rev. Joseph L. Imesch,
Most Rev. Thad J. Jakubowski, Most Rev. Roger L. Kaffer, Most Rev. Gerald F. Kicanas, Most Rev. George J. Lucas,
Most Rev. John R. Manz, Most Rev. John J. Myers, Most Rev. Joseph N. Perry, Most Rev. Michael Wiwchar, CSSR

APRIL 2000

Brothers and Sisters in Christ,

God's wondrous generosity to the human family was made visible in Jesus' welcoming, during his earthly ministry, all that sought the light of truth. Jesus, even before his resurrection, entered the lives of Samaritans, Pharisees, Roman occupiers, tax collectors, sinners, the powerful and very ordinary people. Through love and the healing that comes from love, he redefined their relationship to his Father and to one another by welcoming them to himself.

In the Gospels, Jesus speaks with authority (Mk 1:27). This authority comes from his being anointed with divine Sonship; this authority comes clear in Jesus' speaking divine truth in human words. When he ascended into heaven, Jesus imparted that same authority to the apostles and their successors in the Church, the bishops, telling them to go forth and teach all nations (Mt 28:18-20). Conscious of that charge, bishops teach what the faith tells us is true and, in the light of faith, address those contemporary moral and social issues, which affect the basic human dignity Christ restored. We, with all men and women of faith, look at the world with eyes of Christ.

Some years back, concerned Catholics actively involved in ministry in the African American community asked the bishops of the Ecclesiastical Province of Chicago (the state of Illinois) to speak to the sin of racism in our society. It disturbed us to hear again reports that people of color were sometimes made to feel unwelcome, even in Catholic parishes. In this letter, we, the Catholic Bishops of Illinois, desire to proclaim the Gospel of Jesus Christ by speaking to a grave personal and social evil: the sin of racism.

We begin with three facts. First, racism exists here; it is part of the American landscape. Second, racism is completely contrary to the Gospel of Jesus Christ. Third, all baptized Catholics have a moral obligation to work toward the elimination of racism.

What is meant by racism? Racism is a personal sin and social disorder rooted in the belief that one race is superior to another. It involves not only prejudice but also the use of religious, social, political, economic or historical power to keep one race privileged.

Racism exists, in some form, among all peoples; in any form it is intolerable and unacceptable. This document focuses on racism against African Americans, because the centuries-old Black-White dynamic in this country seems to bear deeper dimensions of prejudice than any other form of racism. Addressing the complexity of the Black-White division, however, will help us address all forms of ethnic and racial injustice, no matter where or how it manifests itself.

Racism is personal, institutional, cultural and internal. Personal racism shows itself in an attitude or action taken by an individual to diminish the God-given dignity or rights of another because of race. An example of personal racism in action is the verbal or mental demeaning of African Americans simply because of their color.

Institutional racism allows racist attitudes or practices to shape the structures of an organization. Institutional racism reveals itself, for example, when promotions are manipulated so that African Americans are not fairly considered for certain positions.

Cultural racism is the extension of this sinful attitude to the mores, standards, customs, language and group life of a whole society. One culture's ways of thinking and behaving are then regarded as the only way to live. All other social patterns are dismissed as deviations or dangers.

Internalized racism is a sense of inferiority or lack of self-esteem because one belongs to a particular race. When an African American child grows up believing that to be Black is inferior, he or she is a victim of internalized racism.

The teaching of the U.S. bishops on racism has been forthright and clear:

> Racism is a sin: a sin that divides the human family, blots out the image of God among specific members of that family and violates the fundamental human dignity of those called to be children of the same Father. (*Brothers and Sisters to Us: U.S. Bishops' Pastoral Letter on Racism in Our Day*; Washington, D.C., 1979, 3)

Racism distorts the word of God in both the Old and New Testaments (Gn 1:26; Gal 3:27-29). The Holy Scriptures insist that every person is formed in the image and likeness of God and that all are one in Christ Jesus. Rather than being built on the firm foundation of divine truth, racism is built on the shifting sands of personal insecurity, self-deception and the idolatry of racial superiority.

Since the publication of *Brothers and Sisters to Us* twenty years ago, some progress has been made in the struggle to overcome the sin of racism. African Americans have been elected to public office and risen to leadership positions, ordained, religious and lay, in the Church and in businesses. The number of African American youth who are attending college is steadily increasing, and the gap between the median income of African Americans and other Americans is slowly shrinking. There are real changes in the growth of a sense of fairness and in levels of attainment by African Americans in the general society.

These and other signs of change in attitudes and behavior have lulled some into thinking that the battle against racism is almost won. That is not the case. Events continue to remind us that racism thrives. Look at the brutal and racially motivated death by dragging last year of an African American in Texas. Consider the more recent aggravated sexual assault on a Haitian prisoner by members of the Brooklyn Police force. Search the websites filled with racially charged hate speech on the Internet. All this is so blatantly racist that it can shock and therefore move us to ask again how to confront more effectively the sin of racism.

Any confrontation cannot ignore the more subtle forms of racist actions: realtors who manipulate sales and steer clients along racial lines; law enforcement officers who routinely profile Black drivers for police checks; department store detectives who automatically follow young Black males; parents who drive past an excellent school to register their children at another because a substantial number of the students in the first school are African American; groups who deliberately avoid contact with racially diverse or culturally different communities.

Almost unconsciously, the sin of racism can touch and stain every aspect of life, from friendships to work relationships, from where people recreate to what programs they watch on television. Given the long history of racism in our country, how can anyone hope to abolish at last this moral plague?

In his apostolic letter, *Tertio Millennio Adveniente (On the Coming of the Third Millennium)*, Pope John Paul II invites us to "broaden our horizons" and so "see things from the perspective of Christ." This vision gives hope. At the beginning of the third millennium, all have an opportunity to be renewed in the Father's everlasting love. We have an opportunity to see the world and its peoples through the eyes of Christ. We are given the chance to open ourselves to the Spirit. The new millennium is a time for us to say with one voice: "We will not live with the sin of racism any longer. Racism must end now." But to make that declaration ring true, we must turn our lives over to the Divine Redeemer who alone can save and transform us. Through Christ's gracious power, we can come to a conversion of heart, commit ourselves to change and live in hope.

## CONVERSION OF HEART

Conversion is the response to God's self-revelation as love. Infinite love calls us to a transformation of mind and heart, a turning away from sin and an embrace of God's way for us. Once converted, our eyes are opened; we see what is truly important. We become, with God's grace, free, responsible and holy.

Conversion changes individuals, and individuals change society. Overcoming the sin of racism begins by opening ourselves to God's Spirit, who draws all to holiness. The Spirit makes each of us a member of the Body of Christ, and this spiritual relationship is the source of our hope for personal and social change. In Christ, we recognize racism as a division contrary to his will for his people, a division the Spirit will heal.

## COMMITMENT TO CHANGE

Relying on God's grace, seeing with Christ's eyes, living in the Holy Spirit, what should we do to dismantle racism? Concrete, visible steps will vary from diocese to diocese, from community to community. Here are some actions, some small and some larger, which all can take:

—Pray for an end to racism.

—Take a personal inventory of your own heart and discover what has to change.

—Seek opportunities to know and learn from a person of a different race.

—Identify racist behavior in our community, speak with others and make plans to oppose it.

—Refuse to use biased language and to tell jokes tinged with racist attitudes.

—Teach children to move beyond mere toleration and to accept open-heartedly people of all races.

—Avoid investing in companies which support or practice racist policies and tell the company why you are withdrawing your money.
—Elect public officials who work for racial justice.

—Join community groups, which nurture relationships of trust among peoples of different races and ethnic groups.

—Be critical of how violent crime is focused on and reported; ask media people to publicize good people and actions in every racial group.

—Have your parish sponsor workshops which both present racism in all its complexity and evaluate it morally.

—Help organize ecumenical prayer services inclusive of different racial and ethnic groups.

—Speak and live the truth that you acquire by seeing with the eyes of Christ.

## LIVING WITH HOPE

The theological virtue of hope is not the same as wishing for the impossible. Christian hope stirs up in us the desire that God's kingdom [will] come, here and in eternity. We place our trust in the promises of Christ and rely on his grace rather than on our own strength.

It would be naive to think that racism will disappear overnight; it is too deeply embedded in the American experience. But change will come if we remain constant and never lose sight of the goal. The goal is visible when we see with the eyes of Christ, for our hope of ultimate victory is the Lord who desires that we be one in him.

As the bishops of the Catholic Church in Illinois, we commit ourselves to speak the truth about racism. We commit ourselves to encouraging dialogue between African Americans and other Americans. We commit ourselves to model in our dioceses a future without racism. Confident in the Lord, we invite all Catholics in Illinois, and all men and women of good will, to join us in the struggle against racism so that, one day, we may all be free.

The springtime for the Gospel which Pope John Paul II prays will mark the new millennium [and] will be a time free of the sin of racism. The time is now; let the place be our dioceses and our state. ■

Most Rev. Edwin M. Conway *is an auxiliary bishop of Chicago, Illinois;* Most Rev. Thomas G. Doran *is the bishop of Rockford, Illinois;* His Eminence Francis Cardinal George, OMI, *is the archbishop of Chicago, Illinois;* Most Rev. Raymond E. Goedert *is an auxiliary bishop of Chicago, Illinois;* Most Rev. John R. Gorman *is an auxiliary bishop of Chicago, Illinois;* Most Rev. Wilton D. Gregory *is bishop of Belleville, Illinois;* Most Rev. Joseph L. Imesch *is bishop of Joliet, Illinois;* Most Rev. Thad J. Jakubowski *is an auxiliary bishop of Chicago, Illinois;* Most Rev. Roger L. Kaffer *is an auxiliary bishop of Joliet, Illinois;* Most Rev. Gerald F. Kicanas *is an auxiliary bishop of Chicago, Illinois, and chairman of the Committee on the Diaconate;* Most Rev. George J. Lucas *is the bishop of Springfield, Illinois;* Most Rev. John R. Manz *is an auxiliary bishop of Chicago, Illinois;* Most Rev. John J. Myers *is bishop of Peoria, Illinois;* Most Rev. Joseph N. Perry *is an auxiliary bishop of Chicago, Illinois;* and Most Rev. Michael Wiwchar, CSSR, *is bishop of St. Nicholas in Chicago for Ukrainians.*

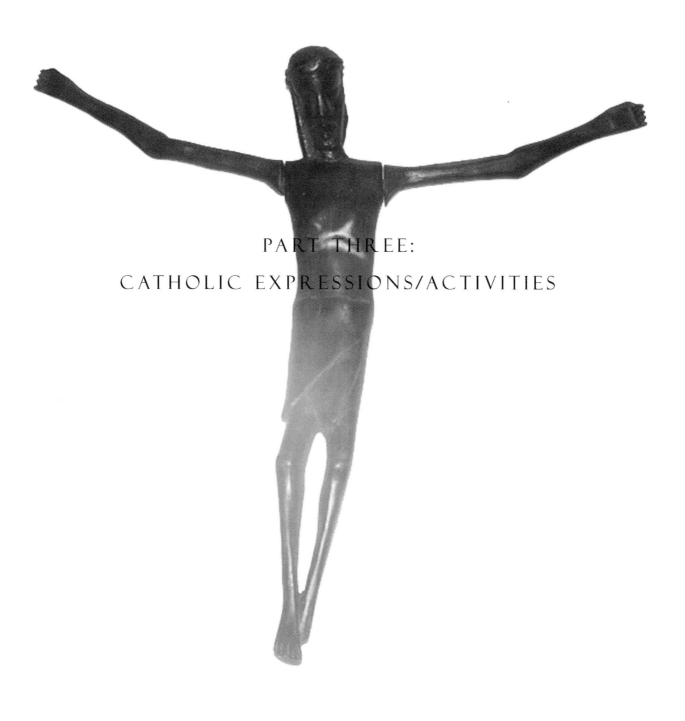

PART THREE:

CATHOLIC EXPRESSIONS/ACTIVITIES

# Homily: Black History Month, St. Patrick's Cathedral, New York

## BY MOST REV. MOSES B. ANDERSON, SSE

FEBRUARY 1998

My most esteemed Brother and Father of the Archdiocese of New York, John Cardinal O'Connor; my brother, Bishop Sheridan; Monsignors; Priests; Deacons; Religious; and my Brothers and Sisters in the Body of Christ, we, from every country, in the islands, North and South America, and Africans in Europe are the African diaspora. God has dispersed us here to the United States.

We have come into this House to glorify, to sanctify, and to praise the person of Christ in our brothers and sisters of the African diaspora. This is not the time for us to imitate Isaiah and cry "Woe is me, for I am a man of unclean lips living among a people of unclean lips." We must be like the Isaiah who saw the glory of God, who heard the angelic hosts, the seraphim who cried out "Holy, Holy, Holy is the Lord of Hosts. All the earth is filled with his glory." We, too, are part of God's glory. Today, all of us must cry out "The Lord has touched us, just as he touched Isaiah." We too have been made clean. All of us can say "we never shall forget that day when Jesus washed our sins away." Yes, He took our feet out of the miry clay and sat all of us at the right hand of the Father. We know the Lord has laid his hands on us! Now, we have the "Blessed Assurance that Jesus is ours!" We have Paul who tells

us, "God in diverse and sundry ways has spoken to *our* ancestors and in the end times he has spoken to us through His Son."

We shall not be like Peter who said, "Leave me Lord, for I am a sinful man." We shall be like the Peter when so many left Jesus and walked with him no more. We shall be like the Peter when Jesus asked him and the Apostles "are you too going to leave me?" We are going to be like the Peter who said, "Lord to whom shall we go. You have the words of eternal life." We must be like Peter and his friends who had fished all night long in their favorite fishing holes and had caught nothing. We imitate them who had faith in the Jesus who made the heavens and the earth, who made the lands and the seas. Certainly He knew the fishing hole where the fish would be biting or ready to be netted.

Our faith must be like that of the Apostle Paul, the Rodney Dangerfield of the Apostles. He too did not get any respect. His faith in who he was, was always unshakable. Christ recognized in him that Paul was a person who had a solid foundation in his personality. He was a citizen of Rome but his personality had many dimensions. He was a Pharisee, a Rabbi, he was schooled in Jewish and Hellenistic thought. He was the universal man of his time. Paul also had the humility to give God the credit for making him to be all the things he was. He appreciated his gifts from God. Paul, like a faithful servant always allowed the glory of God to increase in him through all he was.

We have come here today to celebrate God's gifts to the African diasporas. We whose ancestors worshiped the most high God in Africa and venerated His mes-

sengers have come to know Him by the name of Father and his messengers whom we now know as angels and archangels. We have come to know him as Son, and we have come to know him as Holy Spirit. The Most High God, we have heard him speaking to you and to me, to us in these words, "You are my beloved sons and daughters in whom I take my delight." He gave us a special awareness of Him as He dwells in the place of the ancestors and also the ability to recognize His presence in our daily lives here on earth. He gave us an innate awareness of His holiness in all that He has created and how He has made us caretakers and co-creators with Him. He was always loved and we were always faithful to Him. He gave us a special sense of morality. He allows us to see God

who is invisible made visible through the visible gifts He has given us. His greatest gift is Jesus, His Son, the Messiah. Our goodness to him was always measured by our love and goodness to each other "because we go from the invisible through the visible." He gave us a sense of being a family. We understand that we are also related to other families. We have an awareness that all families have Him as the Father of all.

Today we celebrate the New Pentecost. We now hear God speaking to us, the African diasporas, in *our* languages, in *our* cultures, in all that belongs to us. We call this *Soul*. That is why we refer to each other as *soul brothers* and *soul sisters*. W. E. B. Dubois and, later, makers of the Harlem Renaissance used this term to describe what is the defining element of our life. It is the essence of our being. It is a given which is shared and needs only to be focused on to appreciate its richness. If we, all of us, do not celebrate our gifts from God, while we are looking somewhere else, "someone will walk off with all our stuff." It is the sustaining force which is the cause of our faith and hope and our love. It gives us a sense that all is sacred. It removes all dichotomies. It fashions us to experience the sacred and the profane as one reality with diverse dimensions. It also simultaneously focuses our awareness on the relatedness of what is priestly and what is prophetic. This Harlem Renaissance was not only valuable in defining the African diaspora among the English-speaking communities in the New World. It also found expression in the African diaspora in France and French-speaking lands of the New World. There it was not called *Soul*, but *negritude*. Leopold Senghor and others reappropriated to themselves what was always theirs before the diasporas.

Another people taken into Babylon were taunted by their captors and it is recorded "on the willows there, they hanged up their lyres for their captors required of them song, saying sing us one of those songs of Zion." Their reply was, "How can we sing a song to the Lord in a foreign land?"

We, the African diaspora, who were brought here or who have freely come here have made no statement like that. We have always sung songs, we have played our music, even having to learn to play other musical instruments because our own were taken away. We have danced and made ourselves and others happy. We have been mistreated, abused, demeaned, and killed. Through all of this we built, produced, and improvised with meager resources for ourselves while our lives have enriched us and others. Out of this crucible we have found our real selves.

We stand in the position to understand what our Africans diasporas have always understood. We have always known that we too are creatures of the Most High God. Through our coming to full communion in the Christian faith and the Roman Catholic Church, we have found other ways of expressing the basic notion of family and extended family. We are the Church, God's family, the Body of Christ. We have come to know that God is Triune. The Most High God is now the Father, and the Son, and the Holy Spirit. We too are now aware of our particular being, our diversity, as a gift of the diversity of the Blessed Trinity, Godness or goodness going outside of itself to make humankind in the likeness of the Trinity that is at the same time one and diverse. It is absolutely necessary for all of us of the African diasporas to see how Our Father can let us see our unique diversity and unity. Our ancestors came from many places in Africa. This creates a marvelous diversity and unity. They came from this one continent of Africa. Let all know and affirm this fact, that we are one and diverse. It does not matter when and where they landed—we are all from Mother Africa. This allows us to appreciate our relation to our other mother, Holy Mother, the Roman Catholic Church.

Let all of us go forth from this place with a renewed pledge to be the light of the world so that we may evangelize by showing the Trinitarian revelation of unity and diversity to the world. By our Baptism we have been given the dignity of being the one Christ, of being the one Messiah, who brings us all into the unity and diversity of the Trinitarian life. This allows us all to be the one Catholic Church, which possesses this marvelous relationship among the diversities making them all of us truly one. *We must recognize* our unity and diversity. *We must minimize* our desires to be closed to what the Church really is. *We must optimize* our potentials to be the diverse person of Christ, the Catholic Church. *We must not compromise* our dignity as the African diasporas in the United States. *We must not criticize* each other so that we are all impoverished. *We must not ostracize* those who are diverse yet one with us.

> *Let us accentuate* the positiveness in our unity and diversity in soul and negritude and in the Catholicity and unity of our Church.

> *Let us reappropriate* our soul and negritude. *Let us eliminate* all that is not truly Christ in our lives.

> *Let us cultivate and appreciate* what God has made us all to be.

> *Let us captivate* our young people with our pride in our African diasporas.

> *Let us eliminate* all that does not truly fulfill us.

*Oh, let the Son of God enfold us.* Let us resolve to captivate all with our Dignity, that we will illuminate all with our gifts. That we will integrate the African diasporas. That we will celebrate every day God's gift to the total African diaspora.

*Oh, let the Son of God enfold us.* We can do this, through our arts, music, drama, all of our institutions, our schools, neighborhoods, our colleges, universities, and our Catholic Church. There is only one person who can help us to accomplish this. It is Jesus the Messiah and so let us celebrate our unity and diversity, the unity and diversity of the African diasporas, and our unity and diversity in the Roman Catholic Church. ■

*Let us all sing . . .*

*Oh, let the Son of God enfold you with His Spirit and*
*    His love.*
*Let Him fill your heart and satisfy your soul.*
*Oh, let him have the things that hold you, and His spirit*
*    like a dove will descend upon your life and make*
*    you whole.*

*Chorus:*

*Jesus, oh Jesus, come and fill your lambs.*
*Jesus, oh Jesus, come and fill your lambs.*

*Oh, come and sing this song with gladness as your*
*    hearts are filled with joy.*
*Lift your hands in sweet surrender to His name.*

*Oh, give him all your tears and sadness.*
*Give Him all your years of pain and you'll enter into*
*    life in Jesus' name.*

*Chorus . . .*

Most Rev. Moses B. Anderson, SSE, *is an auxiliary*
*bishop of Detroit, Michigan.*

## BLACK BISHOP URGES AFRICANS IN "DIASPORA" TO REMAIN UNITED

BY TRACY EARLY, CATHOLIC NEWS SERVICE • FEBRUARY 1998

NEW YORK (CNS)—An African American bishop preaching at a Mass celebrated in observance of Black History Month called on members of "the African diaspora" in America to maintain their unity and "celebrate God's gifts."

American Blacks came "from many places in Africa," but "we are one," said Auxiliary Bishop Moses B. Anderson, SSE, of Detroit. "It doesn't matter when or where we landed."

Bishop Anderson was the homilist for a Mass celebrated February 8 by Cardinal John J. O'Connor at St. Patrick's Cathedral in New York. During the Mass, Cardinal O'Connor presented the annual award of the archdiocesan office of Black Ministry to Leon C. Roberts, a prominent Black composer currently based in New York.

The liturgy began with a processional hymn marked by a strong Gospel beat and such loud exuberance that Cardinal O'Connor was moved to joke, "Why are we so gloomy?" Later musical elements of the liturgy included selections from three Masses composed by Roberts, the honoree, as well as compositions by other African Americans. Roberts, who produces and records with Oregon Catholic Press, was a co-founder of Rejoice, a conference on Black Catholic liturgy held for a number of years. He is now artist-in-residence at the Concord Baptist Church of Christ, a large [historically African American] church in Brooklyn, and

director of the Gospel choir at the interdenominational Union Theological Seminary in Manhattan.

The Mass was one of a number of events in New York and across the nation focused on February as Black History Month. The observance was begun in 1926 by the pioneering Black historian, Carter G. Woodson. Among other events was the tenth annual National Day of Prayer for the African American Family February 1.

Franciscan Fr. James E. Goode, a New York priest who initiated the prayer day and is currently president of the National Black Clergy Caucus, told Catholic News Service that it was observed in fifty to sixty dioceses this year. He said thirty thousand brochures for the event were distributed. Fr. Goode said the day of prayer for the African American family is a way to reach out and let Blacks know the Catholic Church is open to them. Many Blacks still do not realize they are welcome in Catholic churches, he said.

At the conclusion of the Mass, Cardinal O'Connor reported briefly on his trip to participate in Pope John Paul II's visit to Cuba. He said the African diaspora included a community descended from a million Blacks brought to Cuba, and they welcomed the pope enthusiastically. After the pope's final mass in Havana, the cardinal reported, some Cubans were saying, "Today the revolution ended."

# Illinois Diocese Participates *in* City's Racial Dialogue

BY DIANE SCHLINDWEIN, CATHOLIC NEWS SERVICE

MARCH 1998

Dominican Sister Mary Clare Fichtner says promoting peace and equality among the races is her life's work. That's why she jumped at the chance to act as a facilitator in the upcoming Springfield Study Circles for Racial Harmony.

The study circles, initiated by the Community Relations Commission of the city of Springfield and Mayor Karen Hasara, are to begin April 12 and meet weekly for six weeks. The groups will consist of ten to twelve individuals from diverse backgrounds and will be hosted in various locations around Springfield.

Springfield Bishop Daniel L. Ryan said he wanted to encourage Catholics to consider being part of the study circles. The Diocese of Springfield, along with the five other Catholic dioceses in Illinois, is in the midst of a multi-year process to address the sin of racism.

Each study circle session will focus on one aspect of diversity and racial harmony. The topics are suggested by *The Busy Citizen's Discussion Guide on Racism and Race Relations*, a study guide produced by the nationally recognized Study Circle Resource Center in Connecticut. Organizers say the study circles will not focus on who is right or wrong but on opening dialogue in a non-abrasive, safe manner.

Facilitators from the Springfield Diocese, including Sr. Fichtner and St. Patrick's parishioner Loraleen Jordan, have been in training for several weeks.

"This certainly fits well with my interest in fighting racism," said Sr. Fichtner, who belongs to the Springfield Diocesan Task Force for Racial Justice. "And I feel becoming a facilitator for the study circles is a wonderful opportunity to talk not only with religious groups, but with the general public as well," she told the *Catholic Times*, Springfield's diocesan newspaper.

Jordan said the study circles will be a positive way to combat the negative experiences she has come across as a young Black woman and as a Black Catholic in Springfield and other parts of the country.

"When I was in glee club in high school," she said, "we had a cast party at my house. Some of the parents wouldn't let the girls come to it because I live on the east side and the party was held after dark."

Jordan said she sometimes feels uncomfortable even at Mass. "Once, when I was in the South, I sat down at a church before Mass to say my prayers. Several people came up to me to tell me the Black church was down the street.

"I asked them if it was a Catholic church and they said it was a Baptist church. I explained that I was a Catholic," she added. "During the whole Mass I felt like I had to say all the prayers from memory, just to prove that I was really a Catholic."

Unfortunately, she said, that same kind of prejudice extends to some Springfield parishes. "I have attended Mass in other parishes [besides St. Patrick's] where people wouldn't shake my hand at the sign of peace; they wouldn't even smile at me."

Sr. Fichtner believes that racial discrimination has increased over the past thirty years and she is determined to find a way to overcome the problems. "I've found, just being a facilitator, that some of the things people say are biased," she said. "However, sometimes you don't realize you are being prejudiced until you really think about what you are saying."

Jordan said although she is too young to have lived through the civil rights movement of the late 1960s, "Springfield has a long history of racial problems. Racism now has ways to disguise itself." In spite of past pains, however, Jordan said she prefers to focus on what can be done now to change things for the better.

"This will be a great learning experience," she said. "I'm happy that the Springfield community now has a way to heal some of the hurts." ■

# Letter: Beyond *the* Boundaries

## BY MOST REV. P. FRANCIS MURPHY

SEPTEMBER 1998

[Following is] a recent article from *The Catholic Review* concerning our efforts on the regionalism project, now called *Beyond the Boundaries*. A group of urban and suburban pastors developed with me this small faith group approach to educating Catholics throughout the Baltimore Metropolitan Region regarding the need for the City of Baltimore and its suburbs to cooperate in addressing issues such as race, housing, economic development and resource sharing. Since that time we have made very significant progress in terms of our pilot programs in parishes, as well as with our symposiums. We are prepared to invite all parishes in Baltimore City, as well as in Anne Arundel, Baltimore, Carroll, Harford and Howard counties to participate. At some point, the religious judicatories should have an agenda to share with the political leaders.

### HEALING THE WOUNDS OF "WHITE FLIGHT": NEW PROGRAM SEEKS CITY-COUNTY DIALOGUE OF UNDERSTANDING

**By Sharon Crews Hare,**
*The Catholic Review*

A seventy-four-year-old woman returning to the city parish where she had raised her family wondered aloud why it was no longer the vibrant congregation that she had known and loved for twenty years. "There's no one left that I know," she said, glancing around the half-empty church as the noon Mass began and remembering the days when both the church and the lower chapel were packed with families.

Like many others, she moved from the city neighborhood of rowhomes and tree-lined streets during the late 1970s after her husband was robbed at gunpoint by two Black men. The episode confirmed the fears that had been gnawing in them since the neighborhood began "changing."

They were part of the decades-long "White flight" that has altered the face of Baltimore City, the exodus that followed as African Americans gradually moved into White neighborhoods.

"White flight" snowballed, leading to suburban sprawl as city residents, many of them Catholic, moved to the suburbs and beyond, abandoning those city parishes that once formed the core of their faith lives and to which they, their parents and grandparents, had held a loyal, parochial attachment for generations.

While some families moved for reasons that were not based on racial fears, the "White flight" was for the most part just what the term implied, an escape from what many Whites saw as an invasion of their neighborhoods by Black people they believed brought with them crime, violence, fear and a dramatic lowering of property values.

That exodus, its related issues and the resulting problems are at the core of a new project being implemented this fall within the Archdiocese of Baltimore.

Called *Beyond the Boundaries: New Challenges of Faith in Metropolitan Baltimore*, two programs have been developed to encourage Catholics throughout the immediate metropolitan area to look at social and economic issues from both a regional and faith perspective.

The first, designed to operate within a parish setting, encourages lay parishioners in small "renew-like" discussion groups to meet for a six-week period. Under the guidance of a facilitator, the group will become familiar with various issues of race, housing and economic development and the way those issues have caused division between the city and its surrounding counties. As they pray and reflect on the newly acquired knowledge, the group can move on to identify ways to actively respond.

A similar program has been designed to reach out to pastoral, institutional and educational leaders through a one-day symposium. In a more condensed version of the six-week program, the leaders will become familiar with the same issues.

The program was initiated more than two years ago under the leadership of Baltimore's previous urban vicar and auxiliary, Bishop John H. Ricard [now head of the Pensacola-Tallahassee Diocese in Florida] along with a committee of suburban and urban pastors. It is now being spearheaded by Bishop P. Francis Murphy. [At the time of the printing of this book—January 2001—the program was being run by Baltimore Auxiliary Bishop Gordon D. Bennett.]

It was conceived, explained Bishop Murphy, as a way to "reflect and discern what our responsibilities are" as pastors and people of the Church to the "complex moral issues of isolating the City of Baltimore from the metropolitan counties of Baltimore."

To Fr. Donald A. Sterling, pastor of New All Saints Church in Baltimore, "White flight" represented a fear of the unknown, and he believes many White Catholics still have it. And, he says, the fear has contributed largely to the problems faced by parishes in the inner city. It is time, he insisted, to address the problems of divisions between city and suburban communities.

"Our behavior patterns are all rooted in the negative and we're dysfunctional," said Fr. Sterling. "We can't continue to run away from one another. We have to internalize the Gospel we proclaim."

Over the past year *Beyond the Boundaries* has been fine-tuned and the materials have been tested as a pilot program in several parishes. One is the Shrine of the Sacred Heart in Mount Washington where Fr. Richard E. Cramblitt, a project team member, is pastor.

Although subjects like segregation, ghetto housing and escalating crime and vandalism are sensitive, the small group discussions were "animated and frankly honest," explained Fr. Cramblitt, primarily because they were within the "safe atmosphere of the church."

Catholics need to talk about problems rooted in racism, he said, because leaving them behind in the city doesn't mean they go away. "We cannot run," said Fr. Cramblitt. "We cannot hide. We have to deal with the problems."

Anne Haley, a pilot group facilitator at Sacred Heart, has only lived in Baltimore for a few years, but sees it as a very alive city despite the serious issues it faces. This program, she said, is an excellent way to force people to discuss subjects they don't really like to talk about. "It makes us step up to the issues," said Mrs. Haley, "and that makes us uncomfortable." Because the issues are sensitive, she emphasized the need for facilitators to be adequately trained. "Conversations can get testy and trigger emotions that are rooted in childhood," she explained.

Another pilot group at St. Andrew by the bay in Annapolis voiced similar concerns. Without well-trained facilitators, one of the team members, Andy Wagner, sees the potential for "intense and heated arguments," as participants bring potentially long-buried prejudices to the surface.

The team at St. Andrew also included Cecilia Walsh, a parishioner at its sister parish in Baltimore, St. Martin. She sees the program as a way to revitalize the inner city and send a wake-up call to the Church that much needs to be done.

While her reaction to the program is positive, she too is worried about the competence of facilitators since training is offered only as an option. "To me, that says it's not necessary," she said. "They has to be an essential part of the program. I don't think a person can come into this without some kind of background. They have to be cognizant of the whole picture."

Fr. Sterling, who presents a portion of the symposium, said he had some of those same concerns, specifically because "understanding the statistics takes development, training and political astuteness. It can be a volatile situation and one of the challenges we face."

As a pastor in an African American community, however, he is hopeful that the *Beyond the Boundaries* will make a difference. Not only is his community being hurt by the exodus of White people, "but in some cases our own peers are running away from us. It's a vicious cycle that has to be stopped."

The pilot portion of the program has accomplished just what the original committee had hoped. The feedback concerning facilitator training, Bishop Murphy said, will enable the committee to continue to improve both the format and process of the program.

During the summer, brochures explaining the small group discussion program "Who Is Welcome at the Table" were mailed to pastors along with information about how to obtain materials. In addition, parish leaders have been invited to attend one of the nine symposia that have been scheduled to begin in September. Their goal is to reach three thousand parishioners and 750 leaders over the next year.

"I am very conscious," said Bishop Murphy, "of the demands that are constantly placed upon pastors, parish staff and the parish community. I see this initiative as an invitation to those people who have the opportunity and the time to engage their faith and their commitment to social justice."

The success of the pilot program at Sacred Heart is just one example of what can be done by faith communities attempting to bridge the gap some thirty years after the mass exodus began. Fr. Cramblitt explained that many of the 150 participants have attended brainstorming sessions to help them identify suitable responses to the issues. They are presently sorting through those ideas to prioritize them.

"That's a unique perspective," he explained, "because as children of God, we are united by faith with the world in which we live. This is not some foreign mission, but right here in our own backyard. No other program has enabled people to unite their faith with the immediate world in which we live. When word about this gets around, I think people will be using it." ■

Most Rev. P. Francis Murphy *is a former auxiliary bishop of Baltimore, Maryland.*

# Fountain *of* Mercy, Wellspring *of* Grace: The Church Between *the* Rivers Looks *to the* Millennium *and* Beyond

BY MOST REV. J. TERRY STEIB, SVD

JANUARY 1999

## INTRODUCTION: THE CALL OF TERTIO MILLENNIO ADVENIENTE

The turning of the year 2000 will be a milestone in the history of our Roman Catholic faith, as well as in the history of the human family. In preparation for this milestone, our Holy Father, Pope John Paul II, has called the Church to consider several important elements of its tradition as we mark the end of the twentieth century and enter the third millennium.

Our Holy Father has asked us to reflect on how we have made the love of Christ concrete in the world—in particular to those who are poor, who have suffered injustice, or who have never heard the Gospel. The Holy Father invites us to reflect on our lives in light of the Gospel and to explore how we have lived our Catholic faith. He urges us to renew our life as church at every level—in the home, in the parish and diocese, and in our witness to the wider community.

What, then, will be our response as members of the Catholic Diocese of Memphis in Tennessee? What particular elements of the Holy Father's message apply specifically to this Catholic community of Western Tennessee? How will we apply the challenges which speak directly to this Church located "between the rivers"?

The intent of this pastoral reflection is to help us make a fitting response to the Holy Father's exhortation by examining the meaning of the Jubilee from its scriptural roots to the present day, by proposing some specific areas of reflection and renewal, and by offering a vision of renewal consistent with our Catholic tradition.

## I. THE MEANING OF JUBILEE

1. In the Old Testament, we find the people of Israel striving to establish a way of life rooted in the justice of God. Led from slavery in Egypt to the promised land, they were of simple origin and humble resources. At first, as they settled in this new land "flowing with milk and honey," they were careful to see that everyone got an equal portion. Even their kings did not take more land than they needed or hoard its riches for themselves (cf. 2 Sm 16:20).

2. This harmonious beginning represented a common life reflective of God's own justice, but it did not last. People gave in to greed. They began to accumulate wealth and land. They even took slaves for debt. Before long,

they found themselves at odds with the God who delivered them from the very injustices they now perpetrated against the lowly of their land. To remedy this, the tradition of a sabbatical year arose. This was a special time during which all debts were forgiven; the land lay fallow; property was returned to the original owners; and slaves were freed (cf. Neh 5:1-5).

3. Just as the Sabbath happened every seven days, so a sabbatical year happened every seven years. Similar in meaning to the Sabbath day, the sabbatical year was given over to the work of God, especially to restoring God's original justice by the relaxation or remission of debt. During the sabbatical year, the people dedicated themselves to renewing their covenant with God and observing God's commands.

4. If the seventh day and the seventh year were significant for remembering God's justice and mercy, all the more crucial would be a sabbatical at the end of sabbaticals—that is to say, the year beyond seven times seven years—the fiftieth year (Lv 25:8-14). This fiftieth or jubilee year anticipated a future age when the world would be brought to perfection. There would be great celebration. The people were to strive, as far as possible, to restore the justice of God by doing even more earnestly all that was ordinarily done in a sabbatical year. However, the perfect reign of justice was never fully realized. So, with each jubilee year came an awareness of the need for a final era when God would make all things new and inaugurate a glorious and lasting period of divine prosperity. This would happen with the coming of a great messiah or king.

5. Our Holy Father in his encyclical *On the Third Millennium* reminds us that Jesus was born of this Hebrew people and that His coming fulfilled the promise of the messiah-king (cf. *Tertio Millennio Adveniente* [TMA], no. 6.1). Whatever else the year 2000 commemorates, we know that it originates first and foremost in the birth of a little child to humble parents in Bethlehem and that this child's birth had changed the world. Jesus is the redeemer long hoped

for by the Chosen People. Jesus is the prophet beyond all others who taught about the Father with authority never known before. Jesus is the king who came to establish the kingdom of justice and mercy. Jesus is the priest who offered His own life on the altar of the cross as the one and eternal sacrifice which redeemed the world.

6. Jesus ushered in God's final era of salvation history, the age beyond all other jubilees, when the fullness of God's presence now dwelt among the human family "as one like ourselves in all things but sin." In Christ, the day of salvation, "the fullness of time," had come (cf. TMA, no. 10.2). The Holy Father reminds us that, "All Jubilees point to this 'time' and refer to the Messianic mission of Christ, who came as the one 'anointed' by the Holy Spirit, the one 'sent by the Father'" (cf. TMA, no. 11.2).

7. The Holy Father continues: "It is he [Jesus] who proclaims the good news to the poor. It is he who brings liberty to those deprived of it, who frees the oppressed and gives back sight to the blind (cf. Mt 11:4-5; Lk 7:22). In this way he ushers in 'a year of the Lord's favour,' which he proclaims not only with his words but above all by his actions. The Jubilee, 'a year of the Lord's favour,' characterizes all the activity of Jesus. It is not merely the recurrence of an anniversary in time" (cf. TMA, no. 11.2).

8. And the Holy Father concludes: "The words and deeds of Jesus thus represent the fulfillment of the whole tradition of Jubilees in the Old Testament" (cf. TMA, no. 12).

9. Jesus knew well, however, that this kingdom of justice, love and peace would require the rest of history to complete. So, just as the Father sent Jesus, Jesus himself sent the apostles and founded the Church to continue his mission through all of time among all peoples. And today, in every corner of the world, a local church exists as the sacrament of Christ's presence. Among all nations and peoples, the Church

extends the mission of Christ to make all things new. Thus, the year 2000 also marks a jubilee for the Church, celebrating a long-standing tradition of bringing the faith to many lands and peoples. In teaching the truth which Christ revealed to us, the Church has enlightened human culture and opened up the mysteries of God's plan for the whole human family.

## II. JUBILEE IN THE CHURCH OF MEMPHIS—THE CATHOLIC COMMUNITY OF WEST TENNESSEE

10. It is significant to know that the very reason pioneers came to this country was for a renewal of faith and for the freedom to express their religion. They were responding to a call, whether it was religious freedom, adventure, a better life, or renewal. They came with faith to an unknown place and trusted that God would provide.

11. It is with this faith and trust in God that the history of Catholicism in Western Tennessee began in 1540. Priests traveling with explorers in the late sixteenth and early seventeenth centuries celebrated Mass on the bluffs where the Mississippi and the Wolf rivers meet. From these times of exploration through settlement, development, and growth, the Catholic Church has played a major role in this community. On November 10, 1839, Fr. Joseph Stokes, a Dominican priest, celebrated the first public Mass within the boundaries of our diocese in Jackson, Tennessee. Seven days later, with the urging and support of Mr. Eugene Magevney, he celebrated the first public Mass in Memphis in a small log school house.

12. The geographic and historic significance of the bluffs of the Mississippi as a place where the Gospel was preached and Mass was celebrated by French missionaries is unique. It is not unlike the high places named in the Hebrew Scriptures. Even a bluff can give one a sense of being close to God and be a place from which one can reach high and teach many.

13. The history of Western Tennessee contains the clear evidence of the movement of God and the response of God's people. This response is seen in so many ways: in the trial of pioneering and settling where hardship was an everyday occurrence, in the development of a relationship with Native Americans, in a new and vulnerable Catholic community amidst a very anti-Catholic milieu, in the American civil war with all its social and political issues, and in the yellow fever epidemics, which brought a heroic response especially from Catholic priests and sisters. God led the Catholic community in Western Tennessee through all of this. Each person in this amazing history, by relying on faith, became a means of hope and a bearer of God's love for all.

14. Eventually, in the latter half of the twentieth century, a new Catholic diocese was envisioned. The new diocese was to encompass the western third of the state of Tennessee, between the Tennessee and Mississippi rivers. Twenty-one counties of this region were to be separated from what was then the Diocese of Nashville. On Wednesday, January 6, 1971, the Catholic Diocese of Memphis was established and its first Bishop, Carroll Thomas Dozier, was ordained and installed.

15. In recent times, we have seen the continued growth of the Diocese of Memphis with individuals coming to us from backgrounds of other faiths and from those with no faith at all. We have seen growth in individuals of many different cultures, not only from other parts of our own country, but from all over the world. Each of these groups has brought its own diverse richness which is part of a Catholic heritage to which we belong, but about which we are often unaware. Along with those of western European descent, men and women from Latin American countries, Asian, African, Native American, Caribbean, South Pacific, and Eastern European cultures—all now belong to this local church. This diversity places us at a new threshold. We no longer live in closed enclaves with similar cultural backgrounds and history. Now we live among each other in a diverse mosaic of color, custom, history, and social diversity.

16. Like the Hebrew people of old who realized that they did not live up to the justice to which God had called them, we must also take stock. As we look over our own history, we realize that, as the Catholic community of western Tennessee, we have not always lived our call to carry out the mission of Christ. We have not always respected or appreciated the differences among us. Some still do not. Sometimes we are even unaware of the moments and times when we offend each other because we are so limited in our scope and vision.

17. We know that the bishops of the Second Vatican Council affirmed that "All people are called to be part of this Catholic unity of the people of God which in promoting universal peace presages it" (*Lumen Gentium*, no. 13). We are called to embody this same Catholic spirit in our diocese. Rooted in the basic virtues of faith, hope, and love, we are called to concrete action. One cannot "play" at this sort of witness.

18. The Holy Father has clearly called the Church to a wider vision of our catholicity. He has emphasized the importance of witnessing to the universality of the Church by appreciating the many nations and cultures which compose our Church, incorporating their traditions and appreciating their unique gifts. How do we live this out? The answer is neither void of challenge nor free of difficulty.

19. But, like the pioneers of our region, our response will require courage. Courage will be needed to overcome the rejection and loneliness we may feel because we did not condone the racial commentary in the coffee break room, or because we are considered odd when we do not laugh at or repeat denigrating jokes or humor.

20. Society's effort toward acceptance and tolerance of diversity remains unfulfilled. The status quo is satisfied that we merely tolerate one another and do not impede one another's chance to have whatever society has to offer. But society does not call, us to appreciate each other's differences, or to love each other as brothers and sisters as Jesus Himself. The Gospel does! We are called to more! We must dare to be different, to be many of the things our world is not!

21. Just as Christ called the Hebrews to accept all peoples as sisters and brothers in faith, just as St. Paul constantly reminded the early Christians that there was in Christ no longer Gentile or Jew, but rather one Body of Christ—we, the Catholic community of Western Tennessee, must accept each member of this local church, each and every person, in the same spirit as Christ Himself. In fact, we are called to that same acceptance and to honest, heartfelt love for everyone—all peoples, of all cultures, races, creeds, and nations.

## III. JUBILEE IN THE FAMILY THE DOMESTIC CHURCH

22. The family, the little church or the church in the home, is the basic unit which, when united to other families, forms the local parish. The local parish, united with other parishes, constitutes the diocesan church. Just as there is great diversity in the universal Church, there are many ways people form families. A husband and wife form a family. A husband and wife and their children form a family. Single parents with their children form a family. In our day, we speak of the extended family, consisting of relatives who are often separated by many miles. The extended family may even consist of close friends who form a new extended family in the local setting. Families are wherever people share their hearts in a common bond of love and support extended over time.

23. Each family, no matter what its make-up, forms a little church. Just as the universal Church is called to manifest within itself the presence of Christ, so is the little church of the home. Just as the universal Church is called to evangelize the world, so is the little church as family called to do the same.

24. One of the strongest challenges offered by the Holy Father in his *Tertio Millennio Adveniente* encyclical

is his call to a new evangelization—an evangelization which involves all of the People of God, making them sharers of the Messianic mission. It is a new awareness which not only points each member toward one another but also to the family itself as it deepens its commitment to Gospel living. It is a mission which points the family out toward the universal Church and the wider world. The family must be a sign of Christ in the world and a privileged place of his presence and action. The family is therefore "the first school of Christian life and 'a school for human enrichment' [no. 169]. Here one learns endurance and the joy of work, fraternal love, generous—even repeated—forgiveness, and above all divine worship in prayer and the offering of one's life" (*Catechism of the Catholic Church*, no. 1657).

25. The ministry of evangelization calls parents to impart the treasure of our Catholic tradition to their children. They are to weave Gospel values into the fabric of everyday life so that their children are literally bathed in the life of faith and virtues which flow from that life of faith. More than anything they can say, it is through their example that parents create this environment of Gospel living.

26. Our children may not easily understand the demands their faith places on them, or easily accept our insistence on certain disciplines. Young people may not easily understand why certain activities common to their peers may not be acceptable. It may not be easy for them to understand that sometimes it is good to say no, even if that which we want seems good or affordable.

27. We may have to explain to them that it is simply not appropriate to belong to groups which tend toward bigotry or elitism, even if some of their friends do. We must help them and support them when they do not readily understand why they are not allowed to go to unacceptable movies. We must walk with them as they struggle with our insistence on sexual abstinence instead of the permissiveness and conve-

nience of contraception. None of this will be quickly taught or easily reinforced. Therefore, families must help each other to find every means for mutual support and the common strengthening of Gospel values.

28. With all that parents are called to do for their children by the Gospel, we must not forget the special role that children have in the domestic church. They should not be seen only as the church of the future, as if only adults really belong to the church. Every person, by reason of baptism, is called to manifest the mission of Christ as priest, prophet, and king. Even as infants, children also become instruments of God's prophetic call by the very demands they place on their parents. Children can and do contribute a great deal in service to their family—their parents, their brothers and sisters, their extended family of relatives and friends, and the wider community in which they live.

29. Each family member, then, has a special role to play. Parents model and teach the life of faith to their children from the perspective of adult life—having weathered disappointments, frustrations, and the stark realization of their own sinfulness as well as the sin of the world. Children model and teach the life of faith through their innocence and simplicity as well as their struggles through the growing pains of life. Everyone in the family, whether adult or child, elderly or young, functional or dependent, must confront his/her own sinfulness as well as the gift of forgiveness and the joy of knowing that he/she is redeemed and loved by God.

30. Each family must be renewed in its vocation to be the "family of God," and the "little church." This renewal becomes a vehicle for the renewal of the world. The Holy Father calls us to renew the justice and mercy brought about through Christ's incarnation. This renewal must radiate within the family, and from each family out toward the wider world in which we live. As Christ's incarnation marked the beginning of the Christian era, this coming millennium, the great Jubilee, marks for us a time of renewal, a time of com-

mitment, a time of discovering anew the graced life to which the vocation to family life invites us.

## IV. JUBILEE IN THE WIDER COMMUNITY OF WEST TENNESSEE—MEMPHIS, SHELBY COUNTY, AND THE JACKSON DEANERY

31. Like the reconciliation and renewal required of us in the church community, and in the families which comprise the church, working toward reconciliation and renewal is asked of us in our relationship with the wider community in which we live. We have a call to bring the wisdom of our faith, the vision of our hope, and the generosity of our love to bear on all the people of Western Tennessee.

32. We hear this call in the words of Jesus Himself. He asks us to preach the Good News by living the gospel call of love in the fabric of everyday life. By living the gospel message, our words will not seem empty. By giving concrete form to Jesus' commands, we become credible witnesses to His word and a means of grace and redemption for the world. This is what evangelization is all about.

33. So the questions arise: What is our specific call as Catholics to serve the wider community of Western Tennessee? How does the challenge of the millennium come to bear on our life as citizens of the land between the rivers?

34. The history of Western Tennessee began as a frontier rich with space and opportunity for the spirited as well as the religiously and politically oppressed. As a fertile center for agriculture, a civilization rooted in farming emerged. The need for labor and the abundance of willing but largely uneducated people converged on the lands surrounding the Mississippi valley.

35. How odd it is that history repeats itself time and time again. We saw earlier how the people of the Old Testament eventually subjected the poor to servitude even though their own ancestors had been held in slavery before being freed from Egypt by God's

mighty power. In similar fashion, those who sought freedom from oppression here, in the land between the rivers, subjected others to a more cruel bondage than they themselves endured. How sad that with the culture of wealth, which grew from large or small but always powerful plantations, came slavery and indentured labor. How sad that a caste system emerged that has strong remnants even today.

36. And the strongest remnant of that caste system which remains to this day has been the devastating division between Black and White peoples. It is better known as racism. Fortunately, the laws which institutionalized racism for such a long time have been changed. Unfortunately, attitudes and other remnants of this past age still remain in the hearts and minds of all of us to some degree or another (cf. *The Church and Racism: Pontifical Commission on Justice and Peace*).

37. Let us strive to overcome those remnants and patterns of racism, not just in the words we use or choose not to use, but also by how we vote, by the neighborhoods we choose to live in or move out of, and by the schools we choose for our children to attend. Let us constantly be alert in our own lives for those moments and times when we are offered the opportunities to overcome racism in our own individual lives.

38. We should not be surprised that the divisions between Black and White bled over into more subtle, but no less destructive, divisions between peoples and cultures here. We see this evident in the marked division between rich and poor, blue and white collar workers, educated and illiterate, those long-established family names and new arrivals. We see other divisions as well—divisions between people of different religions and cultures. We even see sadly the divisions within the Christian communion itself— a division that has been widened by a climate of mistrust, hatred, and fear. We seem incapable of understanding that no matter what is one's state of life, in a divided community, all suffer and all lose.

39. The poor and marginalized of society suffer in a world which often seems devoid of any life and hope. A sense of being abandoned pervades everyday life. Violence and mutual exploitation abound. Human dignity is buried under a rubble of abuse, mistreatment, misunderstanding, and abject poverty. The basic necessities of life in our culture cruelly seem just beyond reach no matter how hard one tries. Being poor or marginalized is not always the result of others' unfair treatment or society's unjust systems; but most of the time, it is.

40. There is no question that the poor of our land have suffered greatly because of our own unjust systems; but they are not the only victims of a divided culture. Those who seem to have the better share of wealth can sometimes be the worst victims because they have the illusion of being "on top." Although they are largely unaware of it, they live every day in fear of not "being successful," as the world defines it. Usually this fear is translated into desperate and compulsive striving for more material wealth and exclusive living. This unhealthy stress plays a major role in much of the life threatening diseases which currently affect all people. These driven ambitions bring death not only to the body, but also to the soul. And all that remains is pervasive emptiness because these aspirations are not rooted in God, whose love is the only real source of happiness and peace.

41. And so, a society based on exploitation and violence breeds more of the same among the rich and poor alike. Such exploitation begins to shape attitudes in every sphere of life. This is especially true in the delicate area of interpersonal relationships. Models of healthy and life-giving friendship have all but vanished. Individuals in all levels of society seek in casual and recreational sex what can only be found in real bonds of intimacy and love. A temporary and false sense of intimacy is created whether for a few weeks or a simple one-night stand. Of course it does not last. Loneliness abounds and the God-given capacity for love is reduced to another addiction.

42. A society molded by a contraceptive attitude toward human sexuality is bound to find itself isolating sex from its source and true end. Efforts are made in every sphere of industry to make sex more available and convenient leading to irresponsible exercise of one of God's greatest gifts to the human family. And because sex is understood as a recreational commodity to which one has a right, abortion is seen as necessary.

43. Everywhere we see the true economy of interpersonal relationship completely out of order. Family life is broken down. The life giving force produced through genuine human love with which God intended to fill our lives has become thin and weak. Instead, we breathe the air of isolation and emptiness. Chemical dependency and depression as well as other psychological ills are at an all time high. The very foundation of human life has eroded and washed away.

44. All of this presents many challenges in the light of the call the Holy Father has given us in the Jubilee Year. There is much to overcome in the prejudice and intolerant behavior so many of us perpetuate. There is much to heal among the poorest of the poor and richest of the rich alike. The restoration of a deeper appreciation of our common humanity and the recovery of true human character seems to be the heart of our task. We as Catholics have much to offer the wider community within which we live, for our heritage of wisdom is rooted in the very source of life itself.

45. To those who live a practical ethic of the survival of the fittest—who feel they must constantly strive for more and more material wealth, who, despite claims to believe in God, live as if they believe merely in the here and now, and who trust only their own ability to survive—to these individuals we must proclaim a renewed faith. Let us make credible the teachings of Jesus about the lilies of the field, about letting tomorrow take care of itself, about being invested in the Kingdom of God first instead of our own kingdom.

46. To those who have been abandoned by a society of wealth and privilege, we must offer hope. This hope in part must be proclaimed by practical help and a commitment to a restoration of justice in the same vein as the Old Testament called for in each jubilee year. Let us work to establish that new Kingdom in the practical order of the society in which we live. Let us proclaim hope in the midst of suffering. Let us demonstrate a life in which acceptance of our human condition replaces the pretense of control. Let us become men and women of serenity, knowing that God comes to us in sorrow as well as joy. Let us be people with a hope which reaches to that final day when all will be made new in Christ when He comes in glory.

47. To the immigrants who are seeking shelter and home, we must be a mirror of the love of God to them. They must see the face of Jesus in us. Let us allow our love to be translated into serving them as would Jesus, welcoming them as would Jesus, making them feel at home as would Jesus.

48. To the sick in body and spirit, we must offer the healing grace of God. We must continue to provide health services through our Catholic health care system—whether it is a hospital, nursing home, or parish setting. Over and beyond that, let us be a comfort to our sick and ailing by our care and concern, by our prayers and good wishes, by our visits and calls. Let us be a healing presence to them by our listening and witnessing.

49. To all peoples we must offer our love. Let us do so by living generously for each other in all aspects of our lives: in our work and business dealings, in our friendships, in the exercise of our sexuality and the gift of procreation, in our family relationships, in our reaching out to those who have been abandoned, especially the poorest of the poor, the sick, and the aged and infirm, and in our loving those who are difficult to love, even our enemies. In loving with the same self-sacrificing spirit which Christ himself showed, we experience the real satisfaction of human belonging and discover that we are all part of a common humanity which in the end, knows no divisions or boundaries.

50. God has given each of us the ability to live this Gospel life. It begins with a heart open to God's love. It grows with the realization that God has a purpose for each of us on this earth. It flourishes with the knowledge that God's will is carried out by human beings as ourselves—human beings open to His love, viewing the world with informed minds.

## CONCLUSION

51. The Holy Father has given us much to reflect on. The Church in our country has taken up this call in many and varied ways. Throughout this land efforts at evangelization, service among the poor, advocacy for justice, and a strengthening of our own Catholic life and identity have all been undertaken with great enthusiasm.

52. We here in the Catholic Diocese of Memphis, amid the land between two rivers, as a people of faith and tradition, embrace this call together with all our Catholic brothers and sisters throughout this land. Let us explore every avenue where our Catholic faith can make a difference in a world so much in need of healing, in our homes so much in need of forgiving, in our lives so much in need of grace.

53. Let us take up the challenge of putting down our old ways and looking toward the new, becoming the new wineskins of a renewed humanity in Christ.

54. Renewed faith, enlivened hope, love beyond measure—these virtues are the hallmarks of the Jubilee. As in past jubilees, may this Jubilee year of 2000 lead us to a stronger resolve to live the Gospel more fully in our lives. ■

Most Rev. J. Terry Steib, SVD, *is the bishop of Memphis, Tennessee, and the chairman of the bishops' Committee on African American Catholics.*

# Black Catholics—On *the* Edge

BY MOST REV. WILLIAM J. LEVADA

FEBRUARY 1999

Last Saturday I joined several hundred other interested folk for the third annual Archbishop John R. Quinn Colloquium on Catholic Social Teaching at the University of San Francisco. The topic was "Black and White in America: A Catholic Perspective." The day was interesting, stimulating and challenging in equal measures.

[San Francisco] Mayor Willie Brown provided some poignant local reminders from recent events in San Francisco that racism is not dead yet, even in this progressive bastion. The nightly news had just rehearsed the events of Jasper, Texas, where a Black man had been viciously dragged to his death behind a pickup, a community faced its own demons as the trial of one of his murderers drew to its conclusion, and news anchors who should know better tried (in vain) to put the word "revenge" on the lips of the dead man's sister, whose noble self-possession in regard to her and her family's feelings won my greatest admiration and respect.

The colloquium speakers—three Black and one White—were each eloquent in their passion for justice and truth. They taught me a lot.

After hearing often that day about the many statements of the U.S. bishops, especially the 1979 pastoral letter *Brothers and Sisters to Us: U.S. Bishops' Pastoral Letter on Racism in*

*Our Day*, I decided to re-read that statement. It too is eloquent and direct, and reminds us that racism is both a fact and a sin. One thing I learned at this colloquium is that in the eyes of African American Catholics today, racism is also alive and well in the United States, including the Church.

I remember last November's testimony by my [African American] brother bishops making the same point. It surprised me then, and it surprised me last Saturday. But I have been able to understand a little better than before that my experience is different than that of my Black brothers and sisters, whose roots in America go back not 150 years but 300 years and more. Whatever economic and cultural, and even religious, hurdles my family and I have had to overcome, they have largely been overcome.

Sadly, this is not yet true for African Americans. They tell us that they are always on edge, waiting for the endemic American racism to surface in some new expression of discrimination, prejudice—or even violence.

Here are some other things I learned. I learned that slavery put its stamp on American society in an all-encompassing way, in the minds of many, maybe most, Blacks. I will have to think and study more before I could agree with one of our speakers that slavery is the primary defining issue of the American story, economic, political and religious. But I will remember in the future not to ignore that voice when I look at cultural, intellectual, political and religious analyses of what shaped the America we live in today.

I also learned that many Black Catholics feel they are being squeezed out of the picture—and the funding—in much of what society does for the poor and marginalized. They look at the new emphasis on "multiculturalism" as a disguised attempt to soften the focus on racism, deriving from the national experience of slavery, by making the African American experience that of all other immigrant groups.

In this context, it was new to me to hear that Black Catholics have feelings which range from concern to resentment about the recent (and in my view necessary) attention given to the rising tide of Hispanics within the Catholic Church. In this view, the focus on Hispanic ministry has come at the cost of the commitment of the past three decades to helping inner-city Blacks through institutional and structural commitments by the Church.

Here one of the greatest stories remains a beacon of hope. Catholic schools in the inner cities of the United States have been a primary source of educational

opportunity for Catholic and non-Catholic African Americans alike.

San Francisco has a right to be proud to be a part of this success story at schools like Sacred Heart, St. Dominic, St. Paul of the Shipwreck and others, where African American children benefit from the sacrifices of their parents and families, of their parishes, and of the entire Archdiocese for support given to their education. From these and other Catholic schools our Black children are prepared for and enter Catholic college-prep high schools, and go from there to college and the competitive educational opportunities that are essential to overcoming the decades and centuries of missed opportunities caused by slavery and segregation.

One of my own personal commitments in beginning our Catholic Education Endowment campaign, "Today's Students, Tomorrow's Leaders," is to guarantee sufficient scholarship and tuition money for present and future children of working class families—Black, White and Hispanic—to enable them to attend Catholic school.

Of course I do not propose Catholic schools as "the" solution to the endemic problem of American racism and its effects on our African American brothers and sisters. But it surely is a part of the solution that is already in place, and the failure of America to support these children's education stands out as another great shame in our land.

In the meantime I have learned again that we have no lack of good teaching and good will as Catholics. But we do need to find more ways to put our theory into practice, in solidarity with the African Americans of our land who truly are "brother and sisters to us." ∎

Most Rev. William J. Levada *is the archbishop of San Francisco, California.*

# National Catholic Gathering *for* Jubilee Justice: Open *the* Doors *to* Christ

BY MOST REV. JOSEPH A. FIORENZA

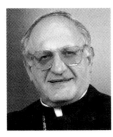

JULY 1999

Thank you for coming to this briefing as we begin the National Catholic Gathering for Jubilee Justice: Open the Doors to Christ. The 2,800 Catholics assembled for this meeting is a milestone in the history of the Catholic Church in the United States. Supported by more than sixty Catholic organizations, it is the largest such gathering to celebrate our efforts for justice in the past two hundred years and to mobilize us for the future as we move into the Third Millennium.

We come together to prepare for a noteworthy crossing. We respond to the call of Pope John Paul II to prepare for this moment by opening the doors to Christ. We do so through prayer, repentance for past wrongs, and a commitment to begin the Third Millennium with a new resolve for justice. We seek to deepen our understanding of jubilee spirituality and Catholic social teaching and to share and learn new skills. We will pledge ourselves to carry the work of charity, justice, and peace forward. This is a challenge we must face if in the new millennium justice, is to be served and peace promoted much better than in the millennium drawing to a close.

All of us here, bishops, priests, religious order Sisters and Brothers, and lay men and women working both within church structures and outside of them, share a common passion: a commitment to the justice mission of the Church.

Pope Paul VI said and Pope John Paul II reiterated "If you want peace, work for justice." Without efforts for justice, the world cannot overcome the disharmony born of inequalities, the rage fired by inability to meet critical needs, and the hopelessness born of oppressive economic systems.

We applaud and recommit ourselves to the efforts for justice which have marked the path of the Church in this country. We are proud of our historic stand with labor, our defense of the unborn, our challenges to those who control economic systems, and our questioning of the reliance on weapons of mass destruction.

We do not rest on past laurels, however. To do so would be to lose the advances we have made. We have particular concerns at this moment in time. We are especially wary of any effort to erode progress in overcoming racism in this nation and urge an openness to immigrants who seek the safety of our shores.

Here in California and at UCLA we are particularly mindful of opposition to affirmative action, a program which attempts to

address the imbalance resulting from our nation's sad history of racist practices. We were dismayed when Proposition 209 abolished affirmative action in California a few years ago, and we are alarmed as other states consider similar legislation.

Make no mistake about it. Racism is a sin: a sin that divides the human family, and violates the fundamental dignity of those called to be children of the same Father.

We hear the sound of racism among those who suggest too much is being given to racial minorities by way of affirmative action programs. At times protestations claiming that all persons should be treated equally reflect the desire to maintain a status quo that favors one race and social group at the expense of the poor and non-White.

The anti-immigrant sentiment moving through the nation, especially in border states, also strikes at the heart of what this country stands for. It threatens to unravel the moral fabric of our nation. The United States is noblest when it defends the weak and has benefitted from the many cultures which have

enriched our society. To reject the immigrant is to kill the spirit of generosity, creativity, and open-heartedness that has made this nation great. A nation such as the United States, which has so much, cannot in conscience turn away those who seek only the opportunity for life, liberty, and the pursuit of happiness.

As we gather here today, we look to revive in people the desire to work for justice. We seek a few sparks of genius and a multitude of sparks of good will to reignite the fire for righteousness. We seek fire-tenders to make this spirit grow so it might illuminate minds, warm hearts, and brighten the paths we must walk. Doing so, we can open the gateways which keep us from full harmony with one another. We can work to right injustice, to rehabilitate oppressive systems, and to set free the captives of ignorance, crushing debt, poverty, fear, and other such blights upon humanity. As we move through these gateways we will be ready to and worthy of opening the doors of the new millennium to Christ. ∎

Most Rev. Joseph A. Fiorenza *is the bishop of Galveston-Houston, Texas, and is the president of the National Conference of Catholic Bishops.*

# Homily: The Multicultural Masses

BY MOST REV. EDWARD J. O'DONNELL

SEPTEMBER 1999

All too often, when we speak of the varieties of racial cultures, national cultures and religious cultures, we do so in terms of problems, of obligations.

Here in Acadiana, though, we don't tolerate such differences, we enjoy them. Every week during the summer in fact we celebrate them. We enjoy the variety of cultures. We enjoy them as we do the spices and flavorings that enrich Southern Louisiana cooking.

It all begins in the Book of Genesis. God's revelation has spoken to the human family for millennia of our relation with God and our relationship with one another. God's ways are not our ways, and the opening chapters of the Bible take us beyond the scientific and even beyond the poetic to understand ourselves, the universe and the God who made them all. The wonder-filled opening chapters of the Scriptures tell us of a God who works like a potter shaping mankind and the whole universe. The narratives tell of snakes who speak, a tower to the heavens and a tree that gives life. The world of our God is as colorful as a painting, as delightful as a fairy tale. Extraordinary those wonders are, but they are also true and tell an ageless story of the human race.

The key idea of the Book of Genesis is a fundamental teaching that there is but one God who is Lord of everything that exists.

And that God, who made all things, looked at what he had made and saw that it was all very good.

In his book *Seeds of Contemplation*, the Trappist writer and mystic [Thomas Merton] poses a question that challenges us to think like God. What do you think when you see a forest of beautiful trees? Tall trees and short trees. Green trees and brown trees. Young growing trees reaching up into the sky and old brown trees falling back to the earth. Can you think that the billions of different trees making up the forests of the earth are each failed models of the one perfect tree that the Creator is trying to create? Certainly not! The beauty is not in creating billions of trees all alike. The very beauty of the trees comes from their diversity. They are not failed attempts to create the one perfect tree but the glorious excess of a loving God giving us yet another cause of our joy and proof of his love in the millions of trees, each unique.

For "He looked at all that he had made and he saw that it was all very good."

Racists would say that only their kind of tree is beautiful—the Arian tree, the Caucasian tree, the African tree. They would say that other kinds of trees are the failed efforts of a clumsy God. But they are wrong. Beauty is in the forest, not in the tree because God made it and as the poster says, "God don't make junk."

No. He looked at what he had made and he saw that it was all very good.

If this is true of the tree, how much more is it true of human beings? In the Creation Story, God took mud from the crust of the earth and fashioned a creature in his own image and likeness—man—and then bone from his bone and flesh from his flesh—woman. He breathed into those mud dolls his own breath, his life. Were Adam and Eve brown? Black? White? Yellow? We don't know. God didn't think it important enough to tell us. But he did look upon every Adam and every Eve and he saw that they were all very good.

Neither were there others than Adam and Eve made by other gods, for there are no other gods. Hitlers who say that Gentiles and Jews are different species are heretics since every Adam and every Eve is made in the image and likeness of the one God. Those who say that brown people and yellow people are not equal are heretics as well, for they are saying that God the Father loves some of his children more than others and blesses them unfairly.

Not only did God create all of us, he sent his Son to become one of us. Most [Roman Catholics] are of a Northern European tradition and see ourselves reflected in the Son and so feel he must be a fair-haired, fair-skinned Barbie or Ken. But that Son who became one of us is also brother to the dark-haired, dark-skinned people of the world. What kind of blasphemy would it be to say that he came only for some of us, leaving the others to sin and death? Since he is the Son of the same God who is our Father, he is brother to us all, and we are brothers and sisters not only of him, but of all our fellow humans as well. Jesus did not attempt to "Lord it over" his human brothers and sisters—although if anyone ever had the right to do so, it was he. In an astounding phrase St. Paul tells us that Jesus did not consider divinity something to be clung to, but that he "disposed himself of the divinity and that he became like us in all things but sin. He had no pride of race or position. Rather he ate with publicans and sinners, he was accused of hobnobbing with prostitutes and tax collectors—the "inferior people" of his day. He called people from the highways and the byways to share his banquet—not only

the clean and rich and beautiful. In him the Scriptures say there was no Greek or Jew, no circumcised or non-circumcised, no free man or slave. Everyone was his brother and sister. All are one family.

So when we celebrate our diversities we celebrate the completeness and beauty of God himself. And Jesus gives us the food and drink for our celebration in the Eucharist. A banquet in which his body and blood are to be shared among all his brothers and sisters, all the children of his one Father. He gave us the Eucharist not so much as something to be worshiped but as something to be shared. It is not a snack, not given to us for ourselves alone. It is a banquet to be enjoyed as a sign of our solidarity. The Council tells us that the Eucharist is the "source and the goal" of the whole Christian life. It is the sign of the love of God and love of our neighbor to which Christ calls us. When we come to the banquet/sacrifice of Christ, we are all invited. *Here Comes Everybody* was the wonderful title of a book by Carrol Houselander. That title says it all. Here comes everybody—all invited to the banquet of the Body and Blood of Christ—a worldwide litany of whom Christ invites: Tax collectors and sinners, prostitutes like the Magdalene and doubters like Thomas, Deny-ers like Peter and people with their own agendas like Simon the Zealot. These are the people with whom Jesus associated. No pride of race or religion. Only pride in being one in Christ with all their sisters and brothers.

Legitimate pride in ancestry is not evil. We should be proud of the accomplishments of our forebears and that is particularly true in Acadiana where our forebears almost universally suffered discrimination and still maintained their faith and their traditions. Our Cajun people were expelled from their Canadian homes by those who would take away their land, their language and most fundamental their religion. Those early Cajuns taught us courage and persistence in maintaining our beliefs. Our Black people from the islands as much as from Africa taught courage even when persecution came from their own church family as from outsiders. Our Vietnamese brothers and sis-

ters are here because they fought Communism in their own country. So too whatever our derivation might be. None of our ancestors came to this country, to this area because they were doing so well at home. As we read in the Book of Exodus, "You shall not molest or oppress an alien for you yourself were once an alien yourself in the land of Egypt."

And so we celebrate our diversity and at the same time our solidarity, recognizing that we are children of the same father, brothers and sisters in Christ, different, not better, not worse. And we thank God for that beautiful diversity of the trees in the forest and of the people of Acadiana.

Our diocese has tried to help celebrate our ethnic diversity. We have encouraged French Masses and Cajun Masses. We have established an office for Black Catholics. And I am happy to announce two more recent steps to help the Church be a partner in the life of ethnic groups. We have for many years been blessed by the presence of Vietnamese people in the diocese and since there have also been a number of Vietnamese priests, their spiritual needs have been met. This year we have widened the Vietnamese apostolate so that there are now two centers of Vietnamese Catholics. The Vietnamese people, like other oppressed people, have been supremely loyal in their faith and we want to help them remain true to the faith in this, their new country, ever loyal to their old church.

We are also trying to reach out to Hispanic members of the Church in Lafayette. The Diocese has contacted several Latino priests to see if any of them would be interested in doing Hispanic ministry here and one in particular has indicated great interest in doing Hispanic ministry here. If all goes well, he will soon be working with our Hispanic people. Although Lafayette does not have a large Hispanic population, demographers tell us that in twenty years the Hispanic people might make up the largest ethnic and national group in the Church. And our Hispanic population here is growing as well. We hope to be

able to establish a Hispanic ministry in the near future.

The diocese welcomes diversity among its people and we find our ethnic population adding to the uniqueness of Acadiana and the strength of the Church here. For us, ethnicity is not a problem but an opportunity. Not a worry but a celebration. We enjoy our diversity and we celebrate our solidarity. We know that the Church is not English or French or German or Greek—it is Catholic. The very word means universal. "Here comes everybody" to the Church in Lafayette. We welcome them all and look forward to working with all of our people to extend God's wonderfully diverse Kingdom of justice and peace and love. ∎

Most Rev. Edward J. O'Donnell *is the bishop of Lafayette, Louisiana.*

## THE MANY CULTURES OF ACADIANA

### SEPTEMBER 1999

**The Chitimacha Tribe**
The Chitimacha Tribe settled in south Louisiana more than 1,500 years ago and once numbered about 20,000. The tribe now has fewer than 1,000 members living in the area of Charenton in St. Mary civil parish. The Chitimachas have begun buying land that was lost over the years, adding to the 260 acres awarded by the United States government.

**The Acadians**
Expelled from their homes in what is now called Nova Scotia, the Acadians were the first White settlers to the area. In the mid-1700s, the Acadians were forced to leave their country by the occupying British forces. They brought with them their skills as trappers, farmers and people who were skilled at living off the land and water. They brought with them also their strong Catholic faith.

**The Creoles**
A people of mixed racial heritage, the Creoles trace their ancestry to African, Caucasian, Native American and Spanish settlers. Creoles in Acadiana enjoy prominence, visibility and respect.

**The African Americans**
Today's African American community in Acadiana is descended from the slaves brought to the United States from Africa and Haiti in the eighteenth century. The African Americans of the Diocese of Lafayette are predominately Catholic and add many elements of their culture to their worship. The Diocese has given heavily of its African American clergy to serve as bishops all over the world.

**The Germans**
German Catholics settled in the area of Roberts Cove in the 1880s. Religious refugees, they were seeking to escape the *Kulturkampf* of Chancellor Otto von Bismarck. Fr. Peter Leonhard Thevis was the first priest to arrive in the area.

**The Italians**
The Italian community has added to the traditions of the Church in Acadiana, most notably the St. Joseph Altar. Italians immigrated to Acadiana over the past century and have settled in all parts of the diocese.

**The Hispanics**
Most of the Hispanic people of the diocese are of Mexican descent, with many other countries of Central and South America also represented. Many Hispanics in the diocese are here temporarily, and will return home after their work is done. Many apply for permanent resident status. They grace many of the parishes with their love for God and the Church.

**The Vietnamese**
In the 1960s and '70s, the war in Vietnam brought many refugees from that country to all parts of the free world, including Acadiana. Today there is a strong and thriving Vietnamese community in south Louisiana. The experiences the Vietnamese people endured in order to worship in freedom are often harrowing and always inspiring. Today, more than 1,000 Vietnamese live primarily in the Abbeville area.

**The Lebanese**
Lebanese Maronite Catholics, like their Acadian brothers and sisters, fled their homeland to avoid religious persecution and to seek the freedom to worship God in their own way. Mostly merchants and professionals, the Lebanese settled in all parts of the nation, but a surprisingly large number settled in the Acadiana area. The traditional friendship of the Lebanese and the French goes back to the Crusades. St. Louis, king of France, fought for the Maronite Catholics against the Muslims, and established an enduring bond between the people of France and Lebanon.

PART FOUR:

DR. MARTIN LUTHER KING JR. CELEBRATIONS

# Some Thoughts *on* Racism *and* Immigration

BY MOST REV. WILLIAM L. HIGI

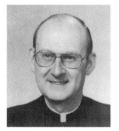

JANUARY 1997

This past week our nation was called to observe the birthday of Martin Luther King Jr. It's even a national holiday. What was your reaction to the media coverage?

How we reacted might well be a barometer of how well we have dealt with racism. There are people in whom there isn't a drop of racist blood, but that is not the case with most of us. Far too often, it's there. It's something that needs to be named and addressed.

In our country, Blacks have long been victims of racism. Blacks do not hold a monopoly: Jews, certainly prior to World War II, Japanese Americans, other peoples of Asiatic origin, not to overlook American Indians. Racism is alive and, it would seem, making a comeback, particularly as the immigrant stream has shifted from White Europeans to peoples of darker skin.

Given this reality, I suggest to you that our parishes would be well served to acknowledge the Martin Luther King holiday. Better yet, it would be a powerful witness to cele-

brate that event as a church community. The purpose would be to foster better understanding, not only of African Americans, but of all people of color. The goal would be to underscore the message of Dr. King that every human being, regardless of race, gender, class or nationality, is fundamentally equal. Each person is a unique creature of God, made in God's image! That is the teaching of the Catholic Church. Any attitude or practice that denies or compromises this fundamental human equality is inconsistent with faith in Jesus Christ. It is wrong!

Would you like to see homilies prior to Martin Luther King Day focus on racism? What if those homilies invited people (each individual) to examine his or her conscience with regard to the degree to which we understand, accept and reach out to all people as sisters and brothers in Christ? Had that happened in your parish this past week (perhaps it did!), what would your reaction have been: joy, irritation, anger?

I would like to see each parish participate in an ecumenical or interreligious celebration of Martin Luther King Day. What would be your "feeling" about participating in such a celebration? What would your reaction be if your parish made a really big deal out of the Martin Luther King Jr. Day?

A belief in human equality and a desire for human dignity are common elements among various faith traditions. The fundamental premise of Jewish ethics is set forth in the first chapter of Genesis: "and God created the human being in the Divine image." In Islam, people are viewed as having been created as equal in the sight of God's law and that there is no superiority of one race over another. We as Catholics should be leaders in ecumenical and interreligious efforts to address issues of social justice. We should witness for justice in our homes, in our neighborhoods and among members of our families.

In a statement titled *Brothers and Sisters to Us: U.S. Bishops' Pastoral Letter on Racism in Our Day* in November of 1979, the bishops of the United States accurately defined racism and located the center of the issue:

> Racism is a sin: a sin that divides the human family, blots out the image of God among specific members of that family, and violates the fundamental dignity of those called to be children of the same Father.

> Racism is a sin that says some human beings are inherently superior and others essentially inferior because of race. It is the sin that makes racial characteristics the determining factor for the exercise of human rights. It mocks the words of Jesus 'treat others the way you would have them treat you.' Indeed, racism is more than a disregard for the words of Jesus; it is the denial of the truth of the dignity of each human being revealed by the mystery of the Incarnation . . . the heart of the race question is moral and religious. It concerns the right of man and our attitude toward our fellow man.

Immigration is another issue that needs reflection. Much is written about immigrants, both documented and undocumented. The overall sentiment is negative, and often based on myths. People migrating to the United States seek to be united with families, seek to provide for families or are fleeing oppression. Unless you are a Native American (Indian), your ancestors did the same. Like the immigrants of today, they struggled against prejudice, survived by working low-paying jobs, overcame poverty and became contributing citizens.

Anti-immigrant attitudes are fueled by fears, frustrations and sometimes by racist prejudices. Frequently, this animosity is directed toward the "other" because they are of a different race, ethnicity or religion.

There is multicultural richness in our local church that needs to be more fully celebrated. As we get into 1998 I would like to encourage parishes to celebrate an annual Eucharistic Liturgy recalling their rich immigrant heritage and diversity. These celebrations could be times to extend special welcome to all newcomers as well as appreciation for the gifts they have brought. Well planned, such celebrations could incorporate and celebrate all of the cultures in North-central Indiana. Selection of music, prayers of petition and dress could add to the celebrations.

The recognition and celebration of our unity in diversity is more than an option. In that 1979 *Pastoral Letter on Racism*, my brother bishops declared: "All men and women are created in God's image, not just some races and racial types, but all bear the imprint of the Creator and are enlivened by the breath of one spirit."

As I was celebrating Mass on the Feast of the Holy Family (December 28) it occurred to me that Holy Family weekend is an excellent time to reflect on immigrants and how we react to the reality of modern-day immigration. Jesus, Mary and Joseph had to flee their country to escape persecution. They were refugees. The Holy Family was a family of immigrants in a foreign land.

The Scriptures say: "When an alien resides with you in your land, do not molest him. You shall treat the alien who resides with you no differently than the natives born among you; have the same love for him as for yourself; for you, too, were once aliens in the land of Egypt" (Lv 19:33-34).

It will be to our credit if we as a local church learn how to celebrate the diversity among peoples, recognizing and appreciating their culture and heritage. It is also important that we name racism where it exists and work to eradicate it.

Conversion from racist attitudes may be a long and slow process for some, one which perhaps is accomplished one heart at a time.

Nonetheless, if we want the world to be a better place in the future, it's a task which must be accomplished. ■

Most Rev. William L. Higi *is the bishop of Lafayette, Indiana.*

## CHURCHES, SCHOOLS, DIOCESES OBSERVE KING BIRTHDAY
### BY CATHOLIC NEWS SERVICE • JANUARY 1999

WASHINGTON (CNS)—Catholic dioceses, churches and schools honored the holiday observance of the Rev. Martin Luther King's birthday with a variety of programs and services, some featuring contemporaries of the slain civil rights leader.

The Rev. Fred Shuttlesworth, 76, who helped organize the Montgomery, Alabama, bus boycott and whose demonstrations helped prompt passage of the Voting Rights Act of 1965, spoke to 450 people of his times with Rev. King at a January 19 prayer breakfast honoring the slain civil rights leader at the University of Dayton, Ohio. He is founder and pastor of the Greater New Light Baptist Church in Cincinnati.

One day, in the lobby of a Whites-only hotel, a young, well-dressed White man approached Rev. King. "I've always wanted to meet you," he told Rev. King just before hitting him in the face.

Rev. King looked at his attacker and asked the man, "Did it help you to hurt me?"

"That's what nonviolence is," Rev. Shuttlesworth said of Rev. King's reaction. "He meant what he said, and most people I know don't."

Rev. Shuttlesworth, who with Rev. King and the Rev. Ralph Abernathy are considered by some historians the civil rights movement's "big three," once survived a Christmas Eve dynamite attack carried out by the Ku Klux Klan against his parsonage in Birmingham, Alabama.

In May 1963, during a demonstration in a White retail district in Birmingham, firefighters used a high-pressure stream of water from a fire hose to pin Rev. Shuttlesworth against a church wall to stop him from protesting.

The United States today is "mired in a quagmire of so many things that keep us from being the country we could be," he said. "We're not dragging the old baggage of segregation, but I don't see a lot of difference between segregation and racism."

Another contemporary of Rev. King's, the Rev. H. Sam Johnson, pastor of Hibben United Methodist Church in Mount Pleasant, South Carolina, knew Rev. King when he was a student in the 1960s. He heard the Nobel laureate ask one searching question that has stayed in his mind ever since, and Rev. Johnson asked that question to the people at a King birthday observance January 14 at Nativity Church in James Island, South Carolina. "Where do we go from here, chaos or community? That's what Martin asked. And we have to know our answer as we approach the new millennium. Our God's will and way must be imbued in our living," Rev. Johnson said.

He railed against failed social justice efforts, saying that "some of us take better care of our animals than we do of God's children." Then he spoke with heat and passion about healing the broken Body of Christ. He called ecumenism God's dream.

"It's an even greater dream than Martin had. You ought to be willing to walk with Jesus. He blesses us so that we might bless others in his name. God calls us, he calls us to be involved in the living of all his people," Rev. Johnson said.

A man who was a teenager when he first met Rev. King told the *Catholic Explorer*, newspaper of the Diocese of Joliet, Illinois, that he was inspired directly, albeit belatedly, by the civil rights leader. When the Rev. Lawrence Carter was a fifteen-year-old high school student in Columbus, Ohio, in the late 1950s, he remembers getting permission from the pastor of Union Baptist Church there if he could peruse the books in his private study.

"I remember there was a wall of books—floor to ceiling—and as I peered past the shelves I saw a man sitting in the corner chair. It was Dr. King, who was a guest speaker at the earlier service," recalled Rev. Carter, 57, now a Baptist minister and professor of philosophy and religion at the country's only all-Black male institution for higher learning, Morehouse College in Atlanta.

Sitting in that tiny, nondescript study, Rev. Carter said, "he asked me my name and then said, 'Did you consider college?'" He told the teen to consider Morehouse College, where Rev. King himself graduated in the early 1940s.

"I said I didn't want to go there because some neighbor said it wasn't up to snuff," Rev. Carter recalled. "He paused and looked at me seriously and then went on about Morehouse. But I didn't go there. It wasn't until my second year at Virginia College (and Seminary in Lynchburg, Virginia) that I knew I made a mistake."

Rev. Carter said when it came time for graduate school, he followed in Rev. King's footsteps. "I went to Boston University (where Rev. King had earned a doctor of philosophy degree) and tried to get as much of the same experience as I could. And I did," said Rev. Carter, who received a doctorate in pastoral care and counseling in 1978 and a master of divinity degree in 1968 from Boston University.

Rev. Carter, also a Fulbright scholar, was recently in Romeoville, Illinois, at Lewis University as part of an exchange with Morehouse.

Before a group of mainly African American students at St. Monica School in Kansas City, Missouri, U.S. Rep. Karen McCarthy, D-Mo., a Catholic, recalled examples of discrimination in her own life. "There were things I couldn't do, and places I couldn't go, because of my religion," McCarthy said. "If some of my friends were Jewish, or if they were of a color other than mine, they couldn't live in my neighborhood."

McCarthy said her parents told her that she could be anything she wanted to be, so she studied hard and earned good grades. "But there were places, no matter how good my grades were, that I couldn't go to become a doctor (as a woman)," she said. "There were institutions that didn't want me, no matter how good a student I was."

In August 1963, when Rev. King articulated his vision of America in his famous "I Have a Dream" speech on the steps of the Lincoln Memorial in Washington, D.C., those closed doors began to open to all people, regardless of gender, race or religion, she said.

"But there were people who didn't agree with Martin Luther King Jr.—people who really were scared about letting others be what they could be. As a result, he was assassinated," McCarthy said. But Rev. King's dream lived on, the congresswoman said.

When McCarthy was a high school teacher some of her students challenged her to put her dreams of a better

world into action. With their help she won a seat in the Missouri General Assembly in 1976 and served there before winning a seat in Congress in 1994.

"Look at me," she told the students. "I'm a Catholic girl, and I am in Congress. And you could be in Congress, too—any one of you because of that dream. Dr. Martin Luther King Jr. is an example to you, as he was to me. He tried to change the world, and he did it. And you can too."

About five hundred gathered at Holy Cross Church in Philadelphia January 10 for the sixteenth annual archdiocesan interfaith commemorative service honoring Rev. King.

Cardinal Anthony J. Bevilacqua of Philadelphia, who presided, said, "We by our presence here bear witness to our belief that Dr. King was called to be God's servant of justice."

He added, "Today, we hear so many reports of acts of violence in our world. People are isolated, injured and even killed because their skin color or ethnic group is not the same as the one who feels superior to them."

"How then," Cardinal Bevilacqua asked, "would Dr. King, a victim of a violent death, respond to the injustices of 1999? I believe that he would have followed the principles of nonviolence which he advocated. This is not an easy path to follow. Living in a peaceful way takes courage and, I believe, must be rooted in God."

# The Catholic Church's Role *in* Combating Racism

BY MOST REV. JOSEPH N. PERRY

SPRING 1998

The Church led the campaign for civil rights in this country, that is, the Protestant church in general and the Baptist tradition in particular under the leadership of Rev. Martin Luther King Jr. King came in contact with the Catholic Church through individual priests, nuns, and religious who joined him with carefully orchestrated marches in racially recalcitrant urban centers of the South and North. Along his campaign, he met great church leaders like Cardinals Spellman, Meyer, and Cushing.

The Catholic Church's role in the race problem in this country is at once remarkable and puzzling. The social Gospel has been our most difficult instrument of evangelization to peddle. The message is, in fact, intellectually received by folks in the pews but loses force with its impact on our privileges of free enterprise and the pursuit of the American dream of material success. Most citizens still find the encroachment of Blacks a disturbing reality. Economics, health, education, and opportunity are some of the thickest walls dividing White and Black in America. Thirty years since the death of King, the interwoven issues of race and affirmative action seem as intractable as ever.

One cannot talk about the race problem in America without treating the intertwine of economics. Poverty and racism are closely related issues in this country because opportunity is divided between White and Black in America. And Catholics, like others, still choose to flee the city for reasons of security and the good life. Problems resulting from poverty are profound and these

tend to register alarm and indifference to the agonies of the minorities left behind. In most instances, the Church followed White flight instead of summoning her faithful to participate in life and church with those left behind.

No one indicts the penchant for seeking a better life in the suburbs. It's just that living in communities that satellite the poor guarantees that one's children seldom interact with peers who are of another race unless the school has some measure of forced integration. Outlying communities, while being symbols of opportunity, also intensify fear of the minority poor. From this social segregation, most citizens, while guarding their prerogatives, tend to look upon Blacks and other poor out of empathy or pity. Our democracy these days is laced with strident conceptions of a meritocracy. Some make it; some don't. And those who don't are often blamed for carrying the largest responsibility for their plight.

Catholics were not there to lead the crusade having just put off, for the most part by the time of the presidency of JFK, the shackles of anti-Catholic prejudice in this country. But we had our quiet heroes and heroines even while on the sidelines; however, the jeerers screaming racial epithets at the marchers were also White Catholics. Parish priests gave way to the cry of "fire" by real-estate moguls and the fear generated by the red-lining of neighborhoods. The clergy were often conspicuous in their silence in face of the summons to social and religious change.

We remain inheritors of an entrenched historical pattern of racial separation in this country that is fixed in our psyches where White and Black are totally out of touch with each other. We operate out of skewed perceptions of each other. Whites, by and large, still experience a visual and emotional dissonance when a Black person enters their space. One wonders whether some inherent psychological barrier premised in racial and color distinctions prevents that understanding people of good will desire.

We cannot rest with what appears to be a better situation for many Blacks we see on television. Integration and some modest gains with affirmative action have taken place not so much as a result of national good will, but by force of the law. Now there is seen retrenchment with these gains. People, by and large, prefer to live and work and worship and recreate and school with their own. People tend to look upon past historical errors and horrors as somebody else's sin, not theirs. Our society simply does not generate nor does it care for checks and balances to ensure equity and justice.

Despite the ethnic and racial variety of Catholicism, Catholics in this country are settled in Euro-American patterns of thought and culture and, like so many institutions in this country, have had to take a second look at Blacks. The social Gospel has not perceptively changed the choices of middle class and upper class American Catholics. The social message simply fell upon infertile soil the closer it was delivered to the threshold of domestic power and survival. Folks in the pews found the theoretics easy enough to stomach. It's the implied attitudinal and lifestyle changes that many have found non-negotiable. The separation of the races does not strike many Americans as an anomaly, but rather is justified as a legitimate option we have in a land of freedom. Despite open housing legislation and the desegregation of institutions, when Blacks encroach on a neighborhood, Whites, in due time, move elsewhere.

The record of the Catholic Church with the race problem is mixed. White Catholics in the United States continue to find Black Catholics an anomaly [even] when the New Testament gives obvious reference to Black presence and leadership in the Church from its beginning. Yet, while Cardinals Ritter and Meyer ordered archdiocesan schools in St. Louis and Chicago to desegregate and Archbishop Cousins tacitly blessed the open housing marches of Fr. Groppi in Milwaukee, the social Gospel fell hard on tight ethnic neighborhood patterns in our cities. Racial struggle is practically indigenous to the American Church, wrestling with becoming a part of the society it serves while being a prophetic voice amidst the social and moral aberrations of our society.

Like all other institutions, the Church has its inspiring figures with the race issue, while deep-seated attitudinal issues of some beg for redemption. After all, in the scheme of social relations heroes and heroines are few. There are dazzling Catholic personalities who broke through all that is sluggish, fearful, and racist in us: people like Dorothy Day, Mother Teresa, and a host of others known only to local communities. Social consciousness is not an easy product to sell in our eucharistic assemblies. It never has been. Going out of ourselves toward another is a courageous act for most of us.

In the meantime, we confess that the Church still has the most persuasive voice appealing to the moral fibers of materially advantaged Americans. The Gospel rescues us from all barriers that prevent us from creating the kingdom here on earth so we can see it in the hereafter. The Gospel, the Church's most effective tool for improving relations among peoples, redeems the broken human situation. This aspect of human brokenness of its nature surfaces saints and martyrs, scoundrels and sinners. Without doubt, the love of neighbor ethic taught by Christ is a profound dialectic.

King's dream of equality of the races is still a dream deferred as we approach the third millennium. Black contributions with art, literature, religion, sciences, and medicine are only begrudgingly mentioned. A Black person cannot drive in certain neighborhoods without being pulled over by the police. Black customers are still watched more closely than others in stores by security guards and owners. Black college and graduate students are presumed to have been given preferential treatment with admissions policies. African Americans are still, today, generalized to be drug addicts, criminally oriented, and welfare recipients even if those generalizing have never known a single Black person who fits the description.

There is much work to be done if the Church's influence will not wane. The Church remains the principal source of healing and hope for people with the race issue. We continue to need from the church prophets and agents of reconciliation, individuals and groups, laity and clergy who make it their responsibility to bring people together despite stubborn differences and the conflicts that would guarantee walls of separation. This task has been the heart of the Christian mission in our society. Issues of race are the most urgent business of Church today to aid in annihilating stereotypes and nurturing mutual respect. Ultimately, our Christian faith is about building bridges between people, not walls. ■

Most Rev. Joseph N. Perry *is an auxiliary bishop of Chicago, Illinois.*

## ASSESSING KING'S LEGACY THIRTY YEARS AFTER HIS DEATH
### BY MARK PATTISON, CATHOLIC NEWS SERVICE • APRIL 1998

WASHINGTON (CNS)—Unerringly, Black Catholics can tell you where they were when they first heard of the assassination of the Rev. Martin Luther King Jr.

They can recall gathering around television sets to hear the news bulletins about the fatal shooting April 4, 1968, in Memphis, Tennessee. They can remember seeing federal troops moving into their neighborhoods. They can still see cities aglow from rioting.

Just as unerringly, they can tell you where America stands today in terms of honoring King's legacy.

For Sr. Patricia Chappell, head of the National Black Sisters Conference, the answer, after thirty years, is "there have been good intentions, but I think we are far from equality for all. I don't believe that discrimination has been erased from our society. Children of color are receiving a substandard education, not being given the skills that they need as they enter the twenty-first century."

Both Sr. Chappell and Joseph Conrad, a permanent deacon who is head of the National Catholic Conference for Interracial Justice, spoke strongly against what they called "systemic discrimination" within the Catholic Church itself.

Sr. Chappell noted the lack of African American vocations and the closure of Catholic schools in the inner cities, "and yet we speak about evangelization."

With the exception of appointing a few more Black bishops, the Church is "hoping the problem is going to go away without the Church doing anything significant," Conrad said. "The Church does business the same way it always does. It banks the same way it always does, it hires the same way it always does."

Conrad said he believed minority bishops are "pressured" to not "make waves if you want to succeed," adding that new leaders of all types face similar pressure.

After King was killed, no one Black leader seemed to step in to fill the void he left. But such a conclusion is inherently false, Conrad said. "We don't expect White America to have one leader," he explained. "But it's easier to deal with one Black leader, one Hispanic leader, one Asian leader. Martin Luther King was the one who got the ink and the TV time."

Ralph McCloud, director of peace and justice for the Diocese of Fort Worth, Texas, said he saw advances for

Blacks in the first twenty years since King's death, but in the last ten years they have been stalled.

"I think we've abandoned a lot of the values Dr. King stood for as relates to being brothers and sisters to each other," McCloud said, pointing to racial polarization and fears stemming from the Million Man March, the Rodney King beating trial and the O. J. Simpson murder trial.

Joseph Hubbard, head of the National Office for Black Catholics, pointed to the voter repeal of affirmative action in California and a similar referendum in Washington state as evidence that King's work will take longer to finish.

Many use King's axiom that "we should judge a man not by the color of his skin but by the content of his character"

to bolster their arguments against affirmative action, but Hubbard said that was an incorrect reading.

"King's thing was, let's make the Constitution work, and the Bill of Rights," Hubbard said. Affirmative action is not about lowering standards but providing opportunity, he added. And without "selective certification" in such fields as law and medicine, Blacks will be indefinitely kept down economically, he said.

Bishop Wilton D. Gregory of Belleville, Illinois, said he saw a correlation between the thirtieth anniversary of the King slaying and the beginning of Holy Week.

"It is a time of prayerful reflection for all of us," Bishop Gregory said, "of the wisdom and the legacy of Dr. King has made for our time," specifically King's philosophy of nonviolence.

Left undone from King's agenda, in Bishop Gregory's view, is "a healing of our racial legacy. We've made progress, though. We can talk about it in certain circumstances. . . . But we have not been able to put it behind us."

The dialogue on race initiated by President Clinton and the subsequent series of public meetings on the topic, he added, are "very good steps, but they're tentative. We should own up publicly and openly where we need to take steps, even as we rejoice where we have made strides."

Jacqueline Wilson, director of the Archdiocese of Washington's Office for Black Catholics, said she has seen economic success for many Black Americans in the thirty years since the slaying. "Some of us have been able to get into the upper middle class," she said, "but the majority are still poor."

She said the work of the thirty-nine-year-old King "is all the greater" thirty years after his death "because he did not ignore the lower classes," according to Wilson. "Today, even in his old age, he'd be out there for us, marching, and galvanizing his people. I don't think he would ever have stopped."

As Catholics, McCloud said, "with our universality, we have an opportunity to be the leaders in race relations as it relates to actually engaging in dialogue, as it relates to advocating for people who are pushed to the edges."

While U.S. society can learn much from King, individuals can—and have.

"Dr. King was a prayerful man in the middle of chaos, racism, etc.," Sr. Chappell said. "My own life has been a prayerful one to provide me the sustenance that I need to keep on keeping on."

# Homily: Mass *for the* Birthday *of* Dr. Martin Luther King Jr.

BY MOST REV. JUSTIN F. RIGALI

JANUARY 2000

Dear Friends in our Lord Jesus Christ,

*It is good to be together today.*

It is hard to believe that a year has passed since last we were here together in this Church, honoring the ideals of the late Dr. Martin Luther King Jr.

It is hard to believe that it is already nearly a year since the historic Pastoral Visit of our Holy Father to St. Louis last January 26-27.

It is hard to believe that after three years of preparation it is already the great Jubilee Year of the Lord, the Holy Year that marks the start of the third Millennium since the birth of Jesus Christ.

We gather today to *give thanks* for all that has happened to us in this year since we last celebrated together. We give thanks to God for the Pastoral Visit of Pope John Paul II. This visit continues to inspire us. We give thanks to God for all His blessings—His blessings on our families, our parishes and our metropolitan area. We give thanks for the safe passage into the Holy Year, this Jubilee of our Lord, and for the great opportunity of grace that this Holy Year affords us. Finally, as we gather here to celebrate

the Eucharistic Sacrifice, which is the source and summit of our Christian lives, we give thanks to the Lord for the gift of His Son Jesus Christ, who became man to save each of us.

We have so much to be thankful for. Indeed, who cannot help but sing out in joy and thanksgiving:

*God is good! All the time!*
*All the time! God is good!*

It is good to be back together *to honor the ideals of Dr. Martin Luther King Jr.,* who was a dedicated Christian, a zealous preacher of the Gospel, a tireless defender of the dignity of the human person, an uncompromising champion of the equal human dignity of all God's sons and daughters, an ambassador of reconciliation and peace. We give thanks and praise to God and to His Son Jesus Christ, in the unity of the Holy Spirit.

It is good to be back together *to celebrate this holy and living Sacrifice* of the Eucharist. In this holy and living Sacrifice, we celebrate and proclaim the absolute truth of those values which informed Dr. King's life. These values were supremely exemplified—and given human form—in the life and ministry of our Lord Jesus Christ. By His dying and rising to new life, Jesus Christ has demonstrated that, for all who live His Gospel, life and love will ultimately be victorious.

In his own life and death, Dr. King challenged Americans to live in pursuit of justice. By his words and work, he inspired so many men and women to bear witness to *the equal human dignity of all people.* He taught Christians *to pursue resolutely the cause of justice.* Although there are many instances in which our society has accomplished much, the work for justice is far from complete.

Right here in our city less than one year ago, we heard our Holy Father challenge us *"to put an end to every form of racism,* a plague which your bishops have called one of the most persistent and destructive evils of the nation." The pope's challenge cannot be ignored.

It is good to be together *to listen to the words of Sacred Scripture.* The inspired words of God never fail to uplift and teach us. Today these readings draw our attention *to the Lord's call for us to follow Him.*

In the First Reading from the Book of Samuel, the Lord calls the young man Samuel to follow Him. Samuel,

who was not familiar with the Lord, is confused by the Lord's call. He mistakes this call for a calling by the priest Eli. But finally Samuel is made to understand that it is the Lord Himself who is calling him.

Samuel's response, so simple and direct, is the response we are all called to make: "Speak, Lord, your servant is listening." This simple act of recognizing the Lord brings Samuel close to Him and sends Samuel on his way to a life of obedience to the Lord.

In the Second Reading from St. Paul's Letter to the Corinthians, the Apostle describes how each person, when joined to Jesus Christ, is linked to His Body, the Church. And St. Paul directs us *to understand the inherent inviolability and dignity of the human body* because of our unity with the Lord in the Spirit.

Finally, in the Gospel according to St. John, we hear the account of the calling of St. Peter. Simon, the brother of Andrew, was brought to Jesus and Jesus named him "Peter," which means "rock." This call of Peter by Jesus is central to the Church: Peter becomes the very rock upon which the Lord builds His Church.

Each of these readings speaks to us *about discipleship.* We must respond like Samuel by allowing the Lord to speak in our lives, and we must serve Him with joy. We must understand the gift of Christ and how we are members of His Body, as St. Paul teaches us. And we must, at all times, build up the Church by our unity with the Successor of St. Peter, the visible head of Christ's Church.

The challenge of discipleship is profound, and we must recognize it as our vocation. *In responding to the Lord's call*—like Samuel and like St. Peter—we glorify God and express the meaning of our lives.

One aspect of our response to the Lord's call is *our pursuit of justice and peace.* As our Holy Father told us during his Pastoral Visit last year:

*If you want peace*, work for justice.
*If you want justice*, defend life.
*If you want life*, embrace the truth—
*the truth revealed by God.*

These words speak of our desire for God, for the truth of our Lord Jesus Christ and for all that His Gospel demands of us.

Some years ago now, the African American bishops of the United States raised their voices in prophetic witness to the truth of Jesus Christ in their Pastoral Letter on Evangelization, *What We have Seen and Heard*. This Pastoral Letter describes the witness of our African American Catholics. For everyone, discipleship involves acknowledging our gifts and putting them to use for the Church. The Bishops cite the words of Pope Paul VI to all sons and daughters of Africa: "You must now give your gifts of Blackness to the whole Church."

Today, the rest of the community greets our African American Catholics and embraces them. *For them and with them we give thanks to God. Their gifts are numerous and enriching.* We are grateful for the values of their heritage, for what they contribute to the Catholicity of the Church and, above all, for who they are.

We give thanks today too for all those in our Church who have accepted the call to discipleship, especially *by embracing the challenge of justice*, which brings forth peace.

One such person was Cardinal Joseph Ritter, Archbishop of St. Louis. In fact, this very celebration is linked to Cardinal Ritter. This celebration, the twenty-fourth annual commemoration, is hosted by the Archdiocesan Commission on Human Rights. The Commission, established by Cardinal Ritter, is a con-

crete example of the effort of the church in St. Louis to accept the challenge of addressing racism and other injustices. Cardinal Ritter led by example, *ordering the integration of Catholic schools* seven years before the Supreme Court mandated this integration throughout the land. In 1963, he founded the Commission and charged its members *to address issues of racism and injustice.* We reverence his memory and express thanksgiving for his witness.

There are so many others—living and dead—who have worked for justice. One of these, our own Msgr. John Shocklee, is an example of selfless dedication to the pursuit of justice and the elimination of racism. For years he served the Church as head of our Human Rights Office. Today, that office continues to work, inspired by his dedication and service. We are grateful to Msgr. Shocklee and pray that his commitment to justice may continue to inspire many others.

In the past year, we have seen other instances of accepting the challenge of discipleship. Their mention is not meant to be exhaustive.

One instance of discipleship was evident in the Freedom Ride 1999. Last June, twenty-five of our

Archdiocesan Catholics rode buses to Mississippi and Alabama to commemorate the anniversary of the tragic murder of three civil rights workers in Meridian, Mississippi, in 1963. This Freedom Ride was educational and spiritual. The group extolled justice in the dedication of civil rights workers of the 1960s, including many Catholic men and women. And the participants prayed together in the celebration of the Eucharist.

With regard to this Freedom Ride, I would mention the witness of Sr. Antona Ebo, FSM. Sr. Antona had been a participant years ago at the marches in Selma, Alabama. She has served the Lord through her religious vocation, a vocation that began in the segregated formation program of her youth. We give thanks for her discipleship and the discipleship of all others dedicated to Christian love and freedom, to all those who testify to *the uplifting and liberating message of Christ*.

During this past year, our own Cardinal Ritter College Prep celebrated the twentieth anniversary of its founding. This celebration took place amidst immense and unprecedented support from the Church and the community in announcing plans to relocate and build a new school in midtown. We give thanks to all the sup-

porters of Cardinal Ritter Prep, to its administrators, teachers and students. The school takes seriously *the call to uplift and serve others through Catholic education.* Today marks the Day for Charity, Justice and Peace as designated by the Church. As part of the program of this day, the Church offers for our acceptance the Pledge for Charity, Justice and Peace. This pledge, with its eight suggestions, serves as *a framework for responding to the call to discipleship*. It serves as a reminder of the many aspects and challenges of discipleship.

Taking inspiration from our Holy Father's challenge to eliminate racism, I lift my voice *to challenge all Catholics and people of good will* in the St. Louis metropolitan area and in the state of Missouri. We must examine our hearts and our lives and see if and when racism or any form of discrimination holds us in bondage. Prejudice and discrimination violently shackle the lives not only of their victims but also of their perpetrators.

Our commitment as the Church is clear: in this Jubilee year, we must seek the reconciliation of all people with God and among themselves. Too often, while we have succeeded in eliminating much racism from our public institutions, we still see tragic traces in our met-

ropolitan area where walls created by racism still isolate and divide. We continue to experience the polarization of hearts still not liberated from prejudice and discrimination—hearts still closed to the fullness of the Gospel of God's love.

With Dr. Martin Luther King Jr. we are convinced that "Love is the only force capable of transforming an enemy into a friend." In pursuing this love, we can—and we must—recommit ourselves day by day, hour by hour, to the removal of all barriers—especially those of the heart—that continue to divide our community. We must build *a civilization of love* which respects the inviolability of each life and the dignity of every person—regardless of race, ethnic origin, culture, sex or religion—because every person shares humanity with the Son of God.

It is good to be together. We have so much to be thankful for. In a few moments, we will celebrate the holy Sacrifice of the Mass. We will participate in the death and resurrection of Jesus Christ, who has given his life for us. We bring to this Eucharistic Sacrifice the whole of our being, for as St. Paul attests: "We are the Lord's."

As we continue to embrace our call to discipleship, with Jesus as our Lord and Savior, and with *a dream of hope* like the one described by Dr. King, we sing out with joy:

> *God is good! All the time!*
> *All the time! God is good!*
> *Praised be Jesus Christ! Amen.* ■

Most Rev. Justin F. Rigali *is the archbishop of St. Louis, Missouri.*

PART FIVE:

HATE CRIMES

# Remarks *to the* Task Force *on* Racism

BY HIS EMINENCE FRANCIS CARDINAL GEORGE, OMI

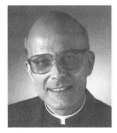

MAY 1997

As I understand it, this is an unprecedented assembly of pastors, principals and other parish and school leaders. I am grateful that Bishop Goedert acted so decisively two months ago [in forming this Catholic task force on racism] in response to the horrible beating of Lenard Clark so that the leadership of the Archdiocese can focus on the problem of racism. Yesterday, the Presbyterial Council also took up this topic, and I expect these will be only the first considerations of how we can best respond to this problem, which the Pontifical Commission on Justice and Peace said "is a wound in humanity's side that mysteriously stays open."[1]

As most of you undoubtedly know, on Tuesday, April 8, I visited Lenard Clark at the Rehabilitation Institute of Chicago just after the news conference announcing my appointment as Archbishop of Chicago. In the few moments that I had with him and with Officer Jim Mullen, the heartbreaking consequences of such senseless violence stood out to me. While the circumstances that put Officer Mullen and Lenard Clark in the Rehab Institute differed greatly, the violence committed against them violated two of the most fundamental principles of Catholic social teaching: the sacredness of each and every human life, and the dignity of every person. The current conditions of these two persons remind us that these

principles have consequences, and that our work together to promote the sacredness of life and the dignity of each person will make our metropolitan area a more peaceful place and a more caring community.

It has been easy to detect that the tragic beating of Lenard Clark has galvanized people throughout Chicagoland. The registrations for [the task-force organized workshops addressing discrimination] today and tomorrow total almost one thousand people. It is apparent that people are altering their usual schedules to respond. Sadly, it too often takes the suffering of the innocent to awaken many of us to the need to act on behalf of social justice. The stark violation of Lenard Clark's basic human dignity, and the assault on his right to life has provoked a necessary and powerful response. It has compelled people of faith to recognize that racism is more than a social problem; it is likewise a spiritual problem. At its root, racism is a sin.

In November of 1979, the National Conference of Catholic Bishops stated this quite clearly. They wrote "racism is a sin: a sin that divides the human family, blots out the image of God among specific members of that family, and violates the fundamental dignity of those called to be children of the same Father."[2] *Brothers and Sisters to Us: U.S. Bishops' Pastoral Letter on Racism in Our Day*, the document from which this declaration comes, is familiar to some but unknown to many. It needs to be a resource for us as we continue on this path of decrying racism and promoting racial justice.

> Compiled from CNN news reports: In March of 1997, thirteen-year-old Lenard Clark was attacked as he and two friends rode their bicycles through the predominantly White Bridgeport area on Chicago's South Side. Clark's friends escaped harm, but he was beaten into a coma. He remained in a coma for days after the racially-motivated attack. Clark spent weeks in the Rehabilitation Institute of Chicago. Pediatrician and psychiatrist Dr. Lisa Thornton said that the frontal lobes of Clark's brain sustained damage, leading to severe traumatic brain injury. Three Bridgeport men, all under the age of twenty-one, were charged with attempted murder, a hate crime, and aggravated battery.
>
> Clark is now back home with his family. His mother, Wanda McMurray, spoke with CNN, after a year of not communicating with the media. She says she won't return hate for hate. "Just because this happened to my son, I don't want me and my kids to say every White person that walks the street, we don't like them. You can't ever say you don't like a person and you don't like them."
>
> In October 1996, Chicago police officer Jim Mullen was responding to a call about a man shooting out an apartment window. The suspect, while fleeing the building, fired a gun on Mullen, hitting him in the face. The bullet lodged in Mullen's spine, leaving him a quadriplegic. "A lot of people would be bitter and angry," says Mullen. "The way I look at it, this is the card I was dealt and I'm just going to have to play it."

I also recommend to you another Church statement entitled, *The Church and Racism: Towards a More Fraternal Society*. This statement from the Pontifical Commission on Justice and Peace situates the problem of racism in a global context. It cites Pope John Paul II who wrote, "Man's creation by God 'in his own image' confers upon every human person an eminent dignity; it also postulates the fundamental equality of all human beings," The Holy Father went on to say, "every form of discrimination based on race . . . is absolutely unacceptable."[3]

I point to these ecclesial declarations so that we may ground ourselves in our tradition as we continue the task that this assembly begins. I have been away from Chicago for thirty years. I do not presume to know the complexities of how this problem manifests itself here today. With your help, and with the help of the ecumenical and interfaith communities, as well as through the civic community, I will become aware of the complex dynamics that engulf the ongoing drive for racial justice in this metropolitan area.

As my starting point, however, I want to affirm the work that has begun, to point to the fundamental church teaching that we have to draw from, and finally, to urge that we not settle for simplistic answers to this complex problem. The roots of racism are deep in our culture. It will take a committed, creative and dynamic effort to move us in the right direction. The best homily or the most brilliant lesson plan alone will not be able to extirpate it. "It is [a] wound in humanity's side that mysteriously remains open," the Pontifical Commission wrote, adding that, "Everyone, therefore, must make efforts to heal it with great firmness and patience."

Our fundamental task is to preach the Gospel, to invite people to love the Lord and to live in His light. The sin of racism challenges all of us to conversion, for it reveals that we have not yet enveloped ourselves fully in God's love. May this assembly empower all of us to experience God's love in a new way, and may it send us forth to help heal this wound. ∎

His Eminence Francis Cardinal George, OMI, *is the archbishop of Chicago, Illinois.*

**NOTES**

1    Pontifical Commission, "Iustitia et Pax," in *The Church and Racism: Towards a More Fraternal Society*, 1988, 44.

2    National Conference of Catholic Bishops, *Brothers and Sisters to Us: U.S. Bishops' Pastoral Letter on Racism in Our Day*, 1979, 3.

3    *The Church and Racism*, 26.

## CATHOLICS TARGET "SIN" OF RACISM

BY FLYNN McROBERTS, *THE CHICAGO TRIBUNE* • MAY 1997

CHICAGO—In a city where some priests, decades ago, were said to have turned away Blacks from the steps of their churches, racism is no stranger to Roman Catholics in Chicago.

But with [the beating of Lenard Clark and shooting of Officer Jim Mullen] fresh in their minds, leaders of the Church are renewing efforts to confront the problem of racism both inside and outside their parishes.

Cardinal Francis George made it clear Wednesday at a workshop in Harvey, Illinois—and during a meeting with archdiocesan priests the day before—that addressing discrimination would be one of his chief priorities.

"The Church brings the Gospel" to the issue of racism, George said during a session that drew several hundred educators, priests and others to a Harvey hotel banquet room. "But we have to see how . . . the gospel can be heard and how it can be applied."

The workshop, followed by a similar one Thursday in Rosemont, Illinois, was organized by a task force created in March by Bishop Raymond Goedert in the wake of thirteen-year-old Lenard Clark's beating. The three accused attackers are current or former students of De La Salle Institute, a Catholic high school.

Earlier in the month, students at Brother Rice, another Catholic high school, taunted a Black basketball player.

After Wednesday's workshop, George said he had asked the task force to look not only at individual racist attitudes but "structural problems" that manifest racism. "Foremost among them are housing patterns."

George was joined by other church leaders, including auxiliary Bishop George Murry.

"We have lingering problems of lack of respect, lack of justice," Murry said. "This is an attempt to find concrete

ways—not just the talk—to help people recognize that to treat people of a different color with discrimination is a sin."

The session was not without voices of dissent. Tirso Villafuerte, a parishoner from St. Kevin Catholic Church on Chicago's South Side, noted the absence of Latino speakers and panelists. "Isn't that showing prejudice?" he asked.

But some of the most outspoken critics of how the Church has dealt with the issue of race expressed confidence in George's willingness to address it.

On Tuesday, the archbishop spoke to the Presbyterial Council, the official body representing priests within the archdiocese, for an hour and a half about racism and ways to combat it in their parishes.

"He has come across to me in the last two days as someone who is not afraid to get his hands and feet dirty on this issue," said Rev. Mike Ivers, pastor of St. Agatha Catholic Church on the city's West Side. "He's really putting himself right out there." Echoing others who attended Wednesday's workshop, Ivers said it was "very unfortunate that it took the Lenard Clark incident to bring together something like this . . . but this is a very serious effort on the part of the Church."

Ivers said the effort was over due. "We've had this problem for a long time," he said. "Historically in the Catholic Church in Chicago, you had priests standing on the steps of parishes telling African Americans that they weren't welcome there. That's forty years ago, thirty years ago."

Since then, strides have been made, but not enough, he said. This time, though, Ivers sees a real difference being made. "I see a real gathering on this issue, a real energy," he said. "I really see the Church coming together on this."

# Dealing With Hate:
# Threat *of* Cicero Rally Raises Questions

BY BILL BRITT, *THE NEW WORLD*

MARCH 1998

Some people hate Mondays. Others hate Midwestern winters. In [Cicero, Illinois], Cubs and Sox fans bask in the folly of the others' shortcomings. But is this really hate?

A true hatemonger, according to Webster's, is a propagandist who seeks to provoke hatred and prejudice, especially against a minority group or groups—a definition that fits the Ku Klux Klan, a group of self-described hatemongers whose actions have disrupted more than one community.

The Klan's heavily publicized plans for a rally in Cicero March 14, which was later cancelled, raised questions of freedom of speech, but also brought civic, community and religious leaders together to take a stand against hate. More than that, the episode has provided Chicago-area Catholics with the opportunity to examine how they deal with hate.

Once a regular target of the KKK, European Catholics no longer receive the brunt of their hate and propaganda. But African Americans, Jews and Hispanics, of whom an overwhelming number are Catholic, still come under attack from the Klan.

How should Catholics deal with hate? Do we confront it and attempt to expose it? Or do we ignore it and do something constructive?

The Interfaith Leadership Project of Cicero, Berwyn and Stickney, Illinois, had proposed a policy of avoiding the Klan rally. Activities had been planned for area families at Morton East High School, 2923 S. Austin Blvd., that included food, entertainment and activities. An interfaith prayer service was scheduled at Mary Queen of Heaven Church, 5300 W. 24th Street.

"The Klan claimed to have never cancelled a rally, but did," said Fr. Richard Prendergast, pastor of St. Mary of Celle, Berwyn. "We, the united ethnic and faith community of Cicero, Berwyn and Stickney consider this a great victory."

Plans for the prayer service and family activities are still scheduled, he said.

Prior to the cancellation announcement, Francis Cardinal George wrote to Prendergast: "In coming together for prayer, you acknowledge our dependence on God to counter hatred with love. In promoting a peaceful response, you are showing the way to defuse the potential for violence."

During the seventy-fifth anniversary of St. Frances of Rome Parish in Cicero, March 8, Cardinal George told the congregation: "We don't have to worry about the KKK. God dwells among his people always. [Hatred] is far more subtle when it shows up in places it shouldn't. Not at some rally."

"This approach [of avoidance] has a proven track record in other communities that have dealt with the Klan," said Servite Fr. John Pawlikowski, professor of ethics at Catholic Theological Union (CTU). "The difficult part is that as Catholics we profess to love everyone. This can be hard to live out."

When confronted with a group that professes hate, Catholics should try to love, but also recognize whom they're dealing with, he said.

"In some circumstances, the best thing to do is to marginalize them," Pawlikowski said. "Create other activities for the residents. Don't give them the audience they so desperately want."

Pawlikowski admits though, when a group of Illinois Nazis proposed to march in Skokie a few years ago, he was personally inclined to counter-protest. The CTU professor is deeply involved in Catholic-Jewish dialogue. "There are so many people in Skokie who were victims and children of victims of the Nazis that I felt I had to take a stand," he said. "This puts freedom of speech in question."

He said he questions the simplistic answer that freedom of speech means any speech, anywhere, anytime.

"People argue with a very rational approach that if people hear hate they will reject it," Pawlikowski said. "They completely ignore the emotional dimension. That argument doesn't take full consideration of a speaker like Hitler who affected rational people's emotions."

Cicero, which has a larger Hispanic population than any other western suburb, may undergo an unforeseen healing transformation, Pawlikowski said.

"This may have the exact opposite effect than the Klan had hoped for," he said. "This may break down some barriers and open relations with people who otherwise may not have been connected."

Jim Lund, director of the archdiocesan Office for the Ministry of Peace and Justice, said the KKK's day has passed.

"There are far more serious and subtle issues of racism in America than whatever the KKK has to say or will do," he said. "Those groups are out in the woods. All the KKK has gained is the disgust of a community."

But does Lund hate the KKK?

"I ignore them. That's the best thing to do." ■

# Letter *to* St. Michael Parish
## *on the* Tragic Death *of* James Byrd

BY MOST REV. JOSEPH A. GALANTE

JUNE 1998

My dear Sisters and Brothers,

I write to you in a time of great sadness and pain to offer you my condolences and my sincere sorrow for the pain that all of you, and especially the Byrd family, have been enduring these days. You are very much in my prayers and in my heart.

There are no words which can bring logic and sense to what is a brutal and sinfully stupid crime. And yet as we, in our hurt and pain, seek to rebuild a sense of hope and a sense of love, to rekindle our faith, we are faced with something that all too often our society does not wish to admit. The reality of sin, our turning away from God's will and from conformity with the will of the Father, as has been expressed to us by His Son, Jesus, continues to bring disruption and pain to so many people.

The horrible event of the death of James Byrd is a vivid reminder that sin does exist, that we human beings are capable of willfully violating God's law and injuring our sisters and brothers.

What are the remedies for sin, for our human weakness? For all people, the mercy and the love of God as shown through His Son, Jesus, is always offered to us. Our need to grow in our relationship with Jesus is brought home again at times like this. For us Catholics we have the wonderful gifts of the sacraments, especially the sacrament of Reconciliation. The opportunity through confession, to acknowledge our sins, to express our sorrow, to open ourselves to God's forgiveness and healing. We also have the wonderful gift of Eucharist, where we gather as a community each week to be present again and to receive the benefits of the suffering, death and resurrection of Jesus. We hear God's word, we are touched by that word, with, in and through Jesus we pray to the Father. Again for us Catholics we have the opportunity to receive the Body and Blood of Jesus in Holy Communion.

This terrible tragedy is a reminder that all of us need to renew our faith, our hope and our love. I pray with you and for you that out of this terrible and evil event that good can and will result. The power of God's love will triumph over the wickedness and disruption of sin. We know by our faith that by the death and resurrection of Jesus sin has been conquered. May all of us reach out and open our lives to that healing power, to that saving grace that Jesus has won for us.

May God bless and strengthen all of you in the community of Jasper. ■

Most Rev. Joseph A. Galante *is the bishop of Dallas, Texas, and the chairman of the bishops' Committee on Communications.*

## COMMUNITY OF JASPER BEGINS HEALING PROCESS AFTER TRAGIC DEATH
### BY KAREN GILMAN, CATHOLIC NEWS SERVICE • JUNE 1998

JASPER, Texas (CNS)—The tragic death of a forty-nine-year-old Black man, apparently at the hands of three White men, serves as "a reminder that all of us need to renew our faith, our hope, and our love," Beaumont Bishop Joseph A. Galante said after the murder.

On June 7, Jasper County sheriffs found James Byrd Jr. dead on a county road outside Jasper. The three men charged with his murder are White, and authorities are calling the murder a hate crime.

La Salette Fr. Ron Foshage, pastor of St. Michael, read the bishop's letter to his congregation during Masses June 13 and 14. He told the parishioners he does not see racism in the community and that violence is not common.

"So much we heard [in the media] is not true, we know it's not true," he said.

Jasper is a town that is about 45 percent Black in a county that is less than 20 percent Black.

A community-wide, ecumenical prayer service sponsored by the Jasper Ministerial Alliance and the Jasper Chamber of Commerce was held June 15 to help with the healing after Byrd's tragic death.

Fr. Foshage, in one of the opening prayers at the service, said the ministers of Jasper have preached of love and forgiveness in their homilies, but that James Byrd's family is living these ideas.

He asked for God to continue to give strength to the community of Jasper and to bless the entire Byrd family.

The group gathered for the service on the Jasper County Courthouse lawn included people of all ages and races. Several participants came from out of town, including fourteen Dominican Sisters from Beaumont who were on

retreat and eight Dominicans who drove over from Houston.

Throughout the prayer service the theme of forgiveness and healing was found. The ministers prayed for forgiveness of sins of commission and sins of omission; for families, the community and for America; for a nation strong in the Lord; for good governmental leadership in the city, county, state and nation; that tragedies such as this would not be repeated; and for the three men charged with the death.

In between each minister, hymns such as "How Great Thou Art," "Amazing Grace" and "God Bless America" were sung.

The service ended with the plea for the healing hand of grace to come upon the community and a call for everyone to turn around and hug someone.

Jasper Chief of Police Harlen Alexander estimated the crowd at 1,500 people, a significant turnout in a community of about 8,000.

A task force has been formed to work within Jasper to help the people and the community at large to get past this tragedy, said Fr. Foshage, who was chosen to be a member.

The task force will be led by Jasper Mayor R. C. Horn. Members will include representatives of the business community, chamber of commerce, religious community and government.

One item that was brought up at the first meeting June 16, Fr. Foshage said, was that although the group felt another citywide service was needed, the community needs more than prayer. Upcoming meetings will focus on suggestions and a timeline for taking Jasper past the tragedy.

"I think the healing has begun," Fr. Foshage told the East Texas Catholic, Beaumont's diocesan newspaper. "I haven't met any bitterness [in the community] throughout the past week."

Members from the entire community of Jasper, Black and White, have turned out in support of Byrd's family. In addition, regional, state and national leaders visited Jasper for the funeral services.

Those attending included the Rev. Jesse Jackson; U.S. Transportation Secretary Rodney Slater; Rep. Maxine Waters, D-Calif., who chairs the Congressional Black Caucus; Houston Mayor Lee Brown; U.S. Sen. Kay Bailey Hutchison, R-Texas; and the Rev. Al Sharpton of New York.

According to a police reconstruction of events, Byrd was walking home in the early morning hours of June 7 after a family gathering, when three men in a truck picked him up. They drove out of town where they beat Byrd. Byrd was then chained by the ankles to the back of the pickup and dragged two miles down a paved county road to his death.

The three men accused of the murder have all served time in prison before. Two of the accused are suspected to have ties to the Ku Klux Klan and the Aryan Nation, White supremacist groups.

# Statement *on the* Killing *of* Mr. Amadou Diallo

BY HIS EMINENCE JOHN CARDINAL O'CONNOR

MARCH 1999

Last Sunday I asked prayers for the soul of Amadou Diallo, for the consolation of his family, for the police officers accused of his death and their families. I have refrained from further comment pending the outcome of appropriate investigations. It will now be the responsibility of a grand jury or other duly appointed authority to determine the fate of the police officers involved.

No grand jury, however, no local or federal authority, can adequately compensate for the death of a human person, made in the image of God, or assuage the suffering and sorrow of his family and loved ones. We can and we must pray. We can and we must weep. We can and we must make whatever restitution is possible. But the only way we can make sense out of this killing—if we *can* make sense out of it at all—is to use it to stop *all* killing. We have created what Pope John Paul II has called a "culture of death." We must reach out, every one of us, whatever our color, our race, our ethnic background, our religion, we must reach out to one another, with God's grace, to restore a culture of life. We have gone mad with violence. It meets us at every turn, in a thousand different ways. Moses told the people before they were to enter the Promised Land: "You have before you life and death. Choose life."

To deny that African Americans, Blacks, have suffered inhuman discrimination in our country would be the height of hypocrisy. To claim that, 223 years after the Declaration of Independence that holds as self-evident the truth that all men are created equal, we who are White truly treat Black brothers and sisters as equal is to deny reality. If I am walking a lonely street at night, do I fear the approach of a White man, as I fear the approach of a Black man? Let us be brutally honest.

Because of more than two centuries of prejudice, so many of us who are White and so many of us who are Black fear one another, question one another, are suspicious of one another. How many of us truly, deeply love one another? The reality is that there can be no love without justice, and justice delayed is justice denied. We must pledge ourselves to a future of liberty and justice for *all*, for *all*, without exception. Pope John Paul II gave us the blueprint in addressing the United Nations here in New York in 1995:

> We must overcome our fear of the future. But we will not be able to overcome it completely unless we do so together. . . . The answer to the fear which darkens human existence at the end of the twentieth century is the common effort to build the civilization of love, founded on the universal values of peace, solidarity, justice and liberty. . . . We must not be afraid of the future. We must not be afraid of man. It is no accident that we are here. Each and every human person has been created in the "image and likeness" of the One who is the origin of all that is. We have within us the capacities for wisdom and virtue. With these gifts, and with the help of God's grace, we can build in the next century and the next millennium a civilization worthy of the human person, a true culture of freedom. We can and must do so! And in

doing so, we shall see that the tears of this century have prepared the ground for a new springtime of the human spirit. (Address to the United Nations General Assembly, October 5, 1995)

Finally, despite the tragedy of the killing of Amadou Diallo, no imperative of political correctness can bring me to denounce the huge numbers of men and women of the New York Police Department who serve us all, day after day, night after night, often in extremely demanding circumstances, with courage, with integrity, with generosity, with self-sacrifice. The mistakes, the follies, the sins, the treacheries, the violence, even the killings perpetrated by some, can not, must not, blind us to the nobility of the vast majority, who themselves abhor whatever makes a mockery of their calling to protect and defend their fellow human beings. In my judgment, the gratitude we owe them can never be discounted by the failure of some.

As we pray once again today for eternal repose of the soul of Amadou Diallo and for the consolation of his family, let us pray for all the families of the police officers involved, who must be suffering indescribably, as well. The officers themselves we entrust to our legal and judicial system and to God.

And now I publicly pledge my own willingness to join, at an appropriate time and in an appropriate place, with representatives of every religious body in New York, to join in a great outpouring of prayer in preparation for the Third Millennium, that we, God's creatures, of every race, color and religious persuasion will commit ourselves to build together a civilization of love. ∎

His Eminence John Cardinal O'Connor *is the former archbishop of New York, New York.*

## CARDINAL CALLS ON NEW YORK POLICE TO ADDRESS CHARGES OF MALTREATMENT

BY TRACY EARLY, CATHOLIC NEWS SERVICE • MARCH 1999

NEW YORK (CNS)—Cardinal John J. O'Connor of New York praised the city's police in a homily March 21, but said perceptions of police injustices against minorities must be addressed. "It is rare that perceptions have no foundation," he said.

With hundreds of police from the Holy Name Society in St. Patrick's Cathedral for their annual Mass, the cardinal spoke of tensions arising over a number of tragedies, but especially the February 4 killing of an unarmed Black man, Amadou Diallo, by four White police officers.

Cardinal O'Connor said "a certain anxiety" was affecting New York, and "to pretend that it doesn't exist would be foolhardy." He said most New Yorkers would want to tell their police, "We deeply believe in you. We trust you. We are grateful for you. We love you." Residents recognize

that the police make "tremendous sacrifices," and that many of them put their lives "at risk every day," he said.

But Cardinal O'Connor noted that police do make mistakes, and a small number of them make "grave mistakes" that are "very damaging" to individuals, families and the city. But he said people need to begin with "the basic premise of widespread goodness in the New York City Police Department," not the premise "that our police department is rotten to the core."

Cardinal O'Connor compared the police situation with past incidents of scandal involving priests. When those occurred in the New York Archdiocese, every priest felt people might look at him with contempt, the cardinal said. He said he asked for an examination of archdiocesan policies, and specialists were brought in, and meetings

were held with priests. He suggested New York needed to handle the police issue with a similar approach of dealing with alleged offenses while supporting the larger group from which any offenders came.

Cardinal O'Connor said he did not consider himself "judge and jury," but had been listening to those who thought they were treated with contempt. "The Church is trying to respond," he said.

The Diallo case has aroused strong and continuing protest in New York. Former Mayor David N. Dinkins and U.S. Rep. Charles B. Rangel, whose district includes Harlem, have been among the Black leaders who have engaged in civil disobedience at police headquarters and got arrested.

The shooting death also was raised during a Lenten day of recollection on Catholic social teaching March 20 at St. Charles Borromeo Church in Harlem. Keynote speaker Auxiliary Bishop Rene A. Valero focused on the history of the Church's social teaching and made no mention of Diallo, but during a question-answer period, his listeners showed that the shooting was boiling in their minds. "We haven't seen one priest or one sister from our church down there [at police headquarters] demonstrating," complained one woman. "I have no answer to that," Bishop Valero responded. He pointed out, however, that Cardinal O'Connor has been involved in some activity related to the case, including announcing plans for an interfaith prayer service.

One man said "now is the time" to tell city officials and police that "this is wrong." "If those four cops who did the shooting were Black, this case would have been solved. Those cops are murderers," he said to applause.

Fr. Theodore K. Parker, a Black priest who is pastor of All Saints Church in Harlem, said afterward that the discussion had inspired him to talk with his parishioners the next day to see if they were ready to join in some kind of demonstration at police headquarters.

The day of recollection also included a number of workshops, and it had been announced that in one of them Black police would be in dialogue with young people. No police showed up, but comments from young people at the workshop indicated that they had serious complaints about the way police treated them.

"I have had a lot of bad experiences," said one boy, complaining of the way police stopped and searched people on the street. "That's affecting the youth a lot."

Christian Brother Tyrone Davis, a Black lawyer who directs the Office of Black Ministry, encouraged the young people to think critically about how they wanted police to act, both in protecting them and in respecting their rights. He pointed out that "it is not easy being police." But he said that "we have a right to expect certain things," and one of those was that the police obey the law.

Msgr. Wallace A. Harris, a Black priest who is pastor of St. Charles Borromeo Church and vicar of Harlem, said in a later interview that the Diallo case had produced "shock and chagrin" among people in his vicariate. But he said police mistreatment of Blacks was "not that unusual." He recalled being stopped by police when he was driving home from a meeting in the Bronx, though he said he was allowed to continue as soon as police saw who he was.

# A Priority: Efforts *for* Justice *for* All

BY HIS EMINENCE JOHN CARDINAL O'CONNOR

APRIL 1999

Some thirty men and women there were and another five or six young men, high schoolers, together with their principal. All were Black, save one Hispanic. All sat at our large conference table, with perhaps fifteen priests, Black and White, taking seats against the wall, silent, listening. It was one of the most moving meetings I have ever experienced.

I do not believe that the many mothers who were present are racists, or that they were fabricating stories about fearing for their sons when they leave their homes for school. The

potential that their sons may have run-ins with police officers—both Black and White police officers—and be humiliated or mal-treated or harmed in some way is in their minds distressingly real. The belief on the part of the high school students present, respectful and well spoken, that they are sin-gled out, asked for documentation, ques-tioned harshly, while engaged in peaceful pursuits is very, very real.

Three police officers were among us in our meeting, Black, self-possessed, experienced, objective. They gave no evidence of axes to grind. All three, one man, two women, are obviously proud of being police officers.

Everyone present was educated, knowledgeable, dignified. They were reasonable people all, not radicals, not bomb-throwers. They have lived their lives as minorities. They are realists. But they want change. They want to help bring it about, calmly, constructively, at a steady pace, but not with endless delay. They are quite in agreement that the vast majority of police officers, Black, Hispanic, White, are thoroughly decent people. They also know that police officers come from and reflect the attitudes of our entire society. They are quite aware that, while at the moment our attention is on police officers, because of the tragic killing of Mr. Amadou Diallo, the real problems are societal. They know that, as a result, as minorities in our society, they are required to bend over backward simply to be seen as standing up straight. And they want all that finally and definitively changed.

It was Br. Tyrone Davis, CFC, executive director, archdiocesan Office of Black Ministry, who brought the group together at my request. It is he who I have asked to bring an action group together from this same group, including priests and others. Their responsibility? To present me with concrete steps open to the Church, to help toward those structural changes in society that can eventually achieve peace with justice for all and true reconciliation.

Many others have come to see me since I issued an invitation to do so, after the death of Mr. Diallo. With each group, each individual, I have discussed my fundamental and passionate conviction: that constructive and lasting change will come in direct proportion to the recognition by each of the sacredness of every human person as made in the image of God. That sacredness transcends color, ethnicity, religion, sex, whatever. Any movement, any program, regardless of its objective, is ultimately useless if not rooted in that fundamental reality.

As I announced this past Sunday in St. Patrick's Cathedral, we will conduct in the cathedral on Tuesday, April 20, at 10 a.m., what I hope will be a packed-to-overflowing prayer service. I hope, as well, that representatives of every religious persuasion, every race and ethnic background and color will participate. Please God, the business community will participate and public officials and, yes, the New York City police and a host of others. There is a time for protest; there is a time for prayer. This will be a time for prayer, not for protest.

Between now and the prayer service (but after Easter), I will continue to meet with as many individuals and groups as may want to meet with me, in whatever time can be made available. Every meeting I have had thus far has been constructive. I believe that trend will continue.

From my perspective, the prayer service will be by no means an ending, but a beginning of efforts toward lasting reconciliation rooted in liberty and justice for all. For whatever time I have left as Archbishop of New York, these efforts will be a priority. I am absolutely certain our priests and religious will join in enthusiastically, and countless other individuals, as well. I have high hopes. We have a great city that can become even greater, and we are not going to give up on it.

A strange column for Holy Week and Easter? Only if we forget that Jesus died for every one of us and rose for every one of us because he loves every one of us. That's what this column is really all about. ∎

His Eminence John Cardinal O'Connor *is the former archbishop of New York, New York.*

## NEW YORK CARDINAL PLEDGES TO ADDRESS CITY'S RACIAL TENSIONS

BY TRACY EARLY, CATHOLIC NEWS SERVICE • APRIL 1999

NEW YORK (CNS)—Cardinal John J. O'Connor of New York reported in his weekly column April 1 that he was continuing to look for ways of addressing tensions connected with the killing of a Black man by four White city police officers.

Writing in the archdiocesan weekly, *Catholic New York*, he commented on a meeting he had with about thirty Black men and women brought together by the director of the archdiocesan Office of Black Ministry, Christian Brother Tyrone A. Davis. The cardinal said he had also asked Br. Davis to lay the groundwork for a continuing church role by forming an action group from among those at the meeting.

New York has been embroiled in controversy since four White police officers in plain clothes killed a young African from Guinea, Amadou Diallo, in the lobby of his apartment building in the Bronx February 4. Diallo was unarmed and not accused of involvement in any crime. Widespread protests have focused not only on the killing but also on allegations that police often engage in abusive practices when dealing with Blacks, especially young Black males.

The police who killed Diallo, reportedly firing forty-one bullets and hitting him with nineteen, have given no pub-

lic explanation of their action. But some unofficial accounts have said they told friends they thought Diallo had a gun and that when one of them fell, the others thought their fellow officer had been shot.

On March 31, Bronx District Attorney Robert T. Johnson announced that a grand jury had indicted the four officers—Kenneth Boss, Sean Carroll, Edward McMellon and Richard Murphy—on charges of second-degree murder of Diallo and reckless endangerment of others. They were released on bail of $100,000 each and suspended from the police force without pay for thirty days.

Bishop Thomas V. Daily of Brooklyn, in a statement, praised Cardinal O'Connor's planned prayer service in which New Yorkers will "join in beseeching Almighty God for wisdom and guidance as we continue to endure the pain caused by the death of Amadou Diallo."

"While the legal system is at work seeking answers, I am left with the hope that justice with mercy is served, that our relations with one another are prompted by Jesus' call to love one another, and that prayer will lead us to the racial harmony that assures a sense of peace which all of us desire," he added.

## "COMING TOGETHER": PRAYER SERVICE LED BY CARDINAL O'CONNOR PROMOTES RECONCILIATION AND HEALING

BY MARY ANN POUST, *CATHOLIC NEW YORK* • APRIL 1999

NEW YORK—The Rev. Calvin Butts, one of New York City's most influential Black clergymen, made a dramatic gesture of reconciliation toward Mayor Rudolph W. Giuliani in St. Patrick's Cathedral April 20, at an interfaith prayer service led by Cardinal O'Connor to promote "human respect and community healing" after the Amadou Diallo police shooting.

In an unexpected move as he was about to lead a prayer, Rev. Butts—who has called Giuliani a racist in the past—thanked the cardinal for inviting his participation and

then stepped down from the sanctuary with outstretched arms toward the mayor who was seated in a front pew.

"Mayor Giuliani," he said, as the mayor stood up to meet him and joined in the offered embrace. There was a moment of stunned silence from those watching from the pews, then a strong burst of applause.

Later, the cardinal set aside his own closing comments to offer the lectern to Giuliani, saying he was moved to do so by "the magnificent gesture of the Rev. Calvin Butts."

Giuliani, whose ratings in the city's Black communities plummeted after the Diallo incident, expressed thanks on behalf of the city to those who prayed for peace and justice "for the Diallo family, . . . for everyone who grieves and has been hurt by this, . . . for the police officers and their families and for everyone else who has been hurt by this."

Calling New York "the most diverse city in the world," he said, "Sometimes that's a source of fear and difficulty for us, sometimes that's a source of great strength."

"We pray to God in many different ways, in many different languages," Giuliani said. "But we do it more often than any other cities. We do it in a way that emphasizes our similarities rather than our differences. Thank you, Cardinal O'Connor, for reminding us that we are children of the same God."

At City Hall that afternoon, the mayor told reporters it was an "appropriate gesture" on the part of Rev. Butts and said, "I reciprocated, in trying to demonstrate that whatever differences we have had should be put aside."

Rev. Butts, senior pastor of the Abyssinian Baptist Church in Harlem and president of the Council of Churches of New York City, spoke to reporters before the service and called for healing.

Afterward, he said that his gesture to Giuliani was unplanned. He said he was inspired by the rousing sermon of Fr. James E. Goode, OFM, president of the National Black Catholic Clergy Caucus and Apostolate for Life and guardian of St. Clare's Friary in Manhattan, which was delivered immediately before Rev. Butts' prayer.

He said he listened to Fr. Goode's challenge, "What will you give? What will you give?" and then decided what he would do.

The cardinal planned the service in response to the February 4 fatal shooting of Diallo, an unarmed African street peddler shot in the doorway of his Bronx apartment building by four White police officers who apparently thought he had a gun.

The officers were indicted on murder charges by a Bronx grand jury. Bronx District Attorney Robert T. Johnson, who is prosecuting the cases, was at the prayer service, which he later called "a meaningful experience."

"Community healing is very important," he told reporters before he left the cathedral. "We have to work on healing, and at the same time we have to focus on our strengths—and I saw a great deal of strength here today."

Noting that he grew up in New York, Johnson said, "There is much that's positive here in the city, and I think today was an affirmation of that. . . . We have to recognize that we're all coming together."

Commenting on Rev. Butts' action, he said, "I think everybody realized that was a powerful gesture, and that's what this is all about."

Br. Tyrone Davis, CFC, director of the archdiocesan Office of Black Ministry, told *Catholic New York* he viewed the gesture as "very consistent with what we're doing" and a "concrete sign of the power of prayer and the prayer service."

The cardinal was joined by Protestant, Jewish, Muslim and Orthodox clergy and Catholic bishops and priests, including Bishop Thomas V. Daily of Brooklyn, in conducting the two-hour Tuesday morning service for a congregation of about sixteen hundred people.

In welcoming remarks, the cardinal recalled his February 14 statement on the killing, in which he said: "We can and we must pray. We can and we must weep. We can and we must make whatever restitution is possible. But the only way we can make sense out of this killing . . . is to use it to stop all killing."

He said it is his hope that the prayer service "will be the beginning of a new look at racial injustice in our society and help all to recognize the sacredness of every human person." He told his listeners he will continue to meet with any individuals and groups to discuss ways to promote healing and reconciliation and repeated his sentiment that there is a time for protest and a time for prayer. "Today is a time for prayer," the cardinal said.

Bishop Daily said in a statement that the cardinal "gave a gift to the city" by calling the prayer service.

"It helped us see differences not as a problem but as a challenge, and it motivated us to continue promoting justice, peace and good will," he said.

Prayers, readings and teachings were offered by Rabbi Moses A. Birnbaum, a veteran of Jewish-Christian dialogue; Dr. Ronald B. Sobel, senior rabbi of Congregation Emanu-El of the City of New York; the Rev. Alistair Drummond, pastor of West End Presbyterian Church in Manhatten and moderator of the New York Presbytery, Presbyterian Church U.S.A.; and Imam Izakel Pasha of Masjid Malcolm Shabazz in Manhattan.

Public officials attending included Police Commissioner Howard Safir, Deputy Mayor Rudy Washington, District Attorneys Robert M. Morgenthau of Manhattan and Richard A. Brown of Queens and Bronx Borough President Fernando Ferrer.

Notably absent, however, was the Rev. Al Sharpton or a representative of his National Action Network. Rev. Sharpton, who led weeks of protests outside Police Headquarters over the Diallo shooting, and who will accompany Diallo's parents on a national speaking tour against police brutality, had met with the cardinal for fifty minutes April 6 with the Diallos.

Rev. Sharpton told reporters waiting for him at that time that he would "definitely" be represented at the prayer service. He apparently was to be represented by the Rev. Calvin Marshall, pastor of the Varrick Memorial AME Zion Church in Brooklyn, who did not show up. He was scheduled to give the invocation and was listed on the program as representing the National Action Network.

Rev. Butts led a communal prayer, during which those present held lighted candles. He said, "We will go from this place, back to our own communities of faith and associations to work for the appreciation of the respect due to every human being. We pledge with God's help, to heal the divisions in our society." Fr. Goode, who started slowly but built to a fever pitch that brought him a standing ovation, challenged his listeners to act on their stated beliefs. "Are we serious today? Are we serious today about justice and peace and the dignity of life?" he asked.

"Let's march together. Let's labor together. Let's pray together. Let's build together. Let's cry together. . . . Let's respect together and heal together."

Four people offered personal testimonies at the service, including Manhattan Borough President C. Virginia Fields, who told of civil rights rallies she attended in the South with the Rev. Martin Luther King Jr. She said she abides by his teaching that "tensions must be brought out into the open, where they can be seen and dealt

with." She expressed hope that the prayer service would serve that purpose.

Lorenzo Laboy, a senior at Rice High School in Harlem, told the congregation he was brought up to respect God and lawful authorities. "I believe this is true of most of my peers," he said, adding that those in authority should ideally be role models.

"The unfortunate reality is that too often this is not the case," he said. He and other minority youths, he said, "don't want to be the scapegoat for society problems. We don't want to be looked upon as criminals because, in the eyes of some authorities, we fit the description. We want to be looked upon with respect."

Others giving testimony were two police officers: Detective Terrance Wansley of One Hundred Blacks in Law Enforcement Who Care and Detective Dan Mackie, president of the Holy Name Society for Manhattan, the Bronx and Staten Island.

Intercessions were given by Sr. Loretta Theresa Richards, FHM, of the Franciscan Handmaids of Mary; Archimandrite Eugene N. Pappas, president of the New York Archdiocesan Clergy of the Greek Orthodox Archdiocese of America; the Rev. Sooren Chinchinian of the Armenian Archdiocese of America; Bishop E. Don Taylor, vicar bishop for New York City of the Episcopal Diocese of New York; the Rev. Stephen Bouman, bishop of the New York Metropolitan Synod, Evangelical Lutheran Church in America; Rabbi Robert N. Levine senior rabbi of Congregation Rodolph Sholom; Shaykh Abd'Allah Latif Ali, general secretary of the Islamic Leadership Council of the New York City Metropolitan Area; and Sr. Angela Perez, OCD, Carmelite nun.

Compiled from CNN news reports: The four White officers—Edward McMellon, Sean Carroll, Richard Murphy, and Kenneth Boss—accused of shooting Amadou Diallo were acquitted of murder February 25, 2000, after a month-long trial in Albany, New York.

The parents of Mr. Diallo have filed a $61 million wrongful death lawsuit against the officers and the city. The suit accuses the police and the city of negligence for intentionally shooting Diallo, and for depriving him of his constitutional rights through excessive force, racial profiling, and inadequate officer training.

PART SIX:

HEALING

# Healing Racism Through Faith *and* Truth

BY HIS EMINENCE ANTHONY CARDINAL BEVILACQUA

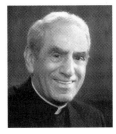

JANUARY 1998

On one occasion when the disciples had been unable to cast out a particularly evil spirit, they asked Jesus why they were unable to do so. "This is the kind," he answered, "that can only be cast out by prayer."[1]

Like these early disciples, we too approach Jesus with the same concern. Why, after all this time and after so much effort, is the grave evil of racism still so much with us? Our Lord's answer remains the same. It is only through a more profound communion with God, achieved through prayer and sacrifice, that we can truly be healed of this evil.

Our Lord has given us a fundamental spiritual truth. How we treat one another cannot be separated from our relationship with God. Unless and until we understand this truth, racism and all other sins against our neighbor will remain.

The Vatican council expressed this teaching of Jesus in these words:

> A person's relationship to God the Father and his relationship with his brothers and sisters are so linked that Scripture says: "He who does not love does not know God." As a consequence, the Church rejects as foreign to the mind of Christ any discrimination against people or harassment of them because of their race, color, condition of life or religion.[2]

It must be remembered that race, color or any other physical trait does not constitute the identity of a person, though it can be integral. Differences in races need to be valued. Jesus, however, calls us to transcend the differences of races and find our true human identity in our unique but common human nature.

This commonality of our human nature binds us as a family not only physically by blood, but also spiritually. Our dignity as human beings is a sacred one, for we are children of God created by him in his own image and likeness.

For Christians, this basic equality of all human persons has been elevated to a special relationship with God. Through baptism, Christians are incorporated into the life of the incarnate Son of God. "For all of you who were baptized into Christ have clothed yourselves with Christ. There is neither Jew nor Greek, there is neither slave nor free person, there is not male and female, for you are all one in Christ Jesus."[3]

A pastoral letter always has first and foremost the intent of fostering a deeper relationship with God. I write this letter with that intention firmly in mind. I pray that all who read it may hear in it the voice of a pastor concerned for his people's closeness to God.

## AN INTRINSIC EVIL

The primary step in effecting a personal and societal relationship with God is to remove from our lives obstacles that separate us from full union with God. Racism is one such obstacle and, indeed, a grave one. Racism is a moral disease, and it is contagious. No one is born a racist. Carriers infect others in countless ways through words and attitudes, deeds and omissions. Yet one thing is certain: The disease of racism can and must be eradicated.

It must be stated clearly that racism is a sin, an evil that can never be justified. It is a sin against fraternal charity. It violates Christ's command to "love your neighbor as yourself." And as Christ showed us, everyone is my neighbor. In short, racism and Christian life are incompatible.

Racism has been condemned as a sin many times. The National Conference of Catholic Bishops[4] and the Pontifical Justice and Peace Commission[5] both have

done so forcefully. Statements, however, are very limited in what they can accomplish. Pope John Paul II, commenting on the teaching of Vatican II, said that the council was always concerned with the truth in people.[6]

For the truth to have an impact, for it really to set us free, it must become our truth. It must be operative within us. It must penetrate and ignite our minds and hearts. The whole mystery of our faith is incarnational. "The Word became flesh and dwelt among us."[7] Our Lord desires that there be alive in each of us the truth that how we treat each other expresses and affects our intimacy with God. Love of God is the only power that can heal the evil of racism within any individual.

## DEEPLY ROOTED IN AMERICAN LIFE

The human condition is one of myriad differences. How we live these differences is the measure of our spiritual growth and maturity. It is deeply significant that the first sin recorded after the fall of Adam and

Eve is the sin of taking the life of a human being. Subsequent human history shows how ingenious human beings have become in continuing and spreading this sin of taking and diminishing human life. All of this is in direct opposition to the spirit of the covenant, which prescribes that we will be God's people and God will be our God only if we respect and nurture life.[8]

Our nation was formed on such a proposition, namely, that all people are created equal. But as Pope John XXIII once wisely noted, a historical movement cannot be completely understood through its founding principles because, while the principles remain the same, the movement itself is subject to constantly evolving historical circumstances.[9]

Our American history from its inception tragically has been influenced by the historical circumstance that an exception was made. The flawed concept that all men except was adopted in practice. Some among us were not to be considered equal. A distinction based on race was set in motion in American life. This distinction in many and varied guises has remained a sin deeply rooted in American life.

## CONSEQUENCES
Like the original sin of Adam and Eve, the sin of racism dulls the conscience, blinds reason, wounds the will and erodes charity. As a consequence, the spiritual immunity built up through grace can be severely weakened, exposing the victim to the onslaught of the viruses of unjust discrimination and racial superiority, breaking out at times into a fever of antagonism and conflict, hatred and violence.

Words are unable to describe adequately the horror of this human tragedy, as evidenced by the unrelenting human toll, the silent weeping of countless mothers inconsolable over the treatment given to their children, the diminished humanity as well as the searing insult of rejection. People are given no admittance, are unwelcome, stereotyped and portrayed as backward and inferior so often that one begins to doubt one's own worth. We witness the quiet suffering, the inner rage, the social pathologies causing shame and helplessness. Such mistreatment amounts to an oppressive weight so heavy as to make it almost impossible to breathe America's air of freedom. An exception indeed! It was an exception so pervasive that it became in all too many ways the very rule of people's lives.

As we step back and look at all of this to the extent we are able, we wonder at it. How could it have happened? Is this really the way things have to be? There has been economic progress as well as new laws and greater admittance to a wide range of American life. Strenuous, often heroic efforts have been made to rectify this nightmare. But it is still so terribly with us. Racism remains the unfinished business of America's freedom.

Whatever may be said about its origins, racism has shown a phenomenal capacity to survive and to affect successive waves of Americans. We Catholics have not been immune. As immigrant peoples, we have been assimilated into American society, which, in turn, has brought us along with others into the destructive atmosphere of racism. It is true that Catholics have experienced the hurtful viciousness of ethnic and religious bigotry. But our experience, for the most part, has been one of dramatic and successful inclusion into all areas of American life and culture. With this inclusion, however, has come a susceptibility to the climate of racism.

In established, low-economic neighborhoods, where large populations of dependent people were housed in projects without consideration of the impact on surrounding communities, racial tension has been and continues to be the pattern. Although there was a real need to provide housing as well as a value to fostering multiracial neighborhoods, the building of these projects, nevertheless, has proven to be a massive social failure. It was inevitable that the problems endemic to them would spill over into the surrounding areas. Our society was not justified in imposing the brunt of the consequences of longstanding racism almost exclusively on the shoulders of working people ill-prepared and inadequately assisted to address them.

Whole populations were thrust upon each other without preparation or warning because integration did not progress in accord with the housing market and the fair housing laws. The result has been episode upon episode of people unleashing their pent-up racial feelings. Who can be proud of that? Who can say this was the right thing to do? Adding insult to injury, the media has highlighted these episodes in such fashion as to brand whole neighborhoods of people as racist. The task that faces all of us is the undoing of these past mistakes that have deepened racial conflicts rather than healed them. These mistakes have brought shame and suffering on all of us. They must not continue.

The Archdiocese of Philadelphia is justifiably proud of the contribution to church life made by our African American faithful. The accomplishments of the parishes, social programs and especially of the schools in the African American communities have been superlative by any measure. The fact remains, however, that the membership of the Catholic Church in this archdiocese is predominantly White. Large numbers of African Americans have not chosen the Catholic Church as their spiritual home. We cannot help but ask why. With much regret, we must confess that often it has been because the Catholic faithful have been guilty of the racism that surrounds us, and for that failure we ask God's forgiveness.

A pastoral letter on the issue of racism does not imply that there are not other serious moral issues. This letter does, however, address the morally destructive force of the ongoing evil of racism and calls upon all Catholics to treat it as such. Concern for what is right and for the spiritual well-being of ourselves and our communities demands an effort of renewal. Not to endeavor actively to eradicate this evil is to be untrue to our deepest selves.

## TRUTHS THAT CAN HEAL

It is my firm conviction that there is within our Catholic teaching, especially in the social doctrine of the Church, much that can be brought to bear in this effort. There have already been reasoned impassioned pleas, particularly from the Catholic Black bishops of our nation.[10] One cannot hear their message without being moved by the depth and longing from which they speak.

Our Holy Father Pope John Paul II, through his teaching and worldwide witness, has personally emphasized the concern for the human person which is the foundational truth of the Church's mission. It has been Pope John Paul's consistent mission to teach that concern for the human person flows from the same mystery that constitutes the life of the Church. He speaks of this concern as the human dimension of the work of redemption. Because of it, there is in the Church a compelling commitment to safeguard the transcendence of the human person and a perpetual watchfulness that life should conform to human dignity.[11]

The Holy Father expresses anew the soaring insight of St. Paul in the Second Letter to the Corinthians:

> He died for all so that those who live might live no longer for themselves, but for him who for their sakes died and was raised up. Because of this we no longer look on anyone in terms of mere human judgment. . . . This means that if anyone is in Christ, he is a new creation. The old order has passed away, now all is new.[12]

It serves us well to recall the explicit words of the Holy Father:

> Out of regard for Christ and in view of the mystery that constitutes the church's own life, the church cannot remain insensible to whatever serves true human welfare. . . .

The human person is the way for the church . . . because the human person—every person without any exception whatever—has been redeemed by Christ, and because with the human person—with each person without any exception whatever—Christ is in a way "leading, even when the human person is unaware of it."[13]

Pope Paul VI had already given this teaching contemporary expression in the encyclical *On the Development of Peoples*, 1967. He spoke of a renewed consciousness of the demands of the Gospel. The theme of this key church document is the dynamic notion of development, which is the transition from less to more human conditions toward a better condition for the entire human family. Pope Paul expressed an urgency for concerted action.

Concern for the human person has been at the heart of Christian life from the beginning. The intimacy of this concern with our closeness to God derives from the words of the Lord:

> I tell you, unless your holiness surpasses that of the scribes and Pharisees, you shall not enter the kingdom of God. . . . Any man who uses abusive language toward his brother shall be answerable to the Sanhedrin, and if he holds him in contempt he risks the fire of Gehenna. If you bring your gift to the altar and there recall that your brother has anything against you, leave your gift at the altar, go first to be reconciled with your brother and then come and offer your gift.[14]

Jesus is clear that this is a matter of holiness and a matter of salvation. Our attitudes and actions toward others enter the mystery of our communion with God. Racism is a sin that weakens and diminishes this sacred union.

Jesus, through his life and death, revealed the mystery of God's life in us as love, which is the giving of oneself for others. Our Christian vocation is to share this mystery by living it. By giving of ourselves for others, we show this mystery of salvation to all who wish to follow the law of God as written in their hearts.[15] Our faith does not turn us away from others, but toward them. In the opening prayer of Mass for the 30th Sunday of ordinary time, we pray, "Give us the love to carry out your command." We need God's love in order to love others. God's love in us and our self-giving love of others are of one and the same mystery. God is love. The apostle John expresses this mystery very forcefully, "Anyone who says he loves God and hates his brother is a liar."[16]

## FAITH MUST LEAD TO ACTION

Bringing this vision of faith to bear upon the evil of racism is the challenge before us. These truths of faith, beautiful as they are, will not bring power to bear unless they are alive and at work in us. I pray that all may see how intimately our attitudes and actions toward others are united with our desire to be closer to God. I encourage and bless all efforts within our educational, social and health institutions as well as our parish communities to bring this message of faith into the hearts and minds of our people. I ask all our priests and deacons to preach with fervor the power of this mystery. I ask most especially all parents, in their desire to give what is best to their children, to create an atmosphere in their homes in which the mystery of self-giving love will grow and be nourished. Let the wretched racial words which bring such hurt never be mentioned among us.

No one says this will be easy. Self-giving love never is. Racism has been too long with us and too ingrained in our way of life. It cannot be overcome without a difficult and sustained struggle. Even though some of the most blatant racist actions have lessened and real progress has been made, the evil persists. It operates silently in strategies of self-interest and in structured patterns of discrimination. Most of all, it is carried forward in the damage it has wrought and the wounds it has inflicted.

Since racism is fundamentally a moral evil against the nature of the human person, its elimination requires ultimately a moral solution. The sin of racism will be eliminated only when every human being acknowledges and respects every other human being as a person made by God to his own image and likeness. At the same time it would be naive not to recognize the enormity of the historical, social and cultural entrenchment of this moral plague. The moral solution is self-evident. The achievement of the remedy regrettably may be more complex than the causes of the disease. In spite of past failures, we must never despair. That would be the greatest sin. We must renew our efforts to end the evil of racism so that the children of the new millennium will inherit a legacy of racial unity and fraternal peace.

In order to be effective, the response to racism must engage the committed efforts of a broad range of experts in many disciplines. Religious leaders with one voice must call on their faithful to end the evil of racism in their own lives through prayer, forgiveness and reconciliation. Public officials, heads of corporations, union officials, the public media as well as other community agencies and leaders will have to act with courage and much wisdom. I call upon all Catholics, whatever their field of endeavor, to cooperate fully in all sincere and prudent efforts to create and carry out those actions which will contribute to the eradication of racism.

Our own city of Philadelphia, along with other communities in the region, has undergone a drastic decrease in the number of jobs available. The manufacturing industries which accounted for a large percentage of jobs as recently as a few decades ago have moved elsewhere or have ceased to exist. Our neighborhoods have suffered. Much of the racial tension we have experienced has grown out of the dislocation and pressures brought on by the loss of economic security.

Surely our nation has learned that restricting people to confined areas, whether they be reservations or ghettos, is a sentence leading to the worst sort of social pathologies. To continue in this path is both a result and a cause of deeper racism. To propose programs suggesting that jobs will become available in these areas is disingenuous and can only lead to deeper resentment and racial tension. The American experience has always been the freedom to move where opportunity exists. Any national effort to overcome racism must ensure this freedom.

## LOVE IN TRUTH AND IN DEED

In the very last scene of the fourth and last Gospel, Jesus is on the shore near a charcoal fire with fish cooking on it. He invites Peter to come sit by him. Peter was in need of healing because of his betrayal. He had accommodated to gain acceptance. Was he any longer worthy to be loved? Peter, blessedly, received the invitation to come sit down by Jesus. Our nation accommodated too in a way that was also a betrayal of our founding proposition. As a tragic result, millions of human beings endured existence as being unwanted. Feeling unwanted was the condition imposed by racism on generations of African Americans and, more recently, on other minority groups coming to this country. This is a wound to the soul which only our compassionate Savior can understand.

There is no greater affirmation than to be told, "I would like you to be with me." This core affirmation is our healing and the beginning of eternal life: to be told we are wanted; to be affirmed as worthy of love. "Do you love me?" Jesus asked Peter. Three times he asked him this. Since love to be real must be mutual, for Peter to be able to say, "Yes, I love you," he would have had to come to believe he now was himself loved. Once again he was made whole. His faith in being loved made him whole.

While the experts and professionals seek solutions and programs in the national effort to repel racism, the presence of the risen Lord invites us to the ministry of affirming one another in our human dignity. It is not enough to profess belief in the dignity of the human

person. We realize our dignity in the experience of being wanted and loved. In this we can all share.

I ask all Catholics to take this teaching of the Church to heart with all seriousness. I ask that all parishes, schools and other Catholic agencies and institutions find innovative and visible ways of ensuring that African Americans and people of all races are welcome. I ask that this be done even if it means reaching out in previously untried ways. It is my hope that each of our institutions will have in place some activity, some program, which makes real the Lord's invitation, "Come, sit beside me. I want you to be with me." I call on Catholics and all people of good will to pray that God will cast out the demon of racism from wherever it exists. I urge that every individual and every organization in our community become united in a renewed serious effort to achieve the eradication of this horrible evil. This is our common task. This was the dream of Rev. Martin Luther King Jr. This is the will of God. ■

His Eminence Anthony Cardinal Bevilacqua *is the archbishop of Philadelphia, Pennsylvania.*

**NOTES**

1    Mk 9:29.

2    Second Vatican Council, *Declaration on the Relationship of the Church to Non-Christian Religions*, no. 5.

3    Gal 3:28.

4    *Brothers and Sisters to Us: U.S. Bishops' Pastoral Letter on Racism in Our Day*, 1979 (U.S. Catholic Conference [USCC]).

5    *The Church and Racism: Toward a More Fraternal Society*, 1989 (USCC).

6    Pope John Paul II, *Redemptor Hominis*, no. 14.

7    Jn 1:14.

8    Gn 9:11-17.

9    Pope John XXIII, *Pacem in Terris*, April 11, 1963, in *The Gospel of Peace and Justice*, 1976 (Joseph Gremillion, Orbis Books).

10   *What We Have Seen and Heard: A Pastoral Letter on Evangelization From the Black Bishops of the United States*, 1984 (St. Anthony Messenger Press).

11   Cf. *Redemptor Hominis*.

12   2 Cor 5:15-17.

13   Cf. *Redemptor Hominis*, nos. 13, 14.

14   Mt 25:20-25.

15   Mt 25.

16   1 Jn 4:20.

# Homily: Black Catholic Men Day of Reflection
## (Jeremiah 1:1, 4-5, 9-10)

BY MOST REV. JOSEPH N. PERRY

SEPTEMBER 1998

The prophet Jeremiah was asked by God to deliver a Word to the nation Israel at the threshold of a very violent turn in the nation's history. The young prophet was called by God to prophesy at the end of the kingdom of Judah. The city would be devastated, the temple destroyed and the people forced into exile.

The call of Jeremiah has some interesting aspects. The powerful words of this passage remind the Jew and the Christian that we are not just accidents of a creation running by itself, but that we existed as a loving thought in God's imagination before we were sired into this vale of tears. Therefore, Jeremiah was known by God in the depths of his being and was appointed to be a prophet to the nations—from the womb. This Biblical teaching feeds into a spirituality that inspires much of what you and I do as believers. We believe God knows all and blesses all from the beginning and that it is our own actions, sometimes misguided, that take creation into a different direction.

Jeremiah, like you and me, experienced his own inadequacy for the divine mission, and he hesitated. He protested in prayer that he could not speak well enough for he was only a boy and that he was too young. Who

would ever take him seriously, he wondered? Notice, the Lord's response was a reemphasis of the Call and an assurance of help to carry out the job of prophet. The words of the Lord himself would compensate for Jeremiah's inadequacy to speak well. Jeremiah's acceptance of the mission was implicit in the fact that he eventually carried out his mission.

WE MUST MAKE SENSE OUT OF OUR EXPERIENCE IF WE ARE TO BE BOTH BLACK AND CHRISTIAN. MORE SPECIFICALLY FOR US, OUR THEOLOGICAL TASK IS TO DETERMINE WHAT IT MEANS TO BE AT ONCE BLACK AND CATHOLIC IN THE CHURCH IN THE UNITED STATES WHERE WE ARE A SMALL NUMBER.

When was the last time you were asked to do the seemingly impossible, yet you managed to rise to the occasion? Perhaps you thought you were too young, did not have the right training or were just asked to do something that stretched you beyond any notion you had of yourself. Yet, each of us, gentlemen, has likely found an inner strength, a sense of purpose we didn't know we had and, thereupon, met the impossible request head on.

The Black man in the United States has undergone a certain kind of treatment which has produced a unique type of spiritual experience both personal and collective, and probably a peculiar second-guessing of [his] own merits. [African Americans] have the witness of our ancestors, many of whom were slaves, and others, who together with us, have been victims of all types of discrimination: open, legal, subtle and violent, even after the so-called emancipation and certain laws passed in our time to end discrimination in housing, employment, eating establishments and educational institutions. The souls of Black men have been tried and tested in the fires of suffering.

We have endured incessant and undeserved infliction of pain due to our blackness. Thus, in moments when we become self-conscious about our Blackness, which accounts for this experience inflicted upon us by those who treat us badly, then we must attempt to make sense of our Black experience. In so doing, African Americans have traditionally turned to religion because it is in religion where we know we find the truth about ourselves, namely, that we are both a sinful but beautiful people.

We must make sense out of our experience if we are to be both Black and Christian. More specifically for us, our theological task is to determine what it means to be at once Black and Catholic in the Church in the United States where we are a small number.

We look for the inclusion of our experience. We look for opportunities for participation and recognition. We beseech the Church to accept our experience as valuable to the life and mission of the Catholic Church in this country.

I wager much of the feeling that prefaces this special day is the frustration we feel that we Black men fall behind other men in opportunity, education and wealth. Sometimes, we feel like Jeremiah, feeling inadequate for the task. And what makes us feel worse is, no one comes seeking our worth or our expertise. Probably our greatest frustration is not so much our lack of this or that or our feelings of inadequacy so much as our hesitation and the hesitation of our brothers who fail to come forward, take up the task because they feel they are too young, lacking education and/or experience and would rather others take up the charge, for to try and fail is our greatest humiliation.

Yes, we could benefit from some leadership training. We could benefit from our own initiative to improve ourselves, to volunteer ourselves, to show that we are interested in this Church we love. These things would certainly help. You see, in accordance with this passage from Jeremiah, it doesn't appear that God accepts excuses and He is not terribly impressed by our complaints.

Prejudice is a prejudgment at sight, and the Black man is highly visible. Whether we live on the Gold Coast or in the dark ghetto, whether we are a first in some distinguished post or a garbage collector—in the estimation of White society the Black man is inferior.

There is one of two ways we can deal with this. We can accept the thesis of White society that we are inferior and take last place, back pew or simply don't show up and cast our vote. Or, we can ignore the thesis and come forward and take up the task.

The Catholic Church's relationship with Black men is at once remarkable and puzzling. The historical periods of slavery and emancipation did not see Catholics out in the forefront winning the hearts and souls of freed Blacks. Baptists, Methodists and other evangelicals were inviting of us and receiving us in generous numbers. Of course, Black clergymen broke with the ranks and formed essentially Black churches out of the outline of many Protestant traditions away from

White governance. This is the larger tradition. Black men are the anchor of the Black Protestant Church tradition. We have not had significant Black clergy numbers in the Catholic Church to posture ownership in our Church. The problem, therefore, is largely historical with effects touching us even today: a situation not easily overturned in this country given the smorgasbord of Protestant Christian religion on every corner of our cities, many of them very soothing to the Black experience.

Despite the historical ambivalence of American bishops with the situation of Blacks in this country, we have had individual heroes and heroines ministering to Blacks in the past: Catholics such as Mother Katherine Drexel, Capuchin Father Stephen Eckert, priests and religious such as the Divine Word Fathers, the Josephite Fathers, the Oblate Sisters and Sisters of the Blessed Sacrament and other clergy, religious and lay persons known only to individual neighborhoods and cities who devoted their lives to our pastoral care.

In the meantime, the larger Church has not hesitated to surface heroic Black Catholic men. Somehow, race prejudice has always been, in ways, a uniquely American problem. So, our Black saints are from elsewhere. We know some of them: Maurice and his legion of militaries, Martin de Porres, Charles Lwanga and his companions, Moses the Black monk, Franciscan Benedict the Moor, New York's layman Pierre Toussaint whose cause is pending for canonization. There are men of the caliber of these saints living among us today. We should surface them. They may be the saints of the calendar of the future.

It occurs to me that there are details of the lives of these real Black Catholic men that provide an outline of what Black Catholic men can be today in the Church we love. We must have the courage not to dismiss the saints as people of the distant past and therefore irrelevant to the contemporary struggle, but extract from the lives of these saintly men what they used to survive the biases and discrimination of their time.

The history of the Hebrew and Christian peoples is full of examples of individuals whose message far outshines their own personal stature, thus making their tidings all the more urgent and profound. This fact was not lost on the Second Vatican Council of the Church, thirty years ago, which reaffirmed that we all are a holy people, called by baptism to announce the Good News in those particular times and places in which we find ourselves.

True, some of us are called in a special way to break open the Word of God for the Christian assembly. Some of us, unfortunately, have skills and education to sit at long tables where taxing meetings take place every other day and plan and strategize and debate about this or that. Whatever your talent, each of us is called to bring God's Word of compassion, love, mercy and forgiveness to our world.

When I think about my own father who never finished grade school but had to work to help support a family that lost their dad in my father's infancy, then Depression followed and after Depression, a war. He feels his own inadequacy. But when I think about it. I see how my father, for all his felt inadequacy and lack of education, gave his first born son to the Church who is a priest and a bishop. Now, that's an accomplishment for which he will probably never be cited in this life. There are many like him—Black men who gave their sons to the Church especially in the 1950s, '60s, '70s and '80s. We could use more of you to do the same in the 1990s which stand to be threatened by a lack of African American clergy for the future because Black fathers are not gently coaching their sons to consider ministry in our Catholic Church. Is this true? We need your help with this important task of the Church with priestly and religious vocations, whether you have a son or not. I encourage you to assist me in this holy endeavor.

Without our representation among the clergy, we have no clout in this Church.

My father will probably never sit at a high-level meeting in the Church and probably will never take up any form of layministry in the Church. But what he has done is equally if not more fantastic. With all that we seek from our Church, gentlemen, I hope we don't forget these Black Catholic men—fathers of priests— fathers who are pretty much like yourselves. This is true participation. This is one among many true apostolates of the layman.

I mention this not to exalt my father nor in any way to suggest that we should simply stay in our pew and pray for vocations. I say this to encourage you to not cut yourselves short. While we examine what the Church has not done for us we should also examine our strengths—what Black Catholic men have done

and are doing in our Catholic Church and coach ourselves to be more proactive than what we are. No one can do it but ourselves. You are more valuable than you estimate yourselves to be. Maybe it is a matter where we must show the Church ourselves how our contribution can be employed and take certain initiatives ourselves in our parishes and our archdiocese in those associations in the Church already doing grand service and strategic planning in the Black Catholic community.

Your presence this day of reflection is one great step in that direction! ∎

Most Rev. Joseph N. Perry *is an auxiliary bishop of Chicago, Illinois.*

## BLACK MEN PONDER THEIR PLACE IN THE CHURCH

### BY ROBERT McCLORY, *NATIONAL CATHOLIC REPORTER* • SEPTEMBER 1998

CHICAGO—An unusual day of reflection held recently here has triggered ongoing efforts to involve Black Catholic men in parish and archdiocesan leadership and has attracted the interest of dioceses around the country. The event, held in mid-September 1998 at St. James Church on the city's near South Side, was directed at Black male Catholics and drew more than two-hundred, many of whom made it clear to Cardinal Francis George that they feel ignored and taken for granted by church decision-makers.

George, who attended most of the day, acknowledged that "a lot of things have to change" and told listeners, "I hope you'll help me as we go along."

The day of reflection was organized by Ralph Shaw, a permanent deacon, and Sheila Bourelly, a student at Loyola University's Institute for Pastoral Ministry. This report is written from extensive videotapes and printed materials from the event. Shaw said the African American deacons have been seriously concerned about the sparse involvement of Black men in their parishes and have noted recent recruiting efforts in the Black community by the Promise Keepers.

He and Bourelly had been discussing these problems as they relate to Black spirituality in the *Deliverance* newsletter they edit, and "it seemed to us the Spirit wasn't

coming alive for our men, wasn't getting integrated into our parish life."

The day featured a Mass, singing and a talk by Fr. George Clements and one (via video recording) by retired Fr. Rollins Lambert, the first Black priest ordained in Chicago. But perhaps the most remarkable moments occurred during the candid oral reports from the twenty-eight small discussion groups that met to consider the "image and role" of Black Catholic men.

"The Church views us as not bringing that much to the table or as having much to offer—and so [doesn't value] our participation . . . as it values other groups," said Jonathan McClure of Holy Angels parish. He added, "Even though we find a lot of fault with the church as it's presently administered, we all still love the Church—it is our Church—and though it may not treat us well, we ain't going nowhere."

#### MONEY IS WELCOME
"Our money is welcome, but not our leadership, not our input," said Opal-Easter Smith of Holy Name of Mary Parish. "Our Black men are not recruited for ministerial roles." It was noted by Smith and several others that there are presently no Blacks in the archdiocesan seminary system.

Robert Miller of Holy Angels reported that among a variety of church images presented to the discussion groups for their consideration, "faithful servant" seemed the most apt. "The powers that be want us to continue to fit into the servant role," he said, "not questioning, not telling the truth, to be of service to them and not to God."

Dexter Watson, also of Holy Angels, said, "This is just ludicrous." That there is not "a Black man in any position in the church in the Archdiocese of Chicago in 1998 is terrible. And I want the archbishop to know there have to be some changes. There are qualified Black men to lead in this church."

In a diocese in North Carolina, said Watson, the chancellor, the assistant chancellor and the vicar for priests are all African Americans. (In fact, Chicago Auxiliary Bishop Joseph Perry is Black, as are two women who hold positions at the archdiocesan level in Chicago: Sr. Anita Baird is George's executive assistant, and Sheila Adams represents African Americans in the Office for Ethnic Ministries.)

"Alleluia for Sister Baird," said Miller, "but, man, where are the brothers?"

There is a consensus that the Church "is not sensitive to the Black man," said Richard Boyd, a permanent deacon from Holy Name of Mary church. "There is no leadership from downtown, no respect. And we want it to stop!" As far as male participation in church structures is concerned, said Boyd, the image "Silent Night" seemed very appropriate to this discussion group.

A written survey conducted during the event revealed that 66 percent of those responding think the Church as a whole does not "convey the message that it is truly a multiracial, multicultural church"; 79 percent think that Black men are overlooked or systematically excluded from positions in the Catholic Church"; and 96 percent said the Church does not involve Black men in "administration and planning that affects the Black community."

Three resolutions were passed unanimously by the assembly:

- That under the leadership of the Black deacons, a commission be formed to establish a "Black men's ministry in local parishes."

- That the archdiocese establish a commission to examine its policies on race, to investigate complaints of racial discrimination and to make recommendations to the cardinal.

- That the archdiocese develop "sensitivity" concerning the images employed in churches and other areas to ensure they reflect the church as multiracial, that it

remove "the preponderance of White images of God, angels and saints still found in many of these areas," and cease perpetuating the notion of Catholicism as " a White man religion."

## UNEXPECTED ANIMOSITY

George said he welcomed the resolutions, though they "will have to be honed a little bit." He told the group he was "somewhat taken aback by the animosity toward downtown." It is "not a transparent organization . . . so we have to revise the structure so that it is more transparent, so people know where decisions are made. . . . Not that much policy is made down here," he said, explaining that many important decision are made at the parish level.

George then challenged the Black deacons to form a corps "to come with me into the White parishes [for confirmation and other visits]. . . . I find it peculiar that I celebrate the Eucharist without a deacon as an assistant . . . so I would welcome the assistance of the Black deacons when I go anywhere in this archdiocese."

In remarks earlier in the day, Fr. Clements said, "The role of the Black man in the Catholic Church is to keep the Church honest, to speak the truth about the Church. I beg you to never allow yourselves to be silenced. Tell the truth! Tell it like it is!"

In a truth-telling spirit, Clements confided there had never been a Chicago bishop "that I have ever liked. . . . Never, never! I have had those I respect. I've had those I obey. I've had those I guess you could say I kind of love." But "I like Francis George. I believe Francis George identifies with us. . . . I believe he's a man you can tell the truth to."

In the two months since the day of reflection, two meetings have been held to implement the resolutions, Bourelly said. Bishop Perry is expected to serve as liaison with George.

# "Take Into Account Various Situations *and* Cultures"

## BY MOST REV. EDWARD K. BRAXTON

JANUARY 1999

### I. INTRODUCTION

Dear Brother Bishops:

Our Holy Father, Pope John Paul II, states in *Fidei Depositum*, his apostolic constitution which introduces the *Catechism of the Catholic Church*, that those who use it must "take into account various situations and cultures." If the *Catechism* is to have any impact on our efforts to preach the Good News of Jesus Christ more effectively to African Americans, we must take the Holy Father's words very seriously. The pope's challenge is unambiguous. We cannot be effective evangelists if we are unwilling to learn firsthand about the fabric of the every-day lives of the people we hope to welcome in the name of the Lord.

I have written and spoken often on the subject of evangelization and African Americans, offering a variety of specific suggestions that might make our ministry of evangelization more effective. Rather than repeating those suggestions in this [National Black Catholic] Congress presentation prepared specifically for fellow bishops, I wish to invite you to reflect at a deeper level. Today I hope to contribute to a radically honest and genuinely realistic evaluation of what we must do at the dawn of the third millennium of Christianity if we

are serious about reaching Black Americans. Knowing that this attempt to suggest implications of John Paul II's instruction to "take into account various situations and cultures" runs the risk of over-simplification, I will be satisfied if I can uncover the roots of fundamental concerns.

This will be done first by visiting a barber shop; second, by reflecting briefly on the meaning of evangelization; third, by examining the cultural divide that separates most potential Black converts from the fundamentally White world of the Catholic Church; and fourth, by offering specific recommendations for bishops to consider that might help create the rapport the Church needs with Black people before we even begin to talk about effective evangelization.

### II. THE BARBER SHOP
The neighborhood barber shop is often the center of life in poor Black communities. The beauty parlor is across the street. A laundromat, a currency exchange, a barbe-cue restaurant, a pool hall and a liquor store are within a few blocks. The vacant lot, where teenage boys play basketball, begins in the alley behind the barber shop. There are several boarded-up apartment buildings in the neighborhood. One is a crack house. The storefront Baptist church and the funeral home are on the corner. The bus to the clinic and the unemployment office stops nearby. The all-Black Catholic school is

outside of the neighborhood. Though they are not Catholics, some parents drive their children there in spite of increasing tuition.

For most of my life as a priest and as a bishop, I have deliberately frequented these "neighborhood centers." Eventually just about everyone comes to see the shop, especially on a Saturday. The atmosphere is congenial. Addressing one another as "Brother Austin" or "Brother Braxton," everyone speaks his mind. Copies of *Ebony*, *Jet*, *Black Enterprise*, *Sports Illustrated*, *Essence* and the local Black newspaper are scattered about. Old, fading pictures of famous Black athletes, politicians, entertainers and civil rights leaders are on the walls. There is also a dramatic painting of a militant Black Jesus Christ, eyes ablaze with righteousness, fist clenched in the Black power salute.

The enthusiastic conversation of the patrons and barbers moves randomly from topic to topic. Listen to what they say: "Biting Evander's ear was wrong and Mike Tyson should have known better. Evander Holyfield is a real class act. I'd like to see them fight again." "How can we keep our children in school, so that they can get good jobs?" "What can we do to get the landlords, the city and the residents to combat the continuing deterioration of housing in our neighborhood?" "White people will never understand the way most Black people feel about the Rodney King beating and the O. J. Simpson trial and that's that!" "Let me tell you about the problems I am having at home with my wife and children." "Do you know what the Man did at my job last night? It was an act of blatant racial prejudice. If I had the seed money or if I could get a loan, I would start my own small business." "We have our share of violence and crime here. But it's nothing compared to the 'White collar' crimes being committed by the invisible criminals, who control the economic system that make it impossible for us to get ahead." "Why did the police come down so hard yesterday on the Black brother, who was a $1,000 crack dealer on the street, and let the $500,000 supplier from outside the neighborhood sleep in a comfortable suburban bed last night?" "What can I do to help my young unmarried granddaughter, now that she is pregnant?" "My eighteen-year-old son was shot and killed last night for his Nike sneakers. Lord, what is this world coming to?"

Someone turns on the television. There are some loud complaints about the many superficial comedies on the Fox TV station featuring all-Black casts. "Sure, they will pay Black people to be on TV as long as we play prostitutes and murderers or make fools of ourselves. It's *Amos 'n Andy* in living color." "Show me one Black character on TV living a normal life, someone you can look up to as a role model for our children." Surfing with the remote, one of the barbers stops at a Catholic program. "The Catholic channel on TV is something else. There is never a Black person on that show. No Black people in the audience. No Black people attending the church services either. And that tired music! They never talk about anything related to being poor or Black. And they wonder why we don't join their church?" The barber cutting my hair informs the speakers that I am a Catholic priest. A relatively young man observes, "Well, well, well, I didn't know there were any Black priests. I didn't think the Catholic Church even allowed them." He asks why he hasn't seen one before. "There are not many of us," I explain. I told him that many priests and sisters, Black and White, do not wear distinctive garb today when they are not directly involved in their ministry. "Then, how are we supposed to recognize them?" he asks.

Brother Austin, who owns the shop, turns on a Black call-in radio station where there is a heated debate about what color Jesus was. One participant argues loudly that Jesus and the apostles were definitely Black. Another says if He was Jewish, He probably was not brown haired and fair skinned the way He is usually pictured. One of the men waiting for a haircut dismisses the radio debate saying, "No self-respecting Black man could fall on his knees before a White Jesus, when the White Man was and is the oppressor."

At that point, a group of basketball players comes in to quench their thirst. They are wearing the jerseys of Michael Jordan, Shaquille O'Neal, Dennis Rodman and other basketball "gods," who, they argue, inspire them more than any religion could. Their astronomical incomes and dazzling feats on the courts convince these teenagers that if they can play great ball, they do not need to go to college. They turn the radio to a rap, hip-hop and gangsta rap station. You may have managed to ignore this "in your face" confrontational and often vulgar music by such famous performers as the late, recently murdered Tupac Shakur, the late, recently murdered Notorious B. I. G., Snoop Doggy Dogg, Ice Cube and Queen Latifah. However, this music idiom is the lifeblood of these young men, more meaningful to them than even the most energetic Black church music. They know the lyrics by heart and sing along, as they pound out the beat with their whole bodies.

As the ball players make their way back to the court, I ponder these rap lyrics and the culture of the streets which they powerfully convey. Sometimes violent, bluntly sexual and almost always anti-White establishment, they feed a smoldering rage and an impatient materialism that dictates how these young men walk, talk, dress, eat and think; yes, even about God and the Christian faith. Because of circumstances too complex for easy analysis, many young Black males and more than a few females believe that everything of value for them can be found in the company of their "homeboys" on the street. Everything truly Black is there. The sometimes searingly brilliant poetry of rap lyrics provides the clearest expression of how they feel.

Two brothers take the chairs on either side of me in the barber shop. They are in a serious conversation about Spike Lee's new documentary *Four Little Girls*, which is about the children who were murdered in the 1963 Birmingham, Alabama, church bombing, and his provocative film *Get on the Bus*, which examined the Million Man March. The Catholic Church had no formal participation in this watershed event in the

Black community, though Black Catholic laymen and priests were certainly there. The conversation turns to John Singleton's powerful movie *Rosewood*, a mythological retelling of the true story of an attempt to annihilate a prosperous Black town in Florida in 1923 by a White mob. One brother who looks directly at me says, "This movie gave me more hope than any church service."

They ask me if I have heard of *Bring In da Noise, Bring In da Funk*, George C. Wolfe and Savion Glover's astounding Broadway phenomenon, in which tap dance is used to tell the story of a people from the slave ships to the present day. When I tell them I have seen it, they hang on my every word. As they are leaving, they give me a flier about Wynton Marsalis's Pulitzer Prize-winning jazz oratorio "Blood on the Fields," which explores the impact of slavery on Black people today.

A group of Black women come in from the beauty parlor, which has no TV, to watch the funeral of Dr. Betty Shabazz, widow of the murdered Malcolm X. They are caught up in a sisterhood of sorrow, as they contemplate the tragedy of this singular light extinguished by the hand of a troubled grandson. Their hearts are broken as they watch Coretta Scott King, widow of the murdered Martin Luther King Jr., comforting Mydie Evers-Williams, widow of the murdered Medger Evers, as poet Maya Angelou tearfully embraces each of Dr. Shabazz's six weeping daughters.

This untimely death caused a great mourning among Black women, including many Black Catholic women. But this death was not lamented in most Catholic churches because it was not a significant event for most Catholics. As they depart, one woman remarks to me, "Reverend, I go to Rev. Hampton's A.M.E. Church myself, but I send my son to the Catholic school for education and the discipline. But I would not want him to become a Catholic and become a priest. You can't get married and you can't have children. As badly as we need good Black husbands and fathers, I think that is such a waste and a shame."

Later, a senior from Howard University settles in for a haircut and turns the public radio station to a round table discussion about Black intellectuals and their books. The session begins [with] praise for a new edition of the writings of James Baldwin. They assert that it's time for Black and White Americans to re-read (or read for the first time) his classic essay *The Fire Next Time* and heed its warning: "God gave Noah the rainbow sign. No more warnings, the fire next time!"

The radio commentator turns to the growing African American intellectual presence at Harvard University. At the W. E. B. Du Bois Institute for Afro-American Research, Henry Louis Gates Jr., the cultural analyst, has assembled such scholars as William Julius Wilson, sociologist and public policy expert; Comel West, philosopher; and Evelyn Brooks Higginbotham, Black women's history expert. Everyone agrees that their new books are having a significant impact on Black thinkers.

The next radio panel gets into an angry exchange about Keith Richburg's *Out of America: A Black Man Confronts Africa*. This largely negative analysis of Black African politics and life brands Black Americans, who have come to identify deeply with Africa, as naive romanticists. Such "Afrocentrism" is laughable in the author's view. Black Americans ought to be thankful that they are not in Africa with its crime, Black political corruption and widespread disease. He urges Black American civil rights leaders to stop praising African politicians indiscriminately. He thinks some should be in prison for their treachery.

Then Martin Bernal's book *Black Athena: The Afroasiatic Roots of Classical Civilization* is briefly discussed. This ambitious scholarly work proposes a more radical Afrocentrism than the one rejected by Richburg. It has as its much debated thesis the belief that the best of ancient Greek and Roman cultures, which are the foundation of western European cultures, is profoundly influenced by even more ancient Egyptian cultures, which in turn have been shaped by sub-Saharan Black African cultures.

When the radio program ends, one of the Howard University students provokes a discussion about Black identity. One man observes that no sooner than White people have adjusted to calling us "Afro-American," they are expected to change to "African American." What are they to make of current expressions such as "Americans of African descent" and "Africans in America"? He says some White people are bewildered. They have begun to think the question of naming has become a tiresome game of political correctness. The university student interrupts him asserting that the matter is not so simple. "It is tied to the story of how our people came to be in the United States against their will and how they have been treated here since the end of slavery." He recommends the W. E. B. Du Bois 1903 classic, *The Souls of Black Folk*, which explores this dilemma of Black identity.

The student continues, "This long history is the reason why different groups and individuals use different designations based upon their experience. As a result, colored people, Negroes, Blacks, Black people, Afro-Americans, African Americans, Africans in America, Americans of African descent, Africans in the Diaspora, Americans, People of Color and yes, even 'niggah' in the world of hip-hop and rap are all used, depending on the context of lived experience. One of the reasons for the emergence of 'Americans of African descent' is the search for an inclusive expression that would be appreciative of the unique history of the various Caribbean peoples." A Catholic gentleman from Haiti spoke up. "Our people think of themselves simply as Haitians, not as African Americans."

One of the barbers asks, "Why can't we let go of all of this tortured history and simply call ourselves—Black and White—what we now all are: proud Americans?" Then he answers his own question. "Sadly, this is not true to what people experience each day. It is similar to asking why the Jewish people cannot put the Holocaust behind them as simply a tragic episode of past history. They cannot do this because it was and is too traumatic. Slavery and its unending aftermath, like the Holocaust, are an unresolved and unreconciled memory of the past that informs how people wish to name themselves today."

As Brother Austin finishes my haircut, I think to myself that not one of the Black authors, artists, scholars, actors, politicians or athletes discussed is a Catholic. I wonder if it is possible that being Catholic inhibits Black women and men from playing pivotal roles in the shaping of Black culture? As I leave, the shop is filled with the rich aromas of soul food. A nearby restaurant chef has just brought dinner for the barbers so that they can take a much-needed break. As you leave the barber shop, you might ask yourselves, as Catholic bishops, how familiar or unfamiliar you are with the "various situations and cultures" that are revealed there.

## III. WHAT DO WE MEAN BY EVANGELIZATION?
There are between 35 and 40 million Americans of African ancestry. By our imperfect count, between 1.3 and 2 million of these are members of the Catholic Church. Millions of Black Americans over thirty are members of Black Christian traditions, especially Baptist. At least half of the total population, or between 17 and 20 million, are under thirty. Many of those under thirty are not members of any faith tradition. Young Black people who are attracted to religious faith, especially if they have been in prison, are far more likely to be drawn to some form of Islam, including Louis Farrakhan's Nation of Islam, than to the Roman Catholic Church. Yet, as in all communities, it is this younger, non-affiliated group that we most urgently need to reach.

Some of the parents, grandparents and aunts of the youthful devotees of popular Black culture may well be Catholics. Though they have found it difficult to pass their faith on to the younger generation, African Americans who are long-standing Catholics are often among the most devout and the most tenacious in holding on to their faith. Some have made their own a traditional Catholicism that makes them long for the

day when the Church was more uniform. They prefer the polyphony of Palestrina over the hand-clapping rhythm of gospel music. They might throw up their hands in disgust at the mere mention of the Black Christ. The majority embraces the reforms of the Second Vatican Council and believe that the Church has only just begun to appreciate the powerful contributions that the cultures and experiences of Black people can make to Catholic worship and to all aspects of Catholic life. They are anxious to do more and be more in the Church.

But how do we reach the millions of younger Black people for whom the Catholic faith seems irrelevant? I am not sure that any of us can answer that question. Before discussing some of the reasons why this question is so difficult to answer, we must ask ourselves what do we, as committed Christians and as bishops, really mean by evangelization. What do we expect to be different about the person who has been evangelized? Surely we expect more than mere church affiliation. We all know people who register in a Catholic parish, identify themselves as Catholics, go to Mass a couple of Sundays a month, put their envelopes in the collection basket, have their children baptized and live lives that seem much more focused on the "gods of secularity" than on the God of Jesus Christ. We would call them members of the Church in a minimal sense. But would we call them evangelized?

I think we mean much more than that. Jesus Christ is at the center of the life of the person who has been effectively evangelized. The whole life and lifestyle of the evangelized person is gradually changed and transformed. This is because true and radical conversion is taking place. When the hearts and minds of women and men are evangelized by the Good News, they become able to affirm the good and gracious nearness of the Mystery of God in their lives, even in the face of pain, suffering and confusion. This Divine mystery, revealed in the depths of their being, in nature, salvation history, tradition, Scripture and uniquely in Jesus Christ and His Church, becomes intimately present in the lives of those who have put on Christ.

The Holy Spirit calls the truly evangelized to participate actively in the life, death and resurrection of Jesus Christ through authentic personal prayer and the sacramental and liturgical life of the Church. This paschal mystery converts their personal lives, calling them, as St. Paul writes to the Romans, to do the things they know they should do and not to do the things they know they should not do. Those for whom the Good News has fallen on rich soil live out their converted lives nurtured by genuine Christian example. As they grasp the radical catholicity of their faith, they seek to live lives of service to others, especially the poor. They strive to purify their hearts, uprooting biases and prejudices against any group or people, because these attitudes are incompatible with the love of God that fills their hearts. As they mature in faith, they develop an intellectual and emotional integration of what they believe, and they become eager to share this faith with others. Rooted in Christ, they look beyond the certainty of death to the "life of the world to come."

If this is what we hope is unfolding in the life of a truly evangelized person, we must acknowledge the painful truth that many Catholic people, like many Christians of other traditions, are not truly evangelized. The Catholic faith, which has come to them as a part of their ethnic and cultural heritage, has never been personally appropriated and made their own. This reminds us that evangelization is an ongoing reality in our own lives as well. An important part of the "new evangelization," to which John Paul calls the Church as we approach the year 2000, must begin with ourselves and our people.

As leaders of the Catholic Church in this country, we are all aware of the fact that the annual increase in the number of Catholics is primarily due to baptism of the children of Catholic couples and to the fact that Christians of other traditions who marry Catholics often decide to join the faith of their spouse. Only a small number of new Catholics are completely new, people who have heard about the faith from a friend or neighbor and want to learn about joining the Church themselves.

Catholic bishops, priests, deacons, religious and the Christian faithful have not, for the most part, been public evangelists. We do not see them visible on street corners, in shopping malls, at neighborhood social events eagerly telling strangers about Jesus and His Church. Nor do we tend to be door-to-door evangelists, knocking on doors for Jesus, putting fliers on car windshields or placing signs on neighborhood bulletin boards with our tear-off phone numbers, so that people call us if they want to know about Jesus. Most of our people do not seem to be inclined to take out their Bibles, Council documents, *Catechisms of the Catholic Church* or rosaries at lunch time in the office, in the warehouse or in the factory where they work, in order to share their Catholic faith. Some Catholics might actually find this offensive.

Several points can be drawn from this. When we speak about evangelization and African Americans, our ultimate hope must certainly be for something more profound than a superficial denominational affiliation. We do not have large communities of Black Catholics with young couples having their children baptized as infants. Nor do we have large numbers of Black Catholics marrying Christians of other traditions, who subsequently become Catholics. As a result, we do not experience a significant increase in White Catholic communities.

Thus, when we say that the Church or Black Catholics must evangelize in Black communities, are we asking that something be done that we are not doing in other communities? Are White Catholics evangelizing in White communities? Are we asking that Catholics open themselves to real changes in the way they see themselves, their relationship to their faith and to others? Are we asking Catholics to become involved with some form of public evangelization, be it on the street, door-to-door or at work? Our people will not become more open to sharing their faith with people of different races until questions such as these are answered.

## IV. WORLDS APART: THE CULTURAL DIVIDE

Even if we could stir up an evangelizing spirit in our people, it might not result in a significant number of Black Americans embracing the Catholic faith in the decades to come. The reasons for this are manifold and as complex as those that have prevented the Church from attracting significant numbers in countries such as Japan, China and India for centuries. The greatest obstacle to the evangelization of Black Americans may be the fact that the cultural, educational, economic and political situations that define the relation between the Catholic Church and most African Americans constitutes a radical cultural divide.

The cultural divide is particularly acute between the Catholic Church as we know it and the culture and lived experiences of the vast majority of poor, younger, urban and rural Black people who usually are not attracted to the Catholic faith. Jesus Christ clearly commanded His followers to teach all nations. Nevertheless, this universal faith as it is embodied by the Catholic Church in the United States has been profoundly shaped by "various situations and cultures" foreign to the contemporary Black experience. These are essentially the cultures of ancient Greece and Rome that became the foundations of western European cultures. The structure of Catholic theological reflection; the aesthetic principles by which religious art, music, literature, architecture, liturgical vestments and the environment for worship are measured; the prism through which Sacred Scripture is read; and the ascetical ideals which inform our understanding of spirituality, prayer, the interior life, the experience of God, our relationship with Christ, sin and the work of God's saving grace in the sacraments; have been primarily shaped by this western European culture. This is inevitable because the Church and the life of faith exist in time and space. The Church trans-

forms and is, in part, transformed by the "situations and cultures" in which it finds itself.

Anthropologists and philosophers of religion have traditionally argued that within the human spirit there are recurring questions of meaning dealing with the purpose and destiny of the human person. For many people, the themes addressed by religion (God, eternity, moral judgments, afterlife, mystery, prayer, sacred time, sacred space, sacred narratives, sacred persons and sacred ritual) have provided the context for seeking answers to these questions. Students of religion are always interested to know why certain religious traditions seem to illuminate these questions more adequately than others for individuals and people in different cultures, ethnic and racial groups, and historical contexts. We bishops also have reason to be interested in this question.

This relationship between the questions human beings ask and the answers provided by a particular faith tradition has sometimes been called the "existential fit." There have always been people who held that the questions themselves were absurd or at best they could not be answered definitively, embracing atheism and agnosticism. Large numbers of young Black Americans say or imply that the questions are irrelevant to the struggles of their everyday existence. Or, if they are relevant, the Catholic Church, looked upon with suspicion as a largely White, racist middle-class reality, has not been able to raise the questions and illuminate the responses of its tradition in a way that touches the minds and passions of Black people. There is no "existential fit." This lack of "fit" does not mean that the truths of faith and the degree of welcome that Catholics convey do not communicate the heart of the faith effectively to potential converts.

The basketball players in the barber shop are not likely to be engaged by an otherworldly apologetic that presents a Catholic Church unwilling or unable to do anything to help alter their present economic, political and social plight. A church that offers little sustained help in the struggle and promises the joy of eternal life after they die is not an "existential fit" for the life experiences of these young people. Any preacher they follow will have to be at their side engaged in the struggle, helping them find a God of the oppressed and an angel of freedom and justice, articulated in a theology that embraces, celebrates and is informed by the Black experience. If God is to really be God for them, He must be God the liberator, who uproots injustice and oppression by His mighty power. A god of the status quo is dead for them.

There are many important, related implications of this cultural divide. Three of them have a negative impact upon evangelization. These are our segregated neighborhoods, our segregated Catholic schools, and, perhaps surprisingly, our segregated Catholic art.

## Segregated Neighborhoods

Since most Catholics are White and since most Black people are not Catholics, the Church's effectiveness in evangelizing Black people would almost certainly be greater if people of both races lived next door to one another as friends and neighbors. But this is rarely the case in the United States. Neighborhoods, like the imaginary one in which the barber shop is located, are all Black as a direct result of the cultural divide. These neighborhoods and the all-Black parishes in them were formed by the systematic segregation and re-segregation of our large urban communities. As Black people moved from the south looking for employment in northern cities in the 1930s, '40s and '50s, many factors fed a xenophobic dread of economic, cultural, religious or racial diversity in city neighborhoods. Because the Catholic Church itself did not know the world of these Black, largely, but not exclusively, Protestant migrants, it does not have a record of prophetic leadership during this time. John T. McGreevy's *Parish Boundaries: The Catholic Encounter with Race in the Twentieth-Century Urban North* documents the rapid movement of White Catholics to the suburbs to escape neighborhoods that were changing racially, economically and culturally. Due in

part to the cultural divide, White congregations and their pastors, often recent immigrants from eastern or western Europe themselves, did not find in their Christian faith an inspiration to welcome their new neighbors.

In spite of this, we must not diminish the enviable record of exceptional service of the White and Black bishops, priests, brothers, sisters and Christian faithful, past and present, who have eagerly committed their entire lives to ministry in African American parishes. We think immediately of the Josephites, the Society of the Divine Word, the Oblate Sisters of Providence, the Sisters of the Blessed Sacrament and the many diocesan priests and others, who have been unselfish in their generosity. In and through God's grace, they have accomplished and continue to accomplish great things in our local church communities.

Nevertheless, we are forced to acknowledge that there are a significant number of White priests today who make it clear that they do not wish to serve in Black parishes at any time during their ministry. This may not be due primarily to racial prejudice. It may be due in part to the real or perceived extreme differences between Black and White neighborhoods and their uneasiness about crossing the cultural divide. These priests may prefer suburban parishes where there are more people, more resources, better parish facilities and more trained personnel because they are more like the communities in which they grew up and because they think it is easier to build post-Vatican II faith communities in such areas.

Some of our Black priests may feel the same way, wondering why they are expected to serve in what others consider undesirable parishes, simply because the parishioners are "their people." Meanwhile, since the need for priests is great, bishops do not have the luxury of sending extra priests to be evangelists in Black parishes where there are only a few Catholics, when they are so needed in the suburban parishes where there are so many Catholics. We are a long way from the day when White Catholics from the suburbs will cross the cultural divide and come eagerly to the city as evangelists and missionaries.

### Segregated Catholic Schools

In the past the all-Black Catholic schools that resulted from our segregated neighborhoods played a central role in the evangelization of African Americans. Black parents, seeking an alternative to the public schools and admiring the value formation for which the Catholic schools were renowned, sent their children to these schools. The pastors required the parents and the children who were not Catholic to study the Catholic faith. These adult "convert classes" resulted in the baptism of significant numbers of children and parents each year for almost a quarter of a century. But this trend was definitely reversed by the mid 1960s.

Today in our all-Black parish schools where most of the students are not Catholics, there may be only one or two religious sisters, if any. There are almost no Black, Catholic, male teachers. Most of the lay teachers are White women who live in other neighborhoods. They may feel ill at ease about going beyond teaching general Christian values to actually enthusiastically urging the students to become Catholics. In some schools, there seems to be an unwritten policy not to evangelize even if the children are unchurched. Many principals and pastors are uncomfortable with the old system of mandatory attendance at religion classes by parents. They also argue that it is un-enforceable.

Even if pastors and catechists sense an openness to the Catholic faith on the part of a student, they may deem it unwise to prepare that child for baptism. Many Black children are brought to Catholic schools by working parents who live a considerable distance from the parish church. When not even one member of the family is committed to the faith, it will be impossible for the sixth, seventh or eighth grader to get to Sunday Mass and participate in the life of the Church. With no support at all, it is unlikely that this fragile faith will survive, especially with the prospect of a public high school. In these circumstances only the smallest number of Black students become Catholic each year.

Real as these difficulties may be, our Catholic schools must never be reduced to mere instruments of social progress. They have the great potential of becoming once again true and effective instruments of evangelization. If we abandon this confidence, we risk undermining the essential nature and purpose of the Church's involvement in the ministry of education, which is to share the light and love of Jesus Christ with all.

### Segregated Catholic Art

When I was the pastor of a parish in the Archdiocese of Chicago, I used to take the children from our all-African American school on a tour of our church three times a year. One of the first questions was always, "Father, why are all angels and saints White? Aren't there any Black people in Heaven?" I thought of these children last month when I had quite a discussion about our beautiful new Mary, Mother of Africa chapel with a young Black man who had recently left the seminary. He asked, "Why should Black Catholics be so grateful for one chapel in our National Basilica while the vast majority of the art in the Basilica and in all of Catholic churches present an image of the Kingdom of Heaven that is exclusively White?"

He continued, "Why can there not be Black angels, cherubs and saints in all of our churches, Black and White? Imagine the impact on Black and White men and women if they saw images of God the Father, God the Son and God the Holy Spirit represented in the deep mystery of what Paul VI called 'the gift of Blackness.' In western iconography, darkness usually represents sin and evil. Demons, devils and Satan are often presented in dark hues. Show me a church in which Satan is pictured as White! Would not our catholicity be well served by the common experience

of seeing Jesus, Mary, Joseph and the saints in different ethnic and racial appearances in all of our churches?"

The former seminarian asserted, "It cannot be argued that it is a matter of historical accuracy. Angels are pure spirits, without race, nationality or gender. Western Christian art has never represented Jesus Christ, Mary or the Apostles as Jewish. God the Father is Absolute Spirit. He has no race or nationality. Scripture never describes Him as an elderly, European-looking man. We know and understand the historical and cultural reasons for what was done in the past. But why should we perpetuate this all-White image of heaven in the present and the future? What would happen if the bishops recommended, even mandated, such diversity in all of our future churches, seminaries, chancery offices and other institutions to convey a more authentically universal vision of the heavenly Jerusalem?"

"Is this an insignificant issue?" asked the former seminarian. "What if the situation were reversed? How would Catholics of European origin feel if, starting tomorrow, all of the images of the Trinity, Jesus, Mary,

Saints, Angels and all the inhabitants of heaven in their churches had Black, Hispanic, Asian or Native American features and none were White? Would they feel fully at home and welcome? Is this not what Black Catholics have lived with for generations? Is this not what they are going to live with for generations to come? Surely, the total absence of images of the holy and the sacred from a Black perspective in our churches has a negative impact on the Church's efforts to evangelize Black Americans. The image of a magnificent Black angel in a cathedral might do more for the evangelization of Black people than handing out copies of a prayer book at the door. Who would want to join a faith, in which all the spiritual 'personalities' are visualized to look like the very people who enslaved and oppressed them?"

The thoughts of this young man are spoken in part from anger, hurt and disillusionment. They may sound too strong and unrealistic to many of us. Nevertheless, we must hear these thoughts because they represent the deep-seated feelings of many Black people, young and old, that we wish to reach. These same feelings are shared by growing numbers of Black Catholics. They are often expressed at gatherings such as this Congress. We must also hear them because they are a painful reminder of talented people like Brother Cyprian Rowe, who left the Catholic Church, in part because of issues dealing with liturgy, art and racial inclusiveness.

This examination of the cultural divide and some of its implications has been attempting to approach a very difficult question from a moving viewpoint. That question is not how do we make existing Black Catholic parishes more vital. Nor is it how can we make the liturgies in which Black Catholics worship more vital or more spiritually nourishing for those who are already coming to church. The question has been how can we reach the Black people, especially young men, who pass by our churches week after week on their way to the barber shop without even noticing them.

## V. SPECIFIC RECOMMENDATIONS

It may be useful to consider specific pastoral recommendations for the American bishops that may aid us in creating a greater atmosphere of openness to Black people on the part of the Church and a greater openness to the Church on the part of Black people. This openness and respect are part of the foundation that is necessary for crossing the cultural divide before the work of pre-evangelization can begin.

Perhaps no private institution has done more than the Catholic Church to secure a more just society. The Church expends large sums of money each year in Black communities subsidizing Catholic schools and in the work of Catholic Charities, and a vast network of social service programs whose positive impact cannot be measured. Yet the Church, as the Church, is not a strong, visible presence to ordinary Black people in their neighborhoods. There are things that we could do, perhaps as a conference, to make our presence better known and make our desires to cross the cultural divide more apparent.

1.  We should give serious attention to our relationship with the Black media. Local dioceses and, where appropriate, the bishops' conference itself should consider preparing press releases tailored for *Ebony*, *Jet*, *Black Enterprise*, local Black newspapers, Black radio stations, the National Association for the Advancement of Colored People, and traditional Black churches. Imaginative advertisements on Black-oriented radio and TV stations would also make the Church more present to people who literally do not know who we are. Visible neighborhood signs directing people to the nearest parish and announcing "THE CATHOLIC CHURCH WELCOMES YOU!" establish immedi-

ate contact with the people on the street. A Catholic invitation to join the Church on the sides of buses and in subway stations in Black neighborhoods would be seen by all.

2.  The bishops of the United States should seriously consider leading the way in the elimination of the practice of calling people "minorities" and "minority groups." Most people of color find these words very offensive. African Americans almost never refer to themselves with these terms except when they are forced to do so by legal language. Editorials in national newspapers, TV documentaries and government studies use these expressions frequently, oblivious of or indifferent to their negative connotations.

    These terms do not simply convey the neutral idea of numerically smaller groups in a given population. We have been conditioned to think of very specific groups in our culture when we hear these terms. Just as we no longer call Christians of other traditions "non-Catholics," which describes them as what they are not, we should also avoid calling people "minority groups," which describes them as what they are not, namely not the majority. The majority of the world's population is not European. Similarly, no particularly European ethnic or national group constitutes the majority of the population in this country. In his call for candid discussions on the topic of race relations in the United States, President Clinton has pointed out that in the coming decades, there will be no majority race, nationality or ethnic group in America. We would do far better to refer to groups of people as who they are.

3.  Think, for a moment, about the chancery offices, cathedrals, bishop's residences, seminaries and parish plants in your diocese and ask yourselves how many Black people are employed as secretaries, custodians, cooks and housekeepers. If our diocesan institutions and parishes hire only

White-owned companies (with all White workers) for building, tuck-pointing, landscaping and painting; if all the electricians, plumbers, carpenters, carpet layers and window washers are White, it is noticed. No matter where our catholic institutions are located, the presence or absence of Black workers is observed and thought about by Black and White people. The only way to ensure racial diversity in these work forces is to have someone who personally oversees and enforces the Church's frequently stated commitment to this diversity. Think also of social gatherings at the bishop's residence. How often do White guests encounter Black guests there?

4. We should feature articles about African Americans frequently in our diocesan newspapers, whether or not we have a significant number of Black Catholics or even Black people in our dioceses. The articles would be primarily for the benefit of our Catholic people who are not African American. These articles need not always be religious in nature. They could challenge stereotypes and help people learn about the Black experience. Many White suburban Catholic teenagers form most of their impressions of Black people from TV and movies, which usually reinforce prejudice and fear.

5. We must go beyond volunteerism. If the vision of this eighth National Black Catholic Congress is to be implemented, additional resources must be provided to support ongoing, organized efforts. If we are to make progress in getting to know the African American communities around us, we must be willing to invest greater resources and personnel over the long run. We cannot propose teams of full-time, well-trained door-to-door evangelists in Black neighborhoods without acknowledging that such persons must be adequately compensated. Very few of our Black parishes, if any, have the income to pay for this training and compensation. Funding will have to come from the larger Church.

6. Our usually imposing parish plants may intimidate many people. Could we consider several strategic experiments with neighborhood store-front community development and self-help centers? These could offer a wide range of recreational activities, social services, counseling, employment guidance, Bible classes and simple non-eucharistic worship services tailored to meet the needs of young Black people right off the street. These experimental centers in three or four dioceses would need to be staffed by trained, paid, full-time deacons, sisters or lay persons.

7. Our Catholic Campaign for Human Development does exceptional work in helping people to help themselves in many situations around the country. Many of us visit these sites and preside at the distribution of funds. Often the beneficiaries of CCHD do not even know what the Catholic Church is and they have no idea that it is the generosity of Catholic people that funds the CCHD. There are obvious pre-evangelization possibilities in the midst of this good work which often takes place in Black neighborhoods. CCHD is not the activity of sincere social workers. It is the work of love of neighbor that flows directly from our commitment to Jesus Christ.

8. The year-long preparation for baptism mandated by the Rites for the Christian Initiation of Adults (RCIA) is an exceptional resource for renewal in the Church. Yet it may need to be adapted to be attractive to poorer, younger people. The RCIA is sometimes experienced as too long and involved. If this becomes discouraging, catechumens tend to drop out. Careful attention needs to be given to appropriate ways to adapt this very important process of entering into the life of the Church, without diminishing in any way the real and in-depth instruction and Christian formation that are essential for a life of faith.

9. Our Episcopal Conference has produced a number of detailed statements containing specific proposals, goals, agendas and resolutions addressing the question of the Church in Black communities and the concerns of this Congress. If you re-read them, you might be surprised and disappointed to note how many excellent ideas have been formulated that have never been systematically implemented. These documents include: *Brothers and Sisters to Us*, our 1979 pastoral letter on the sin and heresy of racism that endures in our Church and in American society; *Here I Am, Send Me*, our 1989 conference response to our mission of evangelizing African Americans and the National Black Catholic Pastoral Plan; *Go and Make Disciples*, our 1992 national plan and strategy for Catholic evangelization in the United States; and our 1997 statement, *A Pastoral Plan for Communication*, with an extensive section on evangelization. While there is no need to say more, there is a great need to do more. Is this really a priority for the Church in the United States?

10. My final recommendation may be the most important. We need to pray. I do not speak of occasional, vague, general prayers. I speak of regular, specific prayers focused on conversion. First we should pray for ourselves and our people that God will bring about a true conversion of our hearts, our attitudes and our way of doing things so as to remove any obstacles that we may unintentionally place in the way of evangelization. We should pray that the Holy Spirit help us announce the Gospel in the way of evangelization. We should pray that the Holy Spirit help us announce the Gospel in ways that speak to Black people who really are brothers and sisters to us. We should pray for vocations from African American families to the religious life, the diaconate and the priesthood. We should pray as well for vocation directors and seminary and convent leadership that they will take special care to nurture potential vocations that come to them. We should also ask our people to pray for these concerns, at home, at Mass and at our chapels of perpetual adoration of the Eucharist.

## V. CONCLUSION

You would not be attending this eighth National Black Catholic Congress unless the relationship between the Catholic Church and Black Americans was a matter of great importance to you. We pray together that the Holy Spirit will guide and inspire us. We can never limit the providential work of the Divine Spirit. While we may not always see in what precise way the Spirit is moving in the work of evangelization, we can be confident that the Spirit whom Christ Himself breathed on the apostles is never working against the authentic efforts of the Church. It is that Spirit who fills us with genuine love for those we wish to call in the name of Christ and fills those who be called with love for us in return.

My brothers, I have spoken to you forthrightly about the challenges that the Catholic Church must face if we are to examine honestly the questions raised by serious reflection on evangelizing African Americans effectively. If the analysis presented here is fundamentally correct, then we can expect no overnight change in the present situation. I firmly believe that we must decide to act in new ways. Otherwise, someone will be giving a similar address ten years from now and the challenge will be greater because the situation will be worse: Why not act now?

Some of what I have said may be discouraging. Let us not be discouraged. When we are discouraged, let us recall the powerful, prophetic words of Pope Paul VI's landmark apostolic exhortation, *Evangelii Nuntiandi*:

> Let us therefore preserve our fervor of spirit, Let us preserve the delightful and comforting joy of evangelizing, even when it is in tears that we must sow. May it mean for us—as it did for John the Baptist, for Peter and Paul, for the other Apostles and for a multitude of splendid evangelizers all through the

Church's history—an interior enthusiasm that no one and nothing can quench. May it be the great joy of our consecrated lives. And may the world of our time, which is searching, sometimes with anguish, sometimes with hope, be enabled to receive the Good News not from evangelizers who are dejected, discouraged, impatient or anxious, but from ministers of the Gospel whose lives glow with fervor, who have first received the joy of Christ, and who are willing to risk their lives so that the Kingdom may be proclaimed and the Church established in the midst of the world. Mary, Mother of Africa and Mother of the Church, pray for us! (63-64) ■

Most Rev. Edward K. Braxton *is the bishop of Lake Charles, Louisiana, and chairman of the bishops' Committee for the American College of Louvain.*

## BISHOP BRAXTON OFFERS IDEAS FOR GREATER BLACK, WHITE OPENNESS

### BY NANCY FRAZIER O'BRIEN, CATHOLIC NEWS SERVICE • JANUARY 1999

BALTIMORE (CNS)—Auxiliary Bishop Edward K. Braxton of St. Louis outlined ten specific "ways to develop greater openness to Blacks by the Church and to the Church by Blacks" in a January 22 talk in Baltimore.

One of thirteen active Black bishops in the United States, Bishop Braxton was addressing a January 21-22 national consultation sponsored by the National Black Catholic Congress.

Bishop Braxton's talk and others at the 1999 meeting were follow-ups to an address he gave two years earlier at the eighth National Black Catholic Congress, also held in Baltimore. In the 1997 talk, he suggested that the Catholic Church's failure to gain substantial membership in the Black community could be due to the fact that "the way the Church articulates its faith and the degree of welcome that Catholics convey do not communicate the heart of the faith effectively to potential converts."

Bishop Braxton noted that his 1999 speech came at the convergence of four very different events: the seventieth anniversary of the birth of the Rev. Martin Luther King Jr., the Week of Prayer for Christian Unity, discussions in the Senate of "grave matters of state" involving President Clinton, and the twenty-sixth anniversary of Roe vs. Wade.

The link among those events, he said, is that "they all have profoundly different meaning for African American Catholics and the Black community in general than for the White community."

Commenting on President Clinton's call for a "serious and sustained national conversation" on racism, Bishop Braxton said it "has not been a very loud conversation" and has been "met with indifference and cynicism" on all sides.

In the Catholic Church, he said, there has not been a "great record of prophetic leadership" in response to what he called "the systematic and systemic segregation and resegregation of our cities."

White Catholics who fled to the suburbs when Blacks began moving in next door "did not find in the Catholic Church the inspiration to welcome their new neighbors," he said.

# Solidarity: The Antidote *to* Resurgent Racism

BY MOST REV. SEAN P. O'MALLEY, OFMCap

JANUARY 2000

Our celebration of a jubilee year is a religious practice that has its roots in the Old Testament. Jesus Christ, our Lord and Savior, went to the synagogue at Nazareth at the beginning of his Messianic mission. He took the scroll and read the passage from the prophet Isaiah in the Old Testament which speaks about the jubilee and the Messiah:

> The Spirit of the Lord God is upon me, because the Lord has anointed me to bring good tidings to the afflicted; he has sent me to bind up the broken-hearted, to proclaim liberty to captives, . . . and release to the prisoners who are bound; to proclaim the year of the Lord's favor. (Lk 4:18-19)

Jesus is the fulfillment of all jubilees. He comes to proclaim a year of the Lord's favor. The jubilee of yore was a time dedicated in a special way to God. It fell every seventh year ("a week of years"). According to Mosaic law, it was a sabbath year during which time fields were to be left fallow and slaves were to be freed. The sabbath year also called for a cancellation of all debts. All this was done in honor of God.

Every fiftieth year (seven times seven, or a week of sabbath years) was an even more solemn sabbatical year of jubilee. Once again, an important part of the celebration was the emancipation of all the dwellers on the land in need of being freed. Even land that might have been lost to a family was restored as part of the jubilee celebration. They could not be permanently deprived of the land because it belonged to God; nor could the Israelites remain in bondage since God had redeemed them for himself by setting them free from slavery in Egypt.

From the prescriptions for the Old Testament jubilee observances, a social doctrine emerges and is developed in the New Testament. Even in Old Testament times, the jubilee was meant to restore equality among all the children of Israel. The jubilee year provided for those in need, slaves, debtors and sharecroppers. The foundations for this tradition were strictly theological, flowing from a theology of creation and of divine providence. God has the Lordship over all creation, over our lives, even our debts. The social doctrine of the Church, our teaching on life issues and justice issues, is rooted in the tradition of the jubilee year.

In calling for the celebration of the jubilee year, the Holy Father reminds us that "the joy of every jubilee is above all a joy based upon the forgiveness of sins, the joy of conversion." He goes on to say, "Hence, it is appropriate that, as the second millennium of Christianity draws to a close, the church should be more fully conscious of the sinfulness of her children, recalling all those times in history when they departed from the spirit of Christ and his Gospel, and instead of offering to the world the witness of a life inspired by the values of faith, indulged in ways of thinking and acting which are truly forms of counterwitness and scandal" (*Tertio Millennio Adveniente*, no. 32).

---

IF WE CLAIM THAT WE LOVE GOD BUT HATE OUR NEIGHBOR, THEN WE ARE "A LIAR"; FOR "ONE CANNOT LOVE GOD WHOM HE HAS NOT SEEN, IF HE DOES NOT LOVE HIS BROTHER, WHOM HE HAS SEEN" (1 JN 4:20).

---

One of the most egregious sins which we often fail to face as individuals or as a community is the sin of racism. It is a sin that has deeply marked the history of our country, where Black people were subjected to forced servitude, not because they were prisoners of war or common criminals, but simply because they were Black. The devastating scars that slavery left on the Black people, the destruction of family life, the economic deprivation and inferior social status have become a painful legacy for generations of African Americans even in our own times. While positive changes have occurred at certain times in various situations, racism not only persists in our world, but also in many places is powerfully resurgent. Hate crimes, church burnings at home and ethnic cleansing abroad are present-day realities.

Racism perpetuates a basic untruth that purports an innate superiority of one group over another because of skin color, culture or ethnicity. This attitude contradicts the biblical understanding of God's action in creation, whereby all human beings are made "in the image and likeness of God." Racism denies the dignity of each human being revealed by the mystery of the incarnation and blasphemes the redemptive act of Christ, who died on the cross to save all people. Indeed, Jesus calls us to lives of discipleship and servanthood without boundaries of race or class. Racism gives false permission for oppression and exploitation that is completely repugnant to the teachings of Christ.

Jesus' ministry is a clear manifestation of the universal love of the Father; for beyond his ministry to the chosen people of Israel, Jesus reaches out to the pagans, curing the centurion's servant. The daughter of the Syro-Phoenician woman as well as the possessed Gerasene man in the Decapolis are also beneficiaries of the Lord's healing power. The apostles themselves are surprised to find the Lord talking to the Samaritan woman at the well and certainly disconcerted by his bold assertion that many would come from the East and the West and would sit down at table with Abraham, Isaac and Jacob when God's kingdom is realized.

The irresistible logic of Christ's teaching allows the Church to be truly catholic and to embrace the universalizing implications of the gospel message. Paul, the apostle of the gentiles, saw the breaking down of the wall of hostility between Jew and gentile as one of the great watersheds in the history of salvation. The Church proclaims our God, who shows no partiality except perhaps for the marginalized and excluded. St. James warns us about being "partial toward persons," about discriminating against those who are poor or different in favor of the rich and famous.

St. James, in his epistle, admonishes us: "My brothers, as believers in our Lord Jesus Christ, the Lord of glory, you must never treat people in different ways according to their outward appearance" (2:1). The sacred writer goes on to condemn this discrimination: "You are guilty of creating distinctions among yourselves and of making judgments based on evil motives" (2:4).

The teaching of Christ is unambiguous in that the whole of our religion, "the law and the prophets," is based on the great commandment of love. No matter how outstanding our talents or contributions, "if I have not love, I am nothing" (1 Cor 13:2). If we claim that we love God but hate our neighbor, then we are "a liar"; for "one cannot love God whom he has not seen, if he does not love his brother, whom he has seen" (1 Jn 4:20).

When asked for a definition of neighbor, our Lord answers with the parable of the good Samaritan. Jesus astonished his audience by making the Samaritan, the member of a despised minority group, the hero and protagonist of the story. In one fell swoop Jesus pops the bubble of ethnic superiority and at the same time challenges us to be a neighbor to all in need and to remove the barriers in our heart that prevent us from seeing our connectedness with every human being.

For when Jesus says neighbor, he is talking about a big neighborhood: first of all anyone who is in need and has a claim on our help, as well as every man, woman and child of whatever religious persuasion, social status, ethnic or linguistic background, liberal or conserv-ative, heterosexual or homosexual, Democrat or Republican, old or young, and all of the above, in all shades, colors and sizes. There is absolutely no room for racism and discrimination in Jesus' concept of neighbor.

We can truly love God only when we truly love our neighbor, made in his image and likeness. Apart from that love, there is no authentic religion. Because love is the essence of our religion, racism is a dangerous heresy that subverts the announcing of the Gospel.

The history of our country has been deeply marked by the sin of racism, which is a betrayal of our Christian faith as well as our democratic ideals. Despite great progress in the area of civil rights since the murder of Dr. Martin Luther King Jr., his dream of racial harmony is still a dream deferred. The "promised land" of integration where "children of for-mer slaves and children of former slaveholders could sit down at the table of brotherhood," so much more

difficult than desegregation, is still very illusive. Church burnings and other hate crimes continue, and motorists are still stopped for "driving while Black." In the last year, 220 articles on racial violence appeared on the pages of the *New York Times*, including the tragic high-profile accounts of the torture of Abner Louima [a Haitian immigrant brutalized by police officers] and the killing of Amadou Diallo [a West African immigrant slain by police officers].

It is with shame and sorrow that we recall the plight of Native Americans and Blacks, the two groups to suffer the most devastating effects of the sin of racism in our country. It is obvious that racism in all its forms and disguises is a dehumanizing force that demeans its victims and renders its perpetrators diminished in their humanity, or to use an expression of Pope Paul VI, "mutilated by their selfishness."

The racial tensions in the United States find a counterpart in the ethnic and nationalistic violence abroad. In fact, of the fifty million people who have died in armed conflicts since the end of World War II, most have perished in "ethnic" conflicts—in Rwanda, Burundi, Angola, Mozambique, India, Pakistan, Bangladesh, East Timor and the former Yugoslavia. The dawn of the new millennium finds the whole world struggling with a legacy of devastating racial and ethnic violence.

The challenge for believers is to build a civilization of love in a world where there is so much division. The ministry of reconciliation is a sacred duty of Christ's Church as we embark on a new millennium. Diversity must be seen as something that can enrich the human family. We must move from fear and suspicion to tolerance, and from tolerance to solidarity. This is not a utopian quest, but a moral imperative for peace and progress on our planet. Indeed, it is probably a question of survival. There will be a civilization of love or no civilization at all.

To combat racism at its root, we must begin with a personal inventory, an examination of conscience and a profound realization of how pernicious racism is. Racial bias profoundly affects our culture. It deforms relationships within and between racial or ethnic groups. It undermines the possibility of true community. In addition, racial bigotry exacerbates unhealthy competition, destroys people's self-confidence and initiative. This sin prevents us from being what God has called us to be.

Racism has many faces, not just a pointed hood of the White supremacists. It is evidenced in one's tendency to stereotype people, in an extreme pride in one's own country or race, in belittling members of other races, in condescending attitudes or behavior, and in not taking peoples of other races seriously. A racist attitude finds expression in a lack of impartiality, in the failure to recognize the negative impact of racism on the victim, by encouraging prejudice in others and by laughing at racist jokes that are hurtful and demeaning.

In the parable of Lazarus and Dives, the rich man goes to Hades not for adultery or murder or robbery, but because he was incapable of seeing Lazarus suffering at his doorstep. In a similar fashion, racism makes one blind to the presence of persons of other races. They become like nameless pieces of furniture that clutter up the landscape. Racism will be banished when we overcome our blindness to the people around us and when instead of being blind, we become colorblind, indifferent to people's complexion but not to their dignity and their feelings.

Desegregation was the process which eliminated discriminatory laws and barriers to full participation in American life. Integration is much more difficult to achieve because it demands a change of heart. Desegregation may unlock doors, but integration is when minds and hearts are opened as well, when the welcome mat is placed at the door.

Integration is so compelling because it is about people, not laws. It is about the way we see each other and treat others; it is about whether there will be room in our hearts and homes and classrooms and clubs and churches to welcome each other naturally as neighbors and friends. Desegregation is about laws; integration is about the Golden Rule.

In the play *South Pacific*, Rodgers and Hammerstein have a song that goes: "You have to be taught to hate and fear. You have to be taught from year to year. It has to be drummed into your little ear. You have to be carefully taught."

Racism is like a disease most often transmitted from parent to child. Its early symptom is the delusion that one's race is somehow superior to others. In advanced stages it leads to hatred, violence and untold suffering. This contagion needs to be checked. The twentieth century was able to entirely eliminate certain diseases like small pox and polio, but this spiritual disease of racism is still menacing our world as we begin a new millennium.

In the fight against any disease it is necessary to recognize the threat. Too often we are in denial about racism. The reality has been driven underground. Because cruder historic forms of racist sentiments and behavior are considered "politically incorrect" and because more laws have been passed, more "concessions" made, there is a false sense of security that the problem has been dealt with. But too often the spiritual problem has not been dealt with: Repentance, change of heart, forgiveness, respect are still needed.

Today's racism is more subtle but no less real. As the U.S. Catholic Conference document *Brothers and Sisters to Us: U.S. Bishops' Pastoral Letter on Racism in Our Day* asserts, racism "is manifest also in the indifference that replaces open hatred. The minority poor are seen as the dross of a post-industrial society—without skills, without motivation, without incentive.

They are expendable. Many times the new face of racism is the computer printout, the graph of profits and losses, the pink slip, the nameless statistic. Today's racism flourishes in the triumph of private concern over public responsibility, individual success over social commitment and personal fulfillment over authentic compassion" (no. 22).

In Catholic social teaching, the antidote for racism is solidarity. It is a concept used by Paul VI in *Populorum Progressio* in his discussion of development. Pope John Paul II expands on this virtue in his encyclical letter *Sollicitudo Rei Socialis*:

> In the light of faith, solidarity seeks to go beyond itself, to take on the specifically Christian dimensions of total gratuity, forgiveness and reconciliation. One's neighbor is then not only a human being with his or her own rights and a fundamental equality with everyone else, but becomes the living image of God the Father, redeemed by the blood of Jesus Christ and placed under the permanent action of the Holy Spirit. One's neighbor must therefore be loved, even if an enemy, with the same love with which the Lord loves him or her; and for that person's sake one must be ready for sacrifice, even the ultimate one: to lay down one's life for the brethren. (no. 40)

Solidarity is an expression of the great commandment that calls us to form a community among people that will enable us to overcome "structures of sin and oppression" that dog humanity. Above the human and natural bonds already so strong, faith leads us o see "a new model of the unity of the human race." The Holy Father insists that solidarity is not sentimentality or a vague compassion or empathy for the suffering of so many, but rather it is a firm and persevering determination to commit oneself to the common good, that is to say, the good of all and of each individual, "because we are all really responsible for all" (*Sollicitudo Rei Socialis*, no. 38).

As we begin the twenty-first century and the third millennium, we must embrace the concept of solidarity as a solution to the racism, as well as to the greed and the competition, that has fractionalized our country and our planet. Solidarity is the virtue we need to instill in the new generation so that racism might become a sad anachronism in our lifetime. Just as racism is contagious, so too solidarity can inspire our young people when they see the witness of men and women committed to social justice and to the good of the entire community.

As we campaign against cigarettes and drugs, we must also launch a campaign of zero tolerance for the intolerance of racism. Parents and teachers need to be the protagonists of this effort. Each of us ought to begin with our own personal conversion and testimony. We also need to create opportunities and space for friendship with people who are of different races and ethnic backgrounds. As a community we should celebrate the gifts and the traditions of all "our neighbors" and work together to build a better community where people care about each other.

Racism thrives on fear, but love casts out fear. Solidarity transforms relationships and connects us with each other. Fear and suspicion are changed into a sense of partnership in a community that truly recognizes the value of each and every person as irreplaceable and as precious in the eyes of God.

The virtue of solidarity is not only an antidote to our racial tensions in our own country, but points the way to a program of development and world peace based on a "new model of the unity of the human race." In his message for World Peace Day, January 1, 2000, Pope John Paul II states:

We can set forth one certain principle: There will be peace only to the extent that humanity as a whole rediscovers its fundamental call to be one family, a family in which the dignity and rights of individuals, whatever their status, race or religion, are accepted as prior and superior to any kind of difference or distinction. (World Day of Peace Message, 5)

Given the U.S. economic, cultural and military power, the Holy Father's dream of humanity becoming "a single family built on the values of justice, equity and solidarity" is in some ways contingent on the ability of Americans of good will being able to bring about Dr. Martin Luther King Jr.'s dream of the promised land of racial integration in our corner of the globe.

As we cross the threshold of hope from a century of violence into a new millennium, our quest is to become what God has called us to be. We make our own the song:

> God of our weary years, God of our silent tears,
> Thou who hast brought us thus far on the way;
> Thou who hast by thy might, led us into the light,
> Keep us forever in the path, we pray.
> Lest our feet stray from the places, our God,
>     where we met thee. . . .
> Shadowed beneath thy hand, may we
>     forever stand
> True to our God, true to our native land.
> —*from "Lift Every Voice and Sing," by James Weldon Johnson and John Rosamond Johnson* ■

Most Rev. Sean P. O'Malley, OFMCap, *is the bishop of the Diocese of Fall River, Massachusetts, and the chairman of the bishops' Committee on Consecrated Life.*

# There Are No "Minority" Americans

## BY MOST REV. EDWARD K. BRAXTON

JUNE 2000

One night recently I was visiting with a group of friends and listening to the music of Billie Holiday, Miles Davis, Nina Simone, John Coltrane and Ray Charles. Our conversation about African American culture turned to a thought-provoking question: Why do more and more African Americans reject the common practice of society, the Catholic Church and many Black people themselves of referring to people of color as "minorities" or as members of "minority groups"? I have never used this term in reference to myself or to any group of American citizens, and I never will, because I believe it is erroneous and counterproductive. Americans and Catholics of African descent are neither "minority" Americans nor "minority" Catholics.

Beginning in the late 1960s the media, the federal government and Americans of certain racial and ethnic backgrounds (especially Hispanic, Asian and Black people) frequently spoke of "minorities" and "minority groups" in solidarity with women and other groups who have experienced justice based upon discrimination. These designations were used to help formulate the argument that, in order to redress the grave injustices caused by systemic prejudices, special consideration should be given to members of these groups in matters related to education, employment, housing, financial assis-

tance and professional advancement. Fair-minded people agree that long-standing practices of discrimination have made it impossible for certain groups of Americans to have equal access to the American dream. Without prejudice to the validity of these important concerns, I believe that the common use of the word "minorities" as the collective designation of these groups of people perpetuates negative stereotypes and is contradicted by what it means to be an American citizen.

It does not take a particularly critical analysis to recognize the fact that words like "minorities" and "minority groups" are used selectively and are not applied consistently in reference to all ethnic groups that make up a statistically small number of U.S. citizens. At times, these expressions seem to be used as code words with subtle racist and negative connotations. They also beg the question, which citizens are the "majority" group. An example may help. In Japan, 99 percent of the residents are ethnic Japanese. However, people from other Asian countries, as well as Europeans, Africans and Americans also live in Japan. However, they are not ethnically and culturally Japanese. Most of them may not even be citizens precisely because of their lack of Japanese identity. Since they are neither politically nor ethnically Japanese, these residents are spoken of, for better or worse, as "minorities."

## UNIQUE SITUATION

The situation in the United States is quite different. Indeed, it is unique. There are no ethnic Americans in the same sense that there are ethnic Japanese. There is no single ethnic, racial or cultural group that constitutes "true" Americans. The simple fact is that every citizen of the United States is fully and equally an American in the exact same sense of the word. Citizens who are descendants of passengers on the Mayflower are not somehow more truly Americans than descendants of "passengers" of slave ships, native people of the Seminole nation or the most recent immigrants from India. If they are citizens, they are Americans, precisely because there are no ethnic Americans. A careful reflection on the meaning of the expression *"E Pluribus Unum"* excludes the possibility of designating "minorities" in this country, unless all citizens are so designated.

Obviously, this truth has not been fully accepted by all sectors of American society or by all members of the Catholic Church in the past or the present. European American Catholics, with roots in Ireland, Germany, Italy or Poland, for example, were once ostracized in this country as "immigrants," "foreigners" and "undesirable minorities." But why are they generally not considered minorities today? The answer is not because any one of these groups now constitutes the statistical majority of the U.S. population. As Matthew Frye Jacobson effectively argues in *Whiteness of a Different Color: European Immigrants and the Alchemy of Race*, the process of gathering together those Americans whose ancestors were from various European countries with very little in common and making them the "majority" group and relegating everyone else to "minorities" is, historically, a rather recent and arbitrary development.

It is a development that at certain junctures excluded even European Americans of certain backgrounds as despicable ethnic minorities. In its present usage, the term "minority groups" often connotes the haves ver-sus the have-nots, the powerful versus the powerless, the assimilated versus the non-assimilated. It may even implicitly advance the argument that some American citizens are "inferior" because they have not assimilated middle-class mores and the cultural heritage of Western Europe. As a result, even when the majority of the residents in a city are African Americans or Hispanic Americans, they are still "minorities." This kind of thinking can become quite convoluted. Americans whose families have come to this country directly from Spain are not generally spoken of as "minorities," as they once were. However, people of Spanish ancestry, who come to this country by way of Mexico, Central or South America, somehow become "minorities." Some sociologists argue that this may be because of their presumed intermarriage with native or African people, which may make it more difficult for them to be "assimilated."

## COMPLEX DIVERSITY

The Catholic Church in the United States cannot be effective in its ministry without being aware of the complex ethnic, racial and cultural diversity that makes up our Catholic population and the larger community. However, an awareness of this diversity must never lead the Church to the uncritical acceptance or even unwitting perpetuation of terms like "minorities" and "minority groups," which are rarely neutral and may contradict what it means to be an American by inviting stereotypes and reinforcing prejudices. Today, Protestant Christians prefer Catholic Christians to refer to them as what they are, "Christians of other traditions," rather than as what they are not, "non-Catholics." Have you ever been called a non-Baptist?

As we enter a new century, I hope we will think of our American sisters and brothers of different racial and ethnic backgrounds as who they are, African Americans, Asians Americans, Hispanic Americans, Native Americans and so on. Speaking of them as "minorities" designates them according to who they supposedly are not. They are not a part of an arbitrary grouping of Americans of certain ethnic groups (those of European ancestry) who are designated as "the majority." The majority of the world's population is not of European origin, and current demographic trends indicate that in the decades ahead Americans of European heritage may become a "minority" of the overall population.

It might be a good thing if the Catholic Church in this country would cease to use the expressions "minorities" and "minority group." Local churches could lead the way by eliminating such expressions from their official statements, diocesan papers and parish bulletins. This is more than a matter of "political correct-ness." Words, as conveyors of meaning, have great power for good and evil. It is clear that, from the prophetic perspective of the Gospel and the redemptive life, teachings, death and resurrection of Jesus Christ, there are no majority/minority groups in any sense of the term. There are simply wonderfully diverse human beings, of equal dignity before God, called by the Holy Spirit to be citizens of the kingdom of heaven. ∎

Most Rev. Edward K. Braxton *is the bishop of Lake Charles, Louisiana, and chairman of the bishops' Committee for the American College of Louvain.*

PART SEVEN:

ECUMENICAL/INTERFAITH ISSUES

# Joint LARCUM Statement *on* Racism

## BY THE BISHOPS OF LARCUM
### [LUTHERAN, ANGLICAN, ROMAN CATHOLIC, AND UNITED METHODIST CHURCHES]

MAY 1997

Jointly we members of LARCUM [Lutheran, Anglican, Roman Catholic, and United Methodist churches] are moving toward the millennium, the year 2000. We do this with firm and loving belief in our Savior Jesus Christ, thanking him for his coming, his saving, his promises. We dare to go to him with our failures, seeking his forgiveness and healing; we ask him now to help us in our struggles to overcome the sin of racism, that powerful prejudice which pits one race against the other to the damage of all. We go to each other, confessing guilt and seeking forgiveness.

This millennium and this 1997 LARCUM dialogue present us with a unique opportunity, namely, to face up to the evil of racism totally united in the belief that God created us all in his own image and likeness, that he created us all equal and that we all have the same inalienable rights. No dogmas, no creeds, no Christian denominations divide us on these beliefs. Arm in arm, heart with heart, calling upon the Lord to assist us, we must, if we deserve to be called Christians, have this love for one another, embrace each other totally and in the firm belief in one Lord, one baptism, one human family, with equal liberty and justice for all. Amen. ∎

Most Rev. David B. Thompson *is the former bishop of Charleston, South Carolina.*

*Rev. Dr. David A. Donges*
*Bishop, South Carolina Synod*
*Evangelical Lutheran Church in America*

*The Rt. Rev. Dorsey F. Henderson Jr.*
*Bishop, Episcopal Diocese of Upper South Carolina*

*The Rt. Rev. Edward Salmon Jr.*
*Bishop, Episcopal Diocese of South Carolina*

*The Rt. Rev. William J. Skilton*
*Suffragan Bishop, Episcopal Diocese of South Carolina*

*The Most Rev. David B. Thompson*
*Bishop, Roman Catholic Diocese of Charleston*

*The Rt. Rev. J. Lawrence McCleskey*
*Bishop, South Carolina Conference*
*United Methodist Church*

## CATHOLICS AT LARCUM DISCUSS RACE RELATIONS

BY *THE NEW CATHOLIC MISCELLANY* • MAY 1997

CHARLESTON, SOUTH CAROLINA—Before the bishops of LARCUM signed their joint statement on May 13 confessing to racism in their churches, each of the four denominations represented broke out into groups to discuss their particular situations and to come up with potential solutions. The groups also talked about their denomination's successes and challenges in the area of race relations.

The Catholics at LARCUM [led by Bishop David B. Thompson of Charleston, South Carolina] thought that racism became institutionalized in the southern church through a lack of concern for promoting a harmony of cultures that are not European. The European Catholic mindset was not necessarily wrong, but it was, and is, too narrow. The Church was slow to appoint Black bishops, they said, and faith communities were regularly segregated by race. Blacks were required for decades to sit either in the back or on the balconies of Catholic churches. Catholic leaders need to be active in welcoming minorities to their parishes and dioceses. Passivity in this regard equates to guilt.

Specific ideas to hasten the healing process among races in the Church included becoming aware of the racism that is still imbedded in the Catholic Church; becoming more sensitive to offensive stereotypes, especially with children; communicating a genuine welcome to minorities; celebrating the common Catholic heritage among peoples of different races; and hiring Blacks and Hispanics to positions of power in the Church.

The Catholics at LARCUM also discussed ways to learn about ending racism from other churches' experiences.

They thought that exchanging religious leaders with other denominations and appointing clergy from outside the South would enable local Catholics to live the Gospel more faithfully with regard to race relations, and they suggested learning from pro-active pastoral leaders of all faith traditions and learning to respect cultural boundaries.

The church leaders also talked about increasing common worship services and working with other denominations in the secular community.

The Catholics said that challenges they still face include poor attendance at joint religious celebrations, an attorney general who is the highest ranking Catholic state official and who does not foster race relations, difficulties in attracting non-White youths to diocesan programs, a pervasive fear of other races that is the result of ignorance and a poor knowledge and appreciation of other cultures.

They numbered among the Catholic successes in race relations: the women of the SCCCW [South Carolina Council of Catholic Women] being fully integrated and working harmoniously since the 1930s; the success of the Southeastern Pastoral Institute (SEPI) in fostering communion with the Hispanic culture, especially the youth; the appointment of the Bishop of Charleston to the National Conference of African Americans; Bishop Thompson's public stands on the Confederate flag and on the death penalty; integrated and successful Catholic schools; the funding from Catholic dioceses to help rebuild Black churches destroyed by arson; and the recommendations of the Synod of Charleston, including the formation of the Office of African American Affairs.

# Statement Given *at* Reconciliation Service Sponsored *by* Ezekiel Project

BY MOST REV. KENNETH E. UNTENER

JANUARY 1998

I stand before you this morning speaking in the name of the White people present—pastors of many denominations, and others of many denominations.

I speak primarily to pastors who are Black, but ultimately to all Black people of this community.

Our entire society has racism in its bloodstream. Saginaw has it too, a long history of racism. It is a shameful thing, and it is a heavy yoke for us to carry, but it is also a fact. In the light of that fact, and with deep sorrow and humility, I acknowledge the following:

—That we have failed to recognize our Black sisters and brothers as equals with whom we walk together from birth to death.

—That we have closed our eyes too often to the racism all around us.

—That we have been silent too often in the face of blatant prejudice.

—That we have preferred our own comfort to simple fairness.

—That we have been unwilling to acknowledge the fact of White privilege, and that we have been unwilling to yield our place of privilege and let it give place to equality.

—That we have often blamed the victims rather than accept our responsibility.

—That we have unwittingly promoted violence by our failure to act for justice.

In a word, we have sinned. We beg God's forgiveness and your forgiveness.

Sin has consequences, and healing them takes time and it takes work. What we are doing this morning may seem a small step, but it is a ritual that has roots in a good work that has already begun in the Ezekiel project. What we are doing this morning is not an empty ritual. It has roots in good soil, and can yield thirty, sixty, a hundredfold.

May God who has begun this good work among us, sustain it along the way, and bring it to its fulfillment. ∎

Most Rev. Kenneth E. Untener *is the bishop of Saginaw, Michigan.*

# BISHOP APOLOGIZES TO BLACK PASTORS FOR SIN OF RACISM

BY DAN DIGMANN, CATHOLIC NEWS SERVICE • JANUARY 1998

SAGINAW, MICHIGAN (CNS)—In what he described as a small step toward ending racial division in Saginaw, Bishop Kenneth E. Untener apologized during a January 17 service at Zion Missionary Baptist Church in Saginaw to the city's Black pastors on behalf of its White pastors for the sin of racism.

More than three hundred people representing several denominations and races attended the healing service sponsored by the Ezekiel Project, an ecumenical and interracial congregation-centered organization in the Saginaw metropolitan area.

The centerpiece of the service was Bishop Untener's statement, made in the name of White people apologizing for racism, and the response from the Rev. Roosevelt Austin, pastor of Zion Baptist Church, on behalf of Black people.

"In a word, we have sinned," Bishop Untener said. "We beg God's forgiveness and your forgiveness."

Rev. Austin then offered forgiveness on behalf of the Black people of Saginaw for the years of White injustices against them. "I forgive you for refusing to accept us as equal brothers and sisters," he said. "For enjoying your supremacy at our expense, I forgive you . . . for accepting racism as status quo, I forgive you . . . Jesus reminds us by this: 'That everyone will know that you're my sons if you have loved one another.'"

Three pairs of Black and White pastors then washed each others' feet and exchanged the kiss of peace, prompting the congregation to give a standing ovation.

The Ezekiel Project began in June 1996 and is aimed at using the unified power of the community to change adverse or unjust conditions on specific issues, directly assisting with the growth of member congregations, and promoting community involvement in planning and implementing its goals.

The organization is similar to Detroit's Jeremiah Project and the Gamaliel Foundation and derives its name from the prophet through whom God promised a new heart, restoration and resurrection to the dry bones of his people.

Fr. Robert Schramm, an Oblate of St. Francis de Sales and pastor of Saints Simon and Jude Parish in Saginaw, chaired the Ezekiel Project's eight-member committee that coordinated the reconciliation service.

"We realized late last year during late spring and early summer that despite our best efforts, many of the Black pastors didn't want to be a part of Ezekiel," Fr. Schramm said. "The Black members of the Ezekiel Project said the other Black pastors were hurt and afraid, and were afraid of being hurt again."

Mary Williams, a parishioner at Coleman Temple Church of God in Christ, said she hopes the service marks the beginning of racial healing and unity in Saginaw. "God has made us all and made us what color he wanted us," she told *The Catholic Weekly*, newspaper of the Saginaw Diocese.

"Promoting superiority over one person because of the color of their skin is wrong because God is over us and he loves all of us equally."

# Interfaith Walk Retraces Steps
# *in* American Slave Experience

BY GARY MORTON, CATHOLIC NEWS SERVICE

JULY 1998

NEWARK, Delaware (CNS)—The steady rhythm of Teresa William's drum helped set the pace July 9 for some sixty walkers participating in the Interfaith Pilgrimage of the Middle Passage.

For Williams, the beat carried yet another message, one that led her to dedicate a year of her life to retrace significant steps in the American slave experience. It was a call for all Americans to examine a largely overlooked part of the American experience—the slavery issue—and face it with honesty.

Drawing her to the pilgrimage, which began May 30 in Leverett, Massachusetts, and will conclude May 31, 1999, in South Africa, is "the need for my personal healing around the legacy of slavery and the suffering of my ancestors in this country," she told *The Dialog*, the newspaper of the Wilmington Diocese.

"We haven't really had much of a dialogue in the United States around this chapter in our history, and what has resulted has been a strong manifestation of racism in different forms," Williams added.

The group was in Delaware July 6-9, visiting local sites important to the Underground Railroad, which helped runaway slaves from the South seek freedom in the North.

On July 7, during an official welcome for the group in Wilmington, a resolution by Wilmington Bishop Michael A. Saltarelli was presented declaring the day Interfaith Pilgrimage of the Middle Passage Day. Bishop Saltarelli said local residents could "draw inspiration" from the example of the pilgrims "to renew our commitment to heal the wounds of racism that exist in our communities, minds and spirits." In the proclamation, he noted "the pilgrimage is designed to be a living prayer of the heart, mind and body for the sons and daughters of the African diaspora that will help heal the wounds inflicted even until today, and will help reconcile the hearts and spirits of all those connected, intimately or distantly, with this history."

It also said the pilgrims would visit "both sites of suffering and death such as slave auctions, slave quarters and lynchings, offering prayers for the spirits of those who suffered and died, and sites of the Underground Railroad, attesting to the monumental courage and conviction of those who worked for freedom and human dignity in the face of slavery and racial oppression."

The bishop's resolution was presented by LaVaida Owens-White, parish nurse at Christ Our King Parish in Wilmington's Ninth Ward, a predominantly Black area. The group had stayed at Christ Our King the night of July 6, after being welcomed to Delaware in a program at St. Helena's Church.

Also July 7, the pilgrims visited four Wilmington sites that were related to the Underground Railroad:

—Peter Spencer Plaza, site of the first independent African American Union Church established by Spencer in 1813. It was a haven for runaways on the Underground Railroad.

—The Old Town Hall, built in 1798, which was the site not only of abolitionist meetings, but housed jail cells in which men, women and children were held who were captured after trying to escape slavery on the Underground Railroad.

—The former site of the Thomas Garrett home. He was Wilmington station master of the Underground Railroad.

—Wilmington Friends Meeting House/Cemetery, built in 1816. Garrett attended the Meeting House and is buried in its cemetery. Following an evening candlelight procession and vigil for peace and reconciliation and a day of rest, the pilgrims left Newark for Elkton, Maryland, just across the state line. From there they were bused to Baltimore.

From [Delaware] participants on the pilgrimage were to go to Washington, and then on to Virginia, North Carolina, South Carolina, Georgia, Alabama and Mississippi.

The pilgrimage will end its U.S. leg in New Orleans in November, when pilgrims board a ship and travel through the Caribbean, Brazil and West Africa. There they will complete the pilgrimage to South Africa.

In Senegal they will link with pilgrims who have made a parallel journey through European countries historically involved in the African slave trade and walk together into South Africa.

What do the pilgrims hope to gain from the venture? Speaking for herself, Williams answered: "Understanding and more dialogue around issues of race and cross-cultural sensitivity, more transparency around history."

She added, "The legacy of slavery affected all of us as American people in this society. And there is no way for us to continue scurrying and dancing around that." ∎

The Interfaith Pilgrimage of the Middle Passage was co-sponsored by the New England Nipponzan Myohoji Peace Pagoda in Leverett and the First Congregational Church in Amherst, Massachusetts. It was the idea of Buddhist Sr. Clare Carter, who is participating along with about ten other members of the Leverett Peace Pagoda.

Among the endorsing organizations are: W. E. B. Dubois Foundation, Fellowship of Reconciliation, Jewish Peace Fellowship, Muslim Peace Fellowship, National Council of Churches of Christ, USA, Refugio del Rio Grande, Sojourners and War Resisters League.

In the metropolitan Washington area, where the pilgrimage stopped July 13-16, local supporters included: the Dorothy Day Catholic Worker House, Pax Christi of Metropolitan DC and So Others Might Eat.

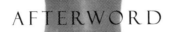

AFTERWORD

# Nine Ways *to* Combat Racism

BY MOST REV. HARRY J. FLYNN

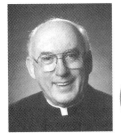

JANUARY 1997

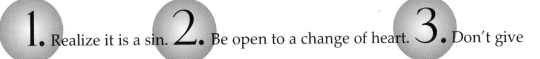

**1.** Realize it is a sin. **2.** Be open to a change of heart. **3.** Don't give

in to xenophobia. **4.** Avoid racial stereotypes, slurs, jokes. Bring the same

to the attention of families and among friends. **5.** Speak out against racial

negatives. **6.** In parishes, make sure all races have positions of leadership.

**7.** Back Catholic schools in minority neighborhoods. **8.** Back legislation

that fosters racial equality. **9.** Keep the dream of a united world alive. ∎

Most Rev. Harry J. Flynn *is the archbishop of St. Paul-Minneapolis, Minnesota.*

# ARCHBISHOP STRESSES DISCIPLESHIP TO BLACKS

BY TERRY KOLB, *THE CATHOLIC SPIRIT* • JANUARY 1997

ST. PAUL, MINNESOTA—"Go and make disciples" is the challenge for Black Catholics as they prepare for National Black Catholic Congress VIII.

And "Go and Make Disciples" was the theme for the reflection day for the Archdiocesan Commission of Black Catholics January 25 at St. Peter Claver, St. Paul, for commission members and guests.

Archbishop Harry J. Flynn's keynote address outlined suggestions for bringing about the full participation of Blacks in the Church, which he said is the first step to making disciples. The archbishop also outlined nine ways to combat racism.

The Church has much work ahead to achieve unity and diversity and to bring together people of different ethnic, cultural and linguistic backgrounds, Archbishop Flynn said.

"Catholic social teachings are bold and uncompromising," he said. "But too often they are unknown, unbelieved and not practiced."

Archbishop Flynn asked audience members to recall that their ancestry is a celebration of life in which people laughed and loved together. "To be a multicultural Church, we need to walk together," he said.

"The Church is a family, and families stay together," he said. "We need to become family with the richness of one another's cultures."

He urged Blacks to encourage vocations to the priesthood and religious life. He said that when he became bishop of the Lafayette, Louisiana, diocese, he invited young Black men to consider becoming priests. The diocese now has five Black diocesan priests, compared to none before.

"You need to pray and invite," Archbishop Flynn said.

The St. Paul Seminary does not have any Black seminarian at the present time, but the archbishop said he personally has extended an invitation to Black men.

Archbishop Flynn asked the audience to share his dream to train Black teachers for Catholic schools. He said he is working on a plan to educate teachers of color, who, with their students, will celebrate the cultures of people of color.

He challenged members of the audience to participate more in the pro-life movement. Talk about reverence for people of different cultures needs to be accompanied with talk about reverence for life, he said.

"Unless we are respecting the child in the womb, and respecting every level of life, we aren't going to get anywhere with asking for respect from others," he said.

Archbishop Flynn said his vision for evangelization is a simple one: "To make the name of Jesus Christ known and loved."

Nedra Robinson, former chair of the Archdiocesan Commission of Black Catholics, said both the reflection day and the national congress, which will be Thursday through Sunday, August 28-31, 1997, in Baltimore, will focus intently on evangelization. This will include more concentrated efforts within individual parishes, she said.

Commission efforts long have been directed toward youths, Robinson said. "Kujenga" has been an ongoing weekend retreat program in which African American Catholic youths and their families develop leadership skills, she said.

Teresa Mardenborough, commission charter member and former chair, said Archbishop Flynn's address spoke to the commission's purpose.

"Its purpose is to address the issues of African American Catholics and the Church at large," she said.

"We must spread the name of Jesus," Mardenborough said. "The challenge he gave us to become more visible in the respect for life movement and his admonishing us to encourage vocations are important."

APPENDIX: CONTRIBUTING BISHOPS

Thanks also to the National Black Sisters Conference, the *Deliverance* newsletter of Chicago, and the National Black Catholic Evangelization Forum for their assistance and contributions to this publication.